POLITICAL REPRESENTATION IN INDIA

POLITICAL REPRESENTATION IN INDIA

Ideas and Contestations 1908–1951

ABHAY V. DATAR

B L O O M S B U R Y

NEW DELHI • LONDON • OXFORD • NEW YORK • SYDNEY

BLOOMSBURY INDIA
Bloomsbury Publishing India Pvt. Ltd
Second Floor, LSC Building No. 4, DDA Complex, Pocket C – 6 & 7,
Vasant Kunj New Delhi 110070

First published in India 2019
This edition published 2019

Bloomsbury Academic
An imprint of Bloomsbury Publishing Plc

ISBN: HB: 978-9-3882-7178-3; eBook: 978-9-3882-7179-0

2 4 6 8 10 9 7 5 3 1

Typeset in Minion Pro by Manipal Digital Systems
Printed and bound in India by Replika Press Pvt. Ltd.

Bloomsbury Publishing Plc makes every effort to ensure that the papers used in the manufacture of our books are natural, recyclable products made from wood grown in well-managed forests. Our manufacturing processes conform to the environmental regulations of the country of origin.

To find out more about our authors and books visit www.bloomsbury.com and sign up for our newsletters

Contents

Acknowledgements

This book is a revised version of the PhD dissertation that was completed under the supervision of Prof. Suhas Palshikar at the Department of Politics and Public Administration, Savitribai Phule Pune University, Pune. Any such work, though ostensibly the outcome of an individual researcher's efforts, is actually in many ways a group activity and a result of a collective endeavour. Many people have contributed in myriad ways to the making of this thesis, and I consider it essential to thank each one of them.

First and foremost, I would like to thank Prof. Palshikar for not only agreeing to supervise a thesis on what was then a rather nebulous topic but encouraging me to pursue it. The numerous and wide-ranging discussions that I had with him have helped me to give a concrete shape to the thesis. His pointed and thought-provoking comments on the draft chapters have helped me hone my arguments and make them sharper.

While the thesis was being written, I joined the People's College, Nanded—an institute with a long tradition of learning. I am indeed thankful to Dr V.N. Ingole, the then Principal of People's College, for continuously encouraging me and taking a keen interest in my research. My colleagues and friends in the Department of Political Science, People's College, particularly Dr Ashok Siddhewad and Dr Vishal Patange, have also helped me in many ways with the thesis. Friends from other departments, particularly Dr Shriniwas Pande, Dr Balaji Chirade, Dr Bajirao Wadawale, Dr Bhagwan Jadhav, Dr Mukund Kawade and Mr Ananda Thorat, among others, have also been of great help and assistance. Their cooperation and encouragement have ensured the completion of the thesis within the stipulated time.

The bulk of the material cited in the bibliography was consulted at the Dhananjayrao Gadgil Library of the Gokhale Institute of Economics and Politics, Pune. I am thankful to the librarian and the staff of the Institute for their assistance, without which the present work probably would have never been materialised in the first place. The facilities and the atmosphere provided by the Institute were indeed conducive to the research. Similarly, the staff of the Jaykar Library of the Savitribai Phule Pune University and the library of the Department of Politics and Public Administration have similarly been helpful. The library of the People's College, long nurtured by eminent scholars like Dr Surendra Barlingay, Dr K.R. Shirwadkar, Dr S.R. Gadgil, Principal Narhar Kurundkar and Dr P.S. Ghare, has been an important source of reference material. I am thankful to Mr Sandeep Gaikwad, the Librarian of the People's College, and his colleagues for their help.

I would also like to thank my friends at the Department of Politics and Public Administration, Savitribai Phule Pune University, namely Dr Shailendra Kharat, Babasaheb Munde, Pandurang Bhoye, Vivek Ghotale, Sominath Gholwe, Shivaji Motegaonkar, Sunil Kankate, Kishor Raktate, Namdev Pawar and Nitin Nipunge, for informally discussing the various aspects of the thesis and, on many occasions, helping me complete various formalities. The administrative staff of the Department has been uniformly helpful in smoothening out what could have been tedious paperwork.

It is a matter of deep regret that two of my revered teachers, Prof. Rajendra Vora and Prof. Yeshwant Sumant, are no longer with us. They would have certainly loved to read this work and would naturally have offered incisive comments, which would have certainly made the thesis a better one. Shravan Modak, who was a dear friend, also passed away while the research was underway. He had always been at the receiving end of whatever I wrote, and patiently lent his ears to many of my ideas. He often brought a refreshing perspective from outside academia to whichever issue was being discussed. Many of the topics in this work, of course, very nebulous then, were discussed with him over many cups of coffee. His expert eye would certainly have helped choose the right word to make my arguments stronger and sharper.

I would also like to thank my parents, Vijaykumar and Sushama Datar, and my grandmother, late Mrs Shanta Ranade, for their encouragement and support. Without them, this thesis would never have happened at all. My wife, Deepali, and parents-in-law, Suhas and Madhuri Bapat, have also supported me, and it also because of them that the thesis could be completed in time.

I would further like to thank Bloomsbury Publishing, India, for agreeing to publish this work and making all efforts to ensure qualitative improvements in it. It is indeed a pleasure to work with a reputed publishing house, whose very name reminds one of a remarkable group of individuals in the history of English literature.

1

Introduction

This study seeks to explore the extensive and wide-ranging debates, marked by contestations as well as the emergence of numerous ideas, about political representation in colonial India and also during the process of constitution-making in India. These debates, hitherto overlooked, are significant, for they helped in shaping the institutional structures of political representation that Indian democracy possesses at present. Such an exploration might provide a tentative answer as to why and, perhaps less importantly, how post-independence India came to adopt these structures.

The starting point for this exploration would be the Indian Councils Act 1909, popularly known as the Morley–Minto Reforms, and the Government of India Act 1919, popularly known as the Montagu–Chelmsford reforms. This study would examine the discussions during the Round Table Conferences, over the Communal Award and the Government of India Act, 1935, as also the debates during the framing of the Indian Constitution. It would conclude with the discussion of the passage of the two Representation of Peoples Acts, those of 1950 and 1951. These events generated the debates in the first place. The Partition of India changed the political situation entirely, and with it, the very context within which the entire debate was taking place changed substantially. Yet, significant continuities remained. The treatment of this issue, however, would not be episodic but thematic.

The key question that ran through these debates, and hence forms the most important element of continuity, was what share of political power would the various communities of India, expressed in terms of religious minorities and caste blocs, have in any scenario, which would be characterised by substantial devolution of power or an imminent transition to independence. Thus, representation continued to be primarily viewed as a means of, and thought of in terms of, access to power, and that of playing a role in decision-making, and hence became a terrain for contestation. During the colonial times, if access to power meant influencing the decisions being made by the colonial regime, then after 1947, it meant controlling the direction of the very process of policy-making.

Each of these aforementioned events generated a flood of discussions. Commissions were appointed, conferences were held, submissions and petitions were submitted, witnesses were summoned and examined and, as a consequence, large amounts of published material came into existence. Thus, these events could be described, for want of a better term, as 'articulatory occasions' as the competing social and political forces in India were, in a sense, compelled to explicitly state and stake out their positions on the ongoing debate about political representation, if they were not to lose out in the entire process. Thus, this provided a fillip to the process by which various communities now started regarding themselves as being politically distinct and hence, worthy of representation.

These debates threw up a wide range of institutional arrangements of political representation in the form of a variety of electoral systems. These alternatives were extensively discussed, yet in the ultimate analysis, the currently prevailing First-Past-The-Post (FPTP) electoral system received broad acceptance. Similarly, these contestations were marked by serious controversy and acrimony over the issue of who deserved representation. These two would form the key themes in this study.

The choice of a given electoral system and whether representation is to be granted on the basis of territorial, sectional/communal or functional considerations cannot be regarded as a question of mere technicalities. More often than not, the electoral system chosen is a reflection of what objectives are sought to be achieved by representation. Similarly, the basis of representation chosen depends on one's opinion about the society that one lives in.

The choices articulated in the Indian debate reflect these considerations. The debate over separate electorates versus joint electorates, which in a sense constitutes the first theme, was not just about fair representation for minority groups but was also about the kind of society India was. Was it a homogenous society, where the social identity of the representative did not matter, or was it a heterogeneous and deeply divided society, where a group could only be represented by one of its own? On the other hand, was it something in between? The choice of the electoral system often was determined by the positions that one took about this issue.

This very issue leads to the second theme—who was to be represented and by whom? This deals with the assertion of sectional, group and communal identities in this debate on representation. The perception of the colonial rulers that India was essentially a heterogeneous society and that any absence of special facilities for minorities would lead to a kind of majoritarianism meant that such concessions would certainly be granted. This, in turn, provided an institutional incentive to a variety of groups, beginning with the Muslim League, which claimed to represent the Muslims of British India, to articulate such demands for special privileges. In the context of political representation, they took the form of separate electorates, reserved seats or functional representation. The process of formation of social identities can be discerned, not always explicitly, in a manner in which these demands were articulated. The very act of granting special kinds of representation to certain social categories entailed that the boundaries of these categories had to be clearly demarcated with very little room left for expansion and/or contraction, as well as definitional certainty of these categories. If the decennial Indian census is credited or blamed for making what were essentially fluid social identities into rigid social categories, then this debate on political representation also contributed to the very same process. This colonial perception was, of course, countered by nationalist spokespersons, who envisaged India as a diverse but, nonetheless, a seamless whole and not a one riddled with social contradictions.

This leads to the third theme of this study—who had the right to vote and, less importantly, who should be the representatives? Adult franchise was ruled out in the early phases of this debate. For the British, the granting of the adult franchise was fraught with logistical difficulties and a concern that such a provision would overload the emergent system. The nationalist movement came to adult franchise rather late—in the 1920s. But was adult franchise advocated as a counter-measure to check the demands for communal representation, rather than as a consequence of a firm belief in the political wisdom of the masses? This issue will also be explored in this study.

Moreover, in the context of separate/communal electorates, the issue of who could be the representatives was not limited to the position that a group should or can only be represented by one of its members. The debate also reveals the technicalities involved in deciding what qualifications should be required for becoming a representative, irrespective of the group to be represented. This debate also spilled over to the postcolonial period. Furthermore, the extent to which the process of delimitation was influenced by the position that Indian society consisted of conflicting interests would also be discussed.

These debates can be framed, albeit at the cost of being reductionist, in terms of two opposing and, to a large extent, mutually exclusive approaches. One saw Indian society as consisting of diverse communities, whose interests were, more often than not, irreconcilable and/or mutually contradictory. Therefore, it was imperative that any system of representation be designed in such a manner that would guarantee political representation for these communities, in order to ensure that their interests were not overlooked in the process of decision-making. This approach could be described as an 'Institutionalist' one, for it emphasised institutional safeguards and arrangements to secure access to political power for all sections of Indian society. This approach seems to have assumed that the various communities of India could, in the ultimate analysis, arrive at a via media as far as the harmonisation of their interests were concerned but that this was possible only if and when they had been granted some share of political representation. The colonial regime and later the Muslim League were the strongest exponents and advocates of this approach.

The second approach did not deny the diverse, and perhaps the divided, nature of the Indian society. But it parted ways with the Institutionalists on the question of whether this diversity would lead to the existence of conflicting interests or that if conflicting interests that already existed could not be easily harmonised. The adherents of the second approach argued that the logic of the democratic electoral process would ensure that such a process of harmonisation would take place effortlessly, for no elected representative could afford to ignore the interests of a significant section of his or her electorate, and thus could be described as 'Processualists'. Hence, for them, there was no need to establish an elaborate institutional structure to ensure the representation of the interests of all communities.

The Institutionalists further argued that in India, one community, the Hindus, preponderated numerically, while the other communities, which were described as minorities, were no match for it. They argued that in the absence of institutional safeguards, any system of political representation in India was bound to lead to majoritarian outcomes to the detriment of the minorities. Hence, they constantly emphasised such safeguards. On the other hand, the Processualists conceded that this logic of electoral politics might lead to majoritarian outcomes but the solution to this was not institutional safeguards; rather it was for the smaller communities to identify themselves with the aspirations of the majority. This would ensure that the minorities would secure representation and have their interests protected.

This study does not claim to explore in detail the ideas or thinking about democracy during this period. Most of those who actively participated in these debates envisaged India, whether independent or self-governing within the British Empire, as some kind of democracy. The idea that the people of India should have some say in how they were being ruled had been articulated since the early nineteenth century. Even later, the leading spokespersons of the Indian nationalist movement articulated their demands in what could be called proto-democratic terms, for they were demanding a share in ruling if not for the people, at least on behalf and in the interests of the people. Their notions of what democracy actually meant must have been diverse, and equally might have evolved as the Nationalist Movement transformed from an elite club to a mass movement. It must be noted that in the mid-nineteenth century, there was a strand of thinking among some Indian figures, notably Sir Syed Ahmed Khan, which saw representation best being achieved through nomination, and not election. However, some form of accountability towards the masses was a continuing common theme. Similarly, there seems to have been a consensus that Indian democracy would be a representative one and not a direct one. Thus, the entire debate on representation took place on the basis of an implicit consensus—one of which was that the India of the future would be democratic to some extent or the other. However, this study essentially confines itself to a discussion of the institutional structures that were being thought of for this future democratic political set-up for India.

The academic exploration of these debates, till date, has been rather fragmentary. A recent work has dealt extensively with Dr Babasaheb Ambedkar's contribution and role in these debates, and the overall making and shaping of the electoral system in India.[1] But there seems to have been no significant exploration of these debates as a whole. The huge mass of printed material wherein the representatives of various communities articulated their demands rarely finds a mention in the relevant literature. These debates of the past are important because they determined the contours of the discussion on the electoral system in India. A recent work has indeed emphasised this point.[2] Also, the fact that the subcontinent simultaneously achieved independence and was partitioned on religious lines has meant that the history and politics of the demands of the Muslims have been explored. While studies of the arguments made by various spokespersons of the Muslim community have received comprehensive treatment, this has not been the case with other social forces and actors—with perhaps the recent exception of the Dalits.

In independent India, there has been almost no discussion as to whether the Indian electoral system needs to be changed. The reason seems to be a sheer lack of political and institutional imagination. Moreover, since the very logic of the Indian democratic and electoral process has in itself led to an enhanced diversity, which is indeed a transformation, in the social background of the country's elected representatives, described with perspicacity as a 'Silent Revolution' or the 'Rise of the Plebeians,'[3] a pressing need to imagine alternatives to the present electoral system has not been felt. The changes that are being suggested do not attempt to alter the basic framework of the FPTP system. The approach towards the demands for reservation for women is a case in point.

Another crucial reason why such discussions did not take place could be cited with some plausibility. The colonial approach to political representation was to make legal–institutional arrangements to ensure the presence of various sections of Indian society in the power structure. This meant providing for separate communal electorates for these sections, a policy vilified as that of 'Divide and Rule'. For many, this institutionalist approach of the British often is responsible not only for thwarting attempts to 'construct' a 'homogenous Indian nation' but for the 'tragedy' of Partition as well. This feeling has perhaps created an atmosphere of distrust towards attempts to seek institutional alternatives to the current electoral system. The space and potentialities given by the electoral process in India in providing for the presence of social groups, hitherto excluded from the corridors of power, also perhaps has put paid to the need to explore institutional alternatives. The unfolding of the democratic process seems to have been regarded as being adequate.

However, an exploration of these debates is intellectually significant, for the issues that it raised seem to be relevant even today as questions about the representative character of the representative institutions, the legislatures, are being raised once again. A variety of social groups, ranging from smaller castes among the OBCs to Dalit Muslims and Dalit Christians, has been demanding that their voices be heard. The means that they desire to achieve their objective is political representation. Concurrently, a debate has been initiated on whether the electoral system in India can be rethought, mainly since a gross disproportionality between votes and seats has been evident in some of the recent state assembly elections. Perhaps, the institutional alternatives discussed in the past might be of some assistance in contributing to these renewed debates, and hence this exploration.

2

The Idea of Political Representation

A system of political representation is an integral component of any democratic political system; or as has been pointed out that 'Representation is Democracy'.[1] In recent times, political representation has been linked to democracy through elections.[2] However, as shall be discussed later, representation, even in its political manifestations, was not necessarily linked to elections and democracy. The present discussion mainly deals with the debates over representation within States that is within the deliberative and decision-making institutions—the representative assemblies—located in the structure of the State.

The earliest and one of the most comprehensive treatments of the concept of 'Representation'—and not just 'Political Representation'—continues to be Hanna Pitkin's *The Concept of Representation.*[3] It seeks to examine the way in which the term 'representation' has been used in different contexts, and makes an attempt to arrive at a specific definition. Pitkin has also given a detailed overview of how the term emerged and was used in history.[4] A recent exhaustive examination of the concept of 'Political Representation'[5] takes mainly a historical overview of its emergence. The origins and emergence of what today is described as a representative government have been also examined in their historical context.[6]

Pitkin offers a rather basic and somewhat nebulous, yet working, definition of what is meant by the act of representation. For her, it means 'the making present *in some sense* of something which is nevertheless *not* present literally or in fact'[7](italics in the original). This definition implies that there exists someone who is being represented, someone who is performing the act of representation, something that belongs to the represented which is being represented, and the context and/or institutional setting in which the act of representation is taking place (i.e. before whom the act of representation is taking place).[8] The former formulation also states that the representative is, in fact, acting in a substantive manner for the person/s whom he or she is representing.[9] Viera and Runciman have further defined political representation as an arrangement where 'representatives ought to resemble and stand in the place of the represented'.[10] Representation has also been thought to be similar to the principal–agent theory, wherein the agent acts according to the instructions and in the interests of the former.

These definitions beg many questions—who is to be represented or who/what deserves to be represented; what are the essential qualifications for being represented; who can represent and what are the essential qualifications in order to represent; what is the mode of representation (the nature of the electoral system); and can there be any criteria to assess whether representation is taking place and if it is, what is its nature, extent, texture and quality. As the following discussion shows, all these questions have been sought to be answered by many.

The first prominent theorist to extensively examine the concept of representation was Thomas Hobbes.[11] For Hobbes, authorisation of any person or persons by the represented is enough to make them the representative. Pitkin calls this view formalistic.[12] The legitimacy of the representative, thus, arises from his or her being regarded as such by the represented. In modern times, most discussions regard some form of election (i.e. methods in which those who are to be represented have some choice in who their representative should be) as being the source of such legitimacy, thus making representation democratic. However, the concept of 'non-democratic representation' has been developed by Andrew Rehfeld to deal with instances where individuals may not be elected but may be regarded both by the represented and the audience before which the act of representation is taking place as being the representatives of the former.[13] Though this formulation has been developed in the context of nation-states being represented in international forums as well the representation of the deprived by non-governmental organisations (NGOs), in the Indian context this would prove useful in the discussions of the representative character of the nominated members of the various councils in colonial India.

Origins

As Pitkin has pointed out, the concept of representation is essentially a modern one arising with the American and the French Revolutions, and that it had tenuous links with ideas of democracy and elections.[14] On the other hand, it has been argued that the idea of representation, in fact, preceded democracy.[15] It has been pointed out that the forerunners of modern democracy, the Greeks and Romans, did not have any arrangements for representation. In fact, representative institutions established after the English, American and the French Revolutions were not regarded as being democratic. Political actors, such as Abbe Sieyes and James Madison, in fact, contrasted democracy and representative government; the first being what the small city-states possessed and the second what modern states required given their large size.[16]

Viera and Runciman offer a synoptic overview of how representation came to mean standing for someone on the basis of authorisation.[17] Furthermore, Friedrich traces the origins of the modern electoral systems to its emergence, which was out of the medieval corporative system that was non-electoral in character.[18]

The necessary connection between being elected and thus being representative of someone, though fundamentally a modern one, did have medieval forerunners.[19] Apart from Hobbes, John Locke and Jean-Jacques Rousseau also discussed the concept of representation. But Rousseau later rejected it in principle. It was in the early nineteenth century that the argument that there was a necessary link between representation and democracy was established, which was strengthened by, among others, Jeremy Bentham, James Mill, Benjamin Constant, Alexis de Tocqueville, Thomas Paine and John Stuart Mill.[20] However, for Tocqueville and Mill, in particular, representation by forging indirect links between the represented and the State could in fact help check democracy, which till then had a negative connotation (which in fact dated back to Aristotle). In the early days, the fact that representation and democracy had nothing to do with each other has been noted by Pitkin in her revisitation of the former concept.[21]

Criticism of representation as being an obstacle, if not being antithetical, to democracy has come from the proponents of direct and/or participatory democracy, such as Rousseau. Recent scholarship has explored this viewpoint and has rejected it. The idea that representative democracies are somehow second-best versions of direct democracies has also been questioned.[22] Similarly, both the necessary equation of elections with authorisation and the belief that elections meant the legitimacy of the representative and consent on part of the represented were established in recent times.[23] This establishment of this link has been termed by Manin as 'the triumph of elections'. Whatever the merits of elections, once the principle that they were an inherent part of representative government and hence of democracy was established, the issues relating to the mode of electing the representatives, who the representatives should be and who is to be represented came to the fore.

Social Composition of the Representative Body

The composition of the body of persons—the representative assembly—that makes binding decisions on the collectivity of persons constituting the State has been a matter of long-standing debate. The viewpoint that argued that the composition of this representative body should reflect the composition of the collectivity that it claimed to represent has been described as 'descriptive representation' has a long history.[24] In recent times, exponents and theorists of this view have included Anne Phillips, Jane Mansbridge and Melissa Williams.[25] However, subtle differences can be discerned within this view. While there would a consensus on the fact that all significant segments of society must be represented in a representative body, there exist differences of opinion on who should represent these segments. Should the representatives belong to the same segment or not?

But the three recent theorists mentioned above, amongst others, have emphasised the need for the representatives to belong to the group/segment/section of society that they represent, especially in the case of those who have been historically disadvantaged and excluded. This debate has mainly been generated in the United States of America out of the concern for low levels of representation for groups like women and Blacks/African-Americans. Phillips has coined the phrase 'politics of presence' in her book of the same title to advocate the representation of historically deprived groups by individuals belonging to these groups.[26] Phillips has argued that the presence of representatives of such groups in representative assemblies would ensure that their viewpoint would be heard and that their interests would be defended in the process of making decisions.

Williams's argument has a similar starting point. It has been claimed that where 'historically marginalised groups are chronically underrepresented in legislative bodies, citizens who are members of those groups are not fairly represented'.[27] The issue of essentialism has been tackled here by conceding that marginalised groups are internally heterogeneous but states that 'the *experience* of marginalisation' is something that they share in common.[28] The possibility that the mere presence of representatives of and from such groups would still not address the problem of marginalisation has been conceded. The thrust of the argument is that descriptive representation will provide marginalised groups with a voice in the decision-making process and make them trust the process as such.

Mansbridge has argued that the fact that the representatives belong to such hitherto excluded groups would enhance their substantive representation (i.e. improve the quality of representation). Such representatives would be able to put forward the viewpoint of such groups in the decision-making process and would also try to ensure that this is incorporated in that process. These representatives, by virtue of their background and characteristics, would naturally enjoy the trust of the represented. Mansbridge has reviewed the empirical investigations of the effects of descriptive representation and has argued it does help in improving the quality of representation.[29] But a viewpoint also holds that the mere fact of the representative and the represented sharing certain characteristics is not enough. If all things are equal, representatives of certain hitherto excluded groups should be those who also represent even more deprived sub-groups within these groups.[30] But there does not seem to have been any explicit debate on what exactly constitutes a group which has been historically excluded. The one working criterion that has been offered is that such groups 'must be subject to long-standing patterns of structural inequality and who share a sense of political identity with group members', and it seems quite nebulous. The point that such groups should not only be objectively discriminated against but also have a subjective sense of being discriminated against is not quite helpful.[31] There also is no clarity on whether with the efflux of time a group ceases to be excluded. If this was regarded as a possibility, then no special efforts would be required to ensure the presence of such a group. These issues do not seem to have been adequately addressed.

Pitkin has expressed reservations about the efficacy of descriptive representation. According to her, this mode of representation would be valid only in instances where the function of the representative assembly is to supply information as an input to future governmental action. If descriptive representation is to form the basis of decision-making, it might lead to issues of accountability[32] as then the presumable representatives would justify their actions not on the basis of their merits or they being taken after due consideration but on the fact that those who took the decisions did so because they were 'representative'. Proponents of descriptive representation have also conceded that the notion has shortcomings. Issues of accountability and the dangers of essentialism have been identified in this context.[33]

At the same time, it is necessary to note that representation being non-electoral is not a notion which has receded in the background. While in the pre-modern era, representation was largely conceived in this manner, it has enjoyed a comeback even in the modern days. Fascists also claimed representativeness for themselves, which was taken seriously enough to warrant a research article.[34] The highly personalistic notions of representative leadership combined with a critique of parliamentary systems, as not necessarily being representative, lent itself to fascist notions of the 'Leader' being the non-elected representative of a country.[35] Recent research has focused on institutional arrangements which are non-electoral in nature but yet it is considered imperative that they be representative in character.[36] However, it must be noted that these arrangements are regarded as supplementary to existing structures of representations. In the Indian context, demands for ensuring the representativeness of institutions like the judiciary and other regulatory agencies are being made from various quarters and angles. The concern is that given the increasing importance of such bodies in governance it is essential that they reflect the opinions of all sections of society in order to arrive at well-considered decisions.

Modes of Election: The Electoral System

The debate over who or what needs representation is extensive. Equally extensive is the one on how representation should be brought about. There seems to be a consensus that the method of election needs to be followed. Carl Joachim Friedrich, a Weimar scholar turned American liberal, offers a pithy rationale for elections. According to him, their purpose is 'to elect the representatives which are to act on the behalf of the electorate, and [...] to review the actions of the government',[37] which introduces both a prospective and retrospective element into them.

The crux of the debate is whether it is individuals who possess certain interests or whether it is the collectivities that possess certain interests who are to be represented. The common factor in both these positions is that there is something called 'interests', in the possession of either individuals or groups, which needs representation. These interests could be economic, political, social and even religious, and in modern times, those of gender and sexual orientation. Burke advocated the representation of collectivities, which he termed interests, which for him had 'an objective, impersonal, unattached reality'.[38] But Burke did not accept that all components of an interest be represented and claims that the representative of trading interests of Bristol (his own constituency) could well represent similar interests from Birmingham. This position of Burke has been described as 'virtual representation and is non-electoral in nature'.[39] Hence, it has been pointed out that this formulation marks a break between the idea of representation on one hand and that of election on the other.[40]

By contrast, James Madison and many other founders of the American Republic primarily favoured representation of individuals. For them, interest-bearing collectivities were the same as factions.[41] For the Utilitarians, led by Jeremy Bentham and James Mill, each person was the best judge of his or her own interest and thus needs to be represented qua individual.[42] One similarity which can be drawn out of these two positions is the recognition of the plurality of interests, collective or individual in nature, and the necessity of all these being represented in the decision-making apparatus. It is this theoretical position that leads to the support and advocacy of Proportional Representation.

The debate over majority/plurality representation and Proportional Representation (PR) has been briefly summed up by Friedrich.[43] The most detailed and exhaustive examination, albeit with a PR bias, of electoral systems is by Enid Lakeman.[44] The selection of the electoral system in a sense depends on what is the desired outcome of elections. Those looking forward to a stable, effective government would prefer a system of majority representation, while those who prefer all sections of society to be represented in decision-making would prefer proportional representation. PR was criticised for leading to the fragmentation and multiplication of political parties and provides an incentive to extremist elements.[45]

The critics of PR have long argued that PR leads to instability and the weakening of democratic institutions.[46] A specially appointed eight-member Royal Commission extensively debated the pros and cons of PR in the United Kingdom in the early twentieth century.[47] Interestingly, three of the members, Sir Courtenay Ilbert, Edwin Montagu and Sir Francis Hopwood (later Lord Southborough), had or would have Indian connections in the future. In the Indian debates in the colonial period, the choice of electoral system to be adopted was contingent on what was one's viewpoint about the notion that India was a nation.

The United States has come up with a distinctive method for ensuring minority representation. This is known as race-conscious districting (or delimitation to use an Indian phrase). Constituencies wherein minorities are in a numerical majority are deliberately created in order to ensure that they achieve adequate representation. Such constituencies are known as 'majority–minority districts' and have been the focus of many academic studies. Phillips, however, warns that such an arrangement by granting a little more than token presence to the minorities might actually end up strengthening majority power[48] and actually prefers multi-member constituencies or PR as means to ensure adequate minority representation.[49] It is a moot point as to why the Americans have not given serious thought to PR or even to the practice of reservations a lá India.

Another mode of representation has been functional. One of its leading modern proponents was the socialist ideologue and political theorist, G.D.H. Cole.[50] Functional representation also was an important component of the doctrine of political pluralism, which recognised that society consisted of groups with varying interests. However, the idea of functional representation predates Cole and has its origins in the medieval town councils of Europe.[51] Functional representation was an important component of the system of representation in colonial India and it exists, albeit in a sharply attenuated form, in independent India as well.

The logic behind functional representation was that individuals should be grouped and represented according to their occupations, rather than their places of residence. It is argued in this context that rather than individuals, it is groups that should have and require representation. Furthermore, the formulation that since individuals have different kinds of interests, they should have different kinds of representatives to serve these interests has been identified as being central to functional representation.[52] However, it seems that this prioritises the economic interests of the individual rather than the non-economic. Whatever the mode of representation, it has been pointed out that 'the representative assembly that it produces can never perfectly reproduce the electorate'.[53]

However, in practically all electoral systems, the territory is the basis for representation. It has been pointed out that a community of interests in any given territory was assumed, and hence geographical representation was advocated. But with increasing social mobility and even stratification within a given geographical area, no such community of interest can be assumed. Hence, it has been argued that there is a need to look beyond mere territorial representation.[54] This is not exactly a recent viewpoint, for in the mid-twentieth century there were suggestions that some kind of functional representation should be considered as being supplementary to territorial representation.[55] However, some have argued for going beyond the principle of territoriality, for it has been claimed that interests are no longer territorial in nature.[56] However, non-territorial representation is bound to create an issue of accountability and, more importantly, that of access on part of the represented to the representative. These issues have not been adequately addressed.

Another neglected aspect of the concept of representation has been the question of who is eligible to be a representative. This issue is distinct from the idea of descriptive representation and deals with the necessary qualifications for the representative. Manin has pointed out that in the early phases of modern democratic politics, efforts were made to ensure that the representatives would be socially superior to the represented. It was expected that the natural elites of the society would be elected and rules were framed to ensure this.[57] It has also been pointed out that as franchise expanded, the qualifications for the representatives started disappearing.[58] A recent study has classified such qualifications into two broad categories—firstly, voter endogenous qualifications, which arise out of voters' preferences; secondly, voter exogenous qualifications, which are externally imposed.[59]

Representation as Activity

Rather than fixing a definition for representation, it has also been looked at in its action-oriented form or through the view that the representative is essentially acting for someone else—in this case, the represented. In one sense, what the representative does and how he or she does it determines what representation would mean.[60] Pitkin argues that an activity-oriented view of representation would enable us to judge the acts of the representative.[61] It has been also argued that the act of representation could help to constitute collective identity or to create new formulations of what interests are being represented.[62] Thus, an important element emphasised here has been the issue as to whether the decisions taken by the representatives are in any way connected with the preferences of the represented. This question links up with the notion of accountability—an issue which been focused on recent discussions on democratic theory.

It is evident from the above examination of the concept of political representation that it has been extensively debated over centuries. This debate shows no sign of abating. But in spite of that, there seems to have emerged some broad consensus on what the term 'political representation' can denote. Pitkin's definition and its cognates still form the basis of the concept. More important than this definitional and analytical certainty, representation is now more than ever firmly linked with elections and democracy. Efforts to delink them, particularly by adherents and proponents of direct democracy, have not been persuasive and certainly not successful. It would certainly take a braver theorist to break them asunder.

3

The Development of Representative Institutions in India

The historiography of the development of representative institutions in India can be broadly divided, at the risk of making too sweeping a generalisation, into two mutually exclusive viewpoints. The first saw the progressive enlargement and strengthening of the all-Indian and provincial councils as a pre-determined outcome of the beneficent nature of British rule, whose ultimate end was to 'train' Indians for self-government. This belief seems implicit in one of the significant studies of the constitutional developments in India, that by Arthur Berriedale Keith.[1]

It is, of course, now recognised that this belief was a mere cloak for imperial ambitions and thus this first view is regarded as being largely outdated. The other view saw this development as a quest on part of the British to draw more and more Indians into the imperial structure as collaborators and junior partners in order to strengthen the Empire.[2] This approach worked but only in the short term. The demands of the Indians for further political reforms became more and more insistent. It must also be emphasised that each installment of reform was preceded by a nationalist upsurge. Moreover, it should be noted that the reforms are in fact both a response to and an attempt to contain this upsurge.

Perhaps, this fact led historians to regard constitutional developments as a mere sideshow to the more intellectually exciting studies of the Nationalist Movement. One pre-independence study[3] seems to have been doubtful of the utility of writing an historical account of such developments and is at pains to justify such a need. Two standard and comprehensive studies of modern India[4] have given these representative institutions their due, albeit with varying emphasis. The point that the very structure and design of these representative institutions influenced the structure of politics and helped shape social identities has been made by one study of the development of these institutions.[5] It laments the small number of studies about these institutions and the electoral processes that they entailed. There also have been almost no studies of the Indian engagement with the idea of political representation, except one about the Muslims.[6] On the other hand, the growth of political consciousness among specific communities has been explored, albeit within the larger framework of social history.[7] The Indian women's struggle for political rights has been examined again within the larger backdrop of the women's movement.[8]

How the Indians viewed and utilised these representative institutions can be debated endlessly. But it must be conceded that these institutions did acquaint Indians with parliamentary procedures and practices and hence can be credited with playing a part in laying the foundations of contemporary Indian democracy.

Early Demands

The history of the development of the representative institutions begins with the Indian Councils Act of 1861. However, the demands that India should have some kind of a representative form of government had preceded it. The atmosphere created by the post-Napoleonic revolutions in France, Spain and Portugal, as well as the Greek war of independence generated these demands. These political developments found an echo in India as well. European radicals and their Bengali counterparts centred in Calcutta started advocating a representative government for India as a consequence of these changes.

The overall progress of democracy in Europe and North America seems to have had an impact on the writings of the mid-nineteenth century Maharashtrian Brahmin government official and social reformer, Gopal Hari Deshmukh (1823–92), better known by his pen-name 'Lokhitwadi' (one who advocates measures for the benefit of the people). In an essay written in the Marathi journal 'Prabhakar', published from Mumbai in 1848, Deshmukh urged Indians to jointly submit a petition to the Queen asking for the grant of a parliament for India since the prevailing system of administration did not benefit the people of India. He suggested that such a parliament should be convened in Bombay and each city and district should be asked to send two representatives each to this assembly. He also noted that representatives should be elected by the people from all sections of society and that they should necessarily possess wisdom and shrewdness as well as tact. Deshmukh added that caste should not be a consideration in the selection of representatives. Interestingly, he added that Brahmins should not be given an excessive share of representation, since they were an arrogant community.[9] Deshmukh's contribution to the early Indian debate on political representation seems to have been completely overlooked.

Constitutional Developments

The Charter Act of 1833 first made a distinction between the executive and the legislative functions of the Governor-General's Executive Council by adding a fourth member to it who would as the Act laid down attend the meetings of the Council only when it met to legislate.[10] The Charter Act of 1853 expanded the Council even further, albeit only for legislative purposes. Demands to include non-official members, both European and Indians, were rejected on the grounds that it would be difficult to select Indian non-officials who were 'properly representative'.[11] The India Councils Act of 1861 provided for the nomination for legislative purposes of not less than six and not more than 12 members to the Council for a period of two years. The Act did not require such persons to be Indians but assurances were given in the House of Commons to this effect.[12] This Act also re-established the legislative powers of the Governors' Councils for Bombay and Madras, which had been abolished by the 1853 Act. The provision was made to nominate non-official members for a period of two years to the local councils. A legislative council was established for Bengal in 1882 and in

1886, for the North-Western Provinces (roughly today's Uttar Pradesh), the Punjab and Burma.[13]

The 1861 Act was obviously a response to the events of 1857. The colonial regime seems to have realised that it was not an easy task to govern India without any participation on part of the Indians. These reforms were implemented, despite opposition, and three Indians were appointed to the Viceroy's Council. The appointment of the Indian members came about largely due to a realisation that if non-official Europeans were to be nominated to the Council, Indians could not be excluded. The purpose of these reforms was, of course, to win over the loyalty of those sections of society who were deemed influential.[14] Thus, it was not surprising that the first three Indians appointed to the Council were landed aristocrats and so were all other Indians appointed to the Council till 1873.[15] It was, of course, widely accepted that the Act of 1861 was in no way the first step in the direction of self-government for India. Equally strong was the belief that the essential purpose of the Act was to strengthen the British rule in India by including some Indians in the decision-making process and thus broadening its support base.

The next installment of political reforms was the Indian Councils Act of 1892. Initiated by the Viceroy, Lord Dufferin, these reforms expanded the all-India and the provincial councils. It was obvious that this expansion was an attempt to contain the increasing nationalist feelings in India, which had become even stronger after the establishment of the Indian National Congress in 1885, which had started making demands for reforms and expansion of the councils coupled with the presence of elected members. Significantly, the Act of 1892 also introduced an element of election. Hitherto all members of the councils had been nominated. The political background of the making of the Act has been discussed in scholarly literature.[16] But more importantly, for the first time, these reforms compelled the colonial regime to explicitly state its opinion about the nature of Indian society.

In 1888, Dufferin had appointed a three-member committee to suggest a scheme for the expansion of the provincial councils. Its report identified three broad social groups in India who deserved representation. They were the hereditary nobility and the landed classes, the trading professional and the agricultural classes, and the planting and the commercial European community. It is interesting to note that in the first instance there is no mention of interests based on religion or caste. Yet the committee did recommend the interests of the religious minorities be safeguarded through a nomination and that the future councils should have a 'fair proportion of members drawn from the two great classes, Hindus and Mahommedans, into which the population is divided'.[17]

This concern for ensuring that all significant sections of Indian society find a place in these new councils was a serious one from an imperialist standpoint. Once it had been decided that representative institutions, in the form of legislative councils, albeit with very limited powers, were to be introduced in India in order to associate the Indians with the colonial regime, it became imperative to ensure that the representativeness of these institutions be ensured. Non-representative councils would not have served the purpose for which they were being introduced. As the powers and size of these councils increased, the debate on representation expanded primarily because they were seen as providing access to political power. However, the introduction of elections to the councils was a half-hearted one. The provincial councils of Bombay, Madras, Bengal and the United Provinces, and the Calcutta Chamber of Commerce, which represented the English commercial interests of Calcutta, were allowed to recommend one name as their representative to the Viceroy's Legislative Council, and the Viceroy could reject this recommendation. The Viceroy was to also nominate five members, all non-officials, to ensure 'the due representation of the different classes of the community'.[18] Similar provisions were made in the provincial councils of Bombay, Madras, Bengal and the United Provinces where local self-government institutions, the senates of universities, and commercial and mercantile associations were given the right to recommend their representative who in turn would be nominated by the provincial government to the provincial legislature. Provision for nomination by the provincial governments was made to ensure 'fair representation of the different classes of the community'.[19] The provincial authorities were empowered to decline to accept the recommendations.

Two features of the 1892 Act can be identified. Firstly, there seems to be a realisation that the provision for elections would not necessarily ensure that the councils would be more representative and that the elected members might, in fact, be unrepresentative of the Indian society at large. Hence, it might have been considered necessary to provide for the provision for nominating non-official members. Secondly, the rules made under the Act allowed the provincial governments to recognise '[a]ssociation or [a]ssociations of merchants, manufacturers or tradesmen' as bodies entitled to recommend a representative to be nominated to the local councils. This meant that the colonial regime now possessed the power to identify, acknowledge and legitimise interests that deserved representation and thus decide who deserved representation. This provision surely must have encouraged the creation of such associations in order to claim representation for themselves.

During this entire period, the Congress had been making demands for an expansion of the legislative councils so as to enable Indians to enter the corridors of power. The colonial regime was not averse to this demand, albeit only as a stratagem to draw conservative sections of Indian society into the imperial structure of government to balance, if not counter emerging nationalist forces. This meant that both the idea of enhancing the numerical strength as well as the powers of the representative institutions and that of ensuring their representative character by devising mechanisms and institutional arrangements were the primary issues of concern. The Congress seemed to emphasise the first, while its Indian opponents and the British rulers seemed to emphasise the second. Indeed, for the colonial regime, the second was often argued as the pre-condition for the first. Indeed, these opposing standpoints governed the entire discourse on representation in India till 1947.

The Morley–Minto Reforms

The Indian Councils Act, 1909, popularly referred to as the Morley–Minto reforms after their principal architects, John Morley, the then

Secretary of State for India, and Lord Minto, the then Viceroy of India, was enacted in the midst of British attempts to severely deal with increasing armed revolutionary activity in India. The reforms are also famous, or notorious, for accepting and translating into reality the demand for separate electorates for the Muslims.[20]

Lord Morley explicitly squashed apprehensions or hopes that these reforms could be regarded as the first step in the long journey to Indian independence.[21] Furthermore, the documents generated by the reforms make it clear the Raj had not changed its views about Indian society. The proposals of the Government of India noted that 'representation by classes and interests is the only practicable method of embodying the elective principle in the constitution of the Indian Legislative Councils'.[22] It added that for the provincial Legislative Councils, representation had to be granted to 'classes, races and interests'.[23] The proposals argued, keeping in line with this conception of Indian society, that the Muslims constituted a distinct interest, which required separate representation.

The stated purpose of the regulations made under the Act was 'to obtain, so far as possible, a fair representation of the different classes and interests in the country'.[24] This was a mere reiteration of previous arguments in favour of granting separate electorates to the Muslims. However, it must be noted in this context that separate electorates also meant direct elections and so the Muslims were now to directly elect some of their representatives to the provincial and all-India legislature rather than through other bodies like municipalities or local boards. The fact that the Morley–Minto reforms, otherwise condemned for their introduction of separate electorates on the basis of religion, also granted, albeit, in a limited manner, the right of direct elections is often overlooked. Furthermore, the Muslims were also granted a double vote, since some members of the community were eligible in the non-communal constituencies as well.

The regulations made under the Act also conceded the primacy of the electoral principle. However, only in those cases where 'a workable electorate' could not be had, the principle of nomination was to be put into practice. It was hoped that once such an electorate could be formed, elections would replace nominations.[25] Furthermore, the regulations also provided for non-official members to constitute a majority over ex-officio and official members in all the seven provincial Legislative Councils. Interestingly, in each of the provincial councils, the number of members provided for by the regulations was less than the maximum number of members permitted by the Act itself.[26] The municipalities, the universities and commercial organisations were to constitute electorates for these councils.[27] The Indian National Congress, however, was not pleased with these majorities. Besides protesting the grant of communal electorates, it described these non-official majorities as 'unsatisfactory' and thus 'ineffective and unreal'.[28] But this dissatisfaction did not stop the nationalist leaders from utilising these expanded councils. The reforms also granted Assam and the Central Provinces provincial Legislative Councils.[29] It was widely regarded that there would be no further advance on these reforms in the near future since they would have the effect of satisfying the aspirations of a significant section of Indian society. However, the outbreak of the First World War radically changed the situation.

The Montagu–Chelmsford Reforms

The requirements of the First World War strained the resources of the British Empire to a considerable extent. Along with other colonies and dominions, India shouldered a significant share of the burden. There were naturally demands that once the war was over, India should be granted a further installment of reforms. Thus, reforms were looked upon by both the British and the Indians as a quid pro quo for the assistance rendered in the War. The real issue at stake was the nature and extent of the reforms.

With the beginnings of the First World War, the British authorities started deliberating of the possibility of a scheme of post-War reforms, mainly due to the pressure exerted by the rising nationalist demands. The sum of these deliberations was that British India was to get the largest measure of self-government, of course, compatible with the overall maintenance of British rule. Rising pressures from within the upper echelons of the Raj led to the British Cabinet agreeing to a formal declaration of policy and a ministerial visit.[30] In August 1917, Edwin Montagu, the Secretary of State for India, made his famous Declaration stating that progressive self-government was the aim of the British policy.[31]

In the meantime, Indian public opinion too had to make plans for a scheme of post-War reforms, initially in response to British requests and then taking initiatives on its own. Earlier, Lord Willingdon had asked Gopal Krishna Gokhale to suggest a scheme of constitutional reform, which the Moderate leader considered essential and immediately practical. Gokhale's scheme, while urging increased Indian participation in the Viceroy's and the Governors' Executive Councils and an element of Provincial Autonomy, also suggested an expansion in the size of the all-India and the provincial legislative councils.[32]

The next proposal was the 'Memorandum of the Nineteen', a proposal for post-War reforms submitted by 19 non-official members of the all-India Legislative Council. It called for a substantial majority of elected members in all legislative councils and the direct elections on a broad and extended franchise. Interestingly, while supporting adequate representation for Muslims, it provided that this should only be done in provinces where Muslims are in a minority. Further, it also advocated a similar proposal for Hindus where they were in a minority.[33] The 'Memorandum' was a result of an initiative taken by M.A. Jinnah.[34] This, in a sense, was an attempt to build a consensus among the nationalists in order to present a 'United Front' towards the British.

The next attempt in this direction, and the best known of them, was the Congress-Muslim League scheme of 1916 (popularly referred to as the Lucknow Pact). By 1916, both the Congress and the Muslim League were committed to evolving a joint scheme of constitutional reforms. After many hectic negotiations, the scheme was adopted by the two political organisations at their respective annual sessions, held at Lucknow in 1916. The Pact envisaged elected majorities in both the provincial councils as well as the all-India Legislative Council. It also accepted the principle of communal electorates for the Muslims at both the levels. In the all-India legislature, the Muslims were to have one-third of the seats allotted to the elected Indian members, while in each of the provinces the community was granted a fixed quantum of representation. All the elected Muslim representatives were to be elected by communal electorates.[35]

The Report on Indian Constitutional Reforms, popularly known and referred to as the Montagu–Chelmsford report, after its principal authors, Edwin Montagu and Lord Chelmsford, the then Viceroy, proposed a drastic overhaul in the constitutional structure of British India at least at the provincial level. These were the Montagu–Chelmsford reforms. The functions of the provincial government were to be divided into two parts—the first which would be handled by Executive Councillors appointed by the provincial Governor; and second which would be entrusted to Ministers appointed from among the elected members of the provincial legislatures. This was the famous scheme of dyarchy. In pursuance of this scheme, the provincial legislatures were to be substantially expanded and were to have a directly elected majority. Communal and special representation was retained at the provincial level.[36] However, no change was proposed in the structure of government at the all India level. But the report did propose an expansion of the Viceroy's Legislative Council, now to be known as the Legislative Assembly, to about 100 members, of which two-thirds were to be elected and the rest being nominated by the Governor-General. In the case of elected members, communal electorates were granted to the Muslims and the Sikhs, and special representation was granted to the landlords as well as the European and the Indian commercial interests. The report generally recommended that these elected members be directly elected by the voters but pointed out the difficulties of doing so in the case of the non-communal constituencies and hence proposed indirect elections for the same. Furthermore, it proposed that not less than one-third of the nominated members were to be non-officials who would represent minorities and special interests.[37] But this elected majority in the Legislative Assembly was nullified by the proposal to create a second chamber, the Council of State. Officials and nominated members were to constitute a majority in the Council of State, which was to have final authority in those legislative matters that the Government of India deemed important.[38]

The report, interestingly, while granting communal representation, declared itself opposed to communal electorates in principle. The grounds for opposition were a refreshing change from the previously expressed opinions about the nature of Indian society. The report did talk of Indian society being a mere collection of castes and communities. While recognising the fact that India was a deeply divided society, it pointed out that communal representation was bound to deepen these divisions further and would hamper India's journey towards self-government. However, it pointed out that since the Morley–Minto reforms had conceded communal representation to the Muslims and that the Muslims regarded this measure as being an important political safeguard, it would be difficult to abolish them. But it opposed communal representation for the Muslims in provinces where they formed a majority of the population, i.e. the Punjab and Bengal. The only other community for whom the principle of communal electorates was agreed to was the Sikh community. The report explicitly conceded that this was a reward for the services rendered during the War. It further suggested the system of nomination in order to secure representation for other minorities for such an arrangement could be easily abolished, unlike the system of communal electorates.[39]

But more significantly, the report explicitly linked representation with elections, at least at the provincial level. However, the report proposed that a committee be appointed to make detailed recommendations regarding the size of the proposed new councils, the franchise qualifications and the division of powers at the provincial level. This was the Franchise Committee, popularly known and referred to as the Southborough Committee after its Chairman, the senior British civil servant Lord Southborough.

The Government of India Act, 1919

The Southborough Committee extensively toured India, examined scores of witnesses and submitted its report in 1919.[40] The Committee was charged with proposing a scheme for the provincial legislative councils with 'as broad a franchise and as representative a council'.[41] It was also asked to examine the best means of securing representation of the minorities, important interests and the backward classes, and to suggest one from the following alternatives—communal electorates, reserved seats in multi-member constituencies, the system of nomination, or any other methods including proportional representation for the same. The Committee further had to examine the feasibility of direct elections to the lower house of the all-India legislature.

The Committee departed from the Report in some significant respects. It recommended communal electorates for the Muslims even in those provinces where the community formed a majority of the population on the grounds that it constituted a minority of the voters. It added that even the Hindus had agreed to this.[42] It also recommended separate electorates for Indian Christians, Europeans and Anglo-Indians, unlike the Report, on the grounds that representatives of the community would find it impossible to get elected by general electorates. But such electorates were not recommended in all provinces. In the case of the Indian Legislative Assembly, the lower house of the central legislature, it did not recommend direct elections citing practical difficulties.[43] Furthermore, it rejected outright the demands by the non-Brahmins of the Bombay and Madras Presidencies for communal electorates, on the grounds that they would constitute a majority of the voters in the general constituencies.[44] It also recommended that the representatives of the 'Depressed Classes' be nominated since it found it impossible to constitute an electorate for the community.[45]

The Committee stated that given the fact that under the proposed reforms many voters would be casting their votes for the first time, the simplest method of voting was required. Hence, it recommended single-member constituencies as a general rule but made an exception for the provinces of Bombay and Madras given differing political circumstances. This seems to be recognition of the fact that multi-member constituencies would be required to accommodate non-Brahmin aspirations if the communal representation was not to be granted. On the grounds of the need for simplicity, it rejected any methods of proportional representation.[46] The scene now shifted to England where a Joint Parliamentary Committee, consisting of members of both houses of the British Parliament, was appointed to examine the reform proposals as embodied in the Government of India Bill. This Committee too examined numerous witnesses and departed significantly from some of the recommendations of the Southborough Committee.

The Southborough Committee had prepared a detailed scheme about the composition of the provincial councils. However, the Joint Committee recommended that while the size of the provincial councils be fixed, their exact composition should be left to be decided by the Government of India. All that it recommended was that 70 per cent of the members of the provincial councils be elected while not more than 20 per cent should be officials.[47] It also fixed the size of the Legislative Assembly and the Council of State.[48] It further recommended that in the provincial councils of Madras and Bombay, the non-Brahmins should be granted reserved seats in multi-member constituencies; the final details to be decided after negotiations between all concerned parties.[49]

The Government of India Bill became an Act of Parliament in 1919. The Act and the Rules, made therein, granted communal representation to various minorities besides reserved seats to the non-Brahmins in Madras, and to some non-Brahmin castes in Bombay. More importantly, provision was made for direct elections to both the houses of the central legislature.[50] With the Act of 1919, the Montagu–Chelmsford reforms were translated into law. This completed the second phase or installment of constitutional reforms and devolution of power in India.

The Government of India Act, 1935

The next phase in the development of representative institutions came with the passage of the Government of India Act, 1935. This was, however, preceded by the appointment of the Indian Statutory Commission (known as the Simon Commission), the holding of the three Round Table Conferences, the announcement of the Communal

Award and the signing of the Poona Pact. The 1935 Act transformed the constitutional structure not only of British India but that of the princely states as well.[51] It envisaged an Indian federation comprising the British Indian provinces and the Indian princely states with the system of dyarchy being introduced in the central government. As far as British India was concerned, provincial autonomy was introduced. The provinces were to have mainly elected legislatures with the executive in the form of popular ministries being responsible to them. This was a major devolution of power with the long-term purpose of bolstering British control over India.

While many Indian nationalists collaborated with the British in the making of this new constitutional structure, most, mainly the Indian National Congress, by then the premier nationalist organisation and one which had the largest mass following, remained largely aloof from the entire process. However, attempts at presenting an alternative constitutional model preceded the Simon Commission. The two noteworthy attempts were the Swaraj Constitution, authored by S. Srinivasa Iyengar, a former Congress president,[52] and the All-Parties Report, which is popularly known as the Nehru Report after its chairman, Motilal Nehru.[53]

The Swaraj Constitution envisaged a federation with a bi-cameral, central federal legislature. Both the houses were to be directly elected with the upper house being a permanent one. The provinces were to have directly elected unicameral legislatures. But, more importantly, the Swaraj Constitution envisaged near adult franchise and the abolition of communal electorates. Literacy was to be the primary criterion for becoming a voter, while proportional representation was proposed to reassure the minorities.[54] The All-Parties Report followed the Swaraj Constitution in proposing a bi-cameral federal legislature and a unicameral provincial legislature. The upper house of the former was to be elected by the provincial legislatures. The Report further recommended the abolition of communal electorates, with the proviso that seats may be reserved for both the majority and the minority communities for a period of 10 years. It also recommended the adoption of adult franchise.[55]

The Simon Commission had been appointed under the provisions of the Government of India Act, 1919, which provided for the appointment of a commission within a decade to review the working of the act. Obviously, the Simon Commission took a more restrained position, as compared to the Swaraj Constitution and the Nehru Report, on the issue of constitutional reforms. This was not surprising since the entire exercise was to devise a constitutional solution that would ensure British control over India while simultaneously accommodating nationalist demands for greater participation in the administration. At the provincial level, the Commission proposed ministries responsible to the legislature with some safeguards.[56] The Commission further recommended an increase in the size of the provincial legislatures[57] and the continuation of communal electorates. It also rejected proportional representation as an alternative to communal representation.[58] While recommending the abolition of reserved seats for the non-Brahmins in Madras, it favoured a continuation of reserved seats for the non-Brahmins in Bombay.[59] As regards to the extension of the franchise, the Commission rejected adult suffrage as 'impracticable'. However, it admitted that the prevailing franchise qualifications had created a limited electorate, and hence recommended its enlargement by broadening the franchise. A committee was to be appointed to examine the issue and it would be charged with making recommendations to expand the electorate to up to 10 per cent of the total population.[60]

In the case of the central legislature, the Commission sought to turn the clock back by proposing that members of the provincial legislatures elect the members of the Federal Assembly, the lower house, by proportional representation.[61] It was claimed that PR would enable the abolition of communal representation.[62] It did not make any firm recommendations regarding the Council of State, the upper chamber of the central legislature.

As a political strategy to satisfy the political aspirations of the Indians, the Simon Commission was a failure. Its all-British character evoked strong protests. Most of the political organisations in India agreed upon a boycott of the Commission. The strength of these protests and boycotts led Lord Irwin, the Viceroy, to suggest that the British government convene a conference to deliberate upon the constitutional future of India and to settle related issues. Thus was born the idea of a Round Table Conference.[63]

Three Round Table Conferences were held in London in the early 1930s. The first and the second conferences saw serious attempts to resolve the communal question plaguing India, which essentially meant how and in what proportion was political power in any future constitutional arrangement going to be shared between the two principal religious communities of India—the Hindus and the Muslims. However, these attempts floundered since no power-sharing formula could be devised.[64] However, despite the failure, the first two conferences led to two concrete outcomes. The first was the idea that British Indian provinces and the Indian princely states should be joined together in a federation. The second was a settlement imposed by the British but only as far as the provincial legislatures were concerned, which spelled out how seats in these legislatures were to be allocated between various religious communities and economic interest groups. This settlement was popularly known as the Communal Award. Apart from reiterating the principle of communal electorates being granted to those communities that had already been granted this concession by the 1919 Act, the Award further granted separate electorates to the Depressed Classes or the 'untouchables' among the Hindus. But unlike other communities, the Depressed Classes were to have two votes. They were to vote along with the caste Hindus in the general electorates, as well as have separate electorates to themselves.[65]

It was this provision in the Award that led to Gandhi embarking on a fast-unto-death against what he regarded as attempts to divide the Hindu society. This led to the Poona Pact that replaced separate electorates for the Depressed Classes with joint electorates with reserved seats.[66] This agreement was largely accepted by the British government.

It had also been decided at the second conference that an expert committee be appointed to recommend the franchise qualifications keeping in mind the Simon Commission's recommendation and the conference's decision to enfranchise a certain stipulated proportion of the population. This was the Indian Franchise Committee, known after its chairman, Lord Lothian, as the Lothian Committee. These developments formed the backdrop to the Government of India Act, 1935. Electorally speaking, the Act was retrogressive. Whereas the 1919 Act had provided for direct elections to the lower house of the all-India legislature, the 1935 Act provided for indirect elections to the same by elected members of the lower house of the provincial legislatures. Furthermore, the representatives in the all-Indian legislature of the princely states were to be nominated by the princes, and the people of these states were to have no voice in who their representatives would be. The provincial legislatures, as well as the upper house of the all-India legislature, was to be largely directly elected, albeit on a restricted franchise. However, the Act granted the right to vote to women, besides providing for reserved constituencies for women. It also provided for upper houses of the legislature in a few provinces. Another committee, the Indian Delimitation Committee, appointed after the passage of the 1935 Act, examined the issue of how the constituencies for the legislatures were to be delimited. It was known as the Hammond Committee after its chairman, Sir Laurie Hammond.

The 1935 Act had stipulated that the federation would come into existence only if a certain number of princely states agreed to accede to it. But this did not happen. As a result, the only part of the Act that related to the provinces was implemented, and thus elections to the provincial assemblies were held in 1937. The provincial executive or the council of ministers then became responsible to the elected provincial legislatures. However, this marked the beginning of a period of constitutional stagnation, which was broken by the exigencies of the Second World War. This was not quite surprising, as the 1935 Act was designed in a sense to contain the nationalist aspirations.

As the War wound down, it was widely realised that an agreement over power-sharing between the Congress and the Muslim League was the key to any feasible constitutional settlement for India. The period of the 1940s saw renewed attempts to sketch out the contours of such a settlement. The most well-known and note-worthy attempt was the Sapru Committee, known after its chairman, the distinguished lawyer and Moderate leader, Sir Tej Bahadur Sapru.[67] It framed a skeletal constitutional framework for India that it described as interim proposals. It further recommended that if the Muslims agreed to abandon their insistence on separate electorates, the lower House of the all-India legislature would have an equal number of caste Hindu and Muslim representatives elected by a system of joint electorates with reserved seats from non-princely areas.

Another such constitutional proposal was that of a committee consisting of members with Hindu Mahasabhaite affiliations. It recommended adult franchise as a solution to the vexed question of communal electorates, weightages for minorities and reservations of seats. The committee recommended that none of the constituencies for the provincial legislature be a single-member one.[68] Another proposal for a constitutional proposal was contained in Dr B.R. Ambedkar's address to the Scheduled Caste Federation, popularly known as the 'Communal Deadlock and a Way to Solve it'. This proposal could be politely described as fantastically unrealistic. It recommended that the representation of the majority community at the all-India level and in the provinces be capped at 40 per cent, irrespective of its share in the population, on the grounds that the character of a majority in India was communal rather than political. This fact, in Ambedkar's opinion, made majority rule 'untenable in theory and unjustifiable in practice'. But more importantly, Ambedkar recommended as an alternative to separate electorates, multi-member constituencies so as to enable the minorities to elect what he described as 'real and not nominal representatives'.[69]

The Constituent Assembly and After

With the transfer of power imminent, a Constituent Assembly was formed in 1946. The first meeting of the Assembly was held in 1946 and was boycotted by the Muslim League, pending a satisfactory and mutually acceptable constitutional settlement.[70] As the Assembly commenced its work, the thorny question of electoral representation naturally made itself felt within the broader framework of a political settlement. Dr Ambedkar was perhaps the only leading political figure to come up with a proposal of a constitutional framework. He proposed that all minorities be granted seats in the legislatures in proportion to their share of the population. Where the share of the majority community in population was huge, all minorities would be granted weightage—i.e. a share of legislative seats in excess of their proportion in the populace, in order to check the possibility of the majority community abusing its numerical dominance. This weightage was to be granted in inverse proportion to a community's educational, economic and social standing. Ambedkar also strongly argued for separate electorates and adult franchise. Curiously, he also proposed a system of cumulative voting.[71] Generally, cumulative, voting is regarded as an arrangement that ensures the representation of minorities without recourse to any specific institutional arrangements, such as reserved seats or separate electorates. This necessarily has to be applied in multi-member constituencies. Here, Ambedkar recommended cumulative voting within a system of separate electorates. He seems to have assumed the existence of political minorities within communities, and hence perhaps this proposal of his.

The June 3 Plan which announced the division of British India into two separate dominions, India and Pakistan, resolved the deadlock created by the League's boycott of the Constituent Assembly. But despite the deadlock, the various sub-committees of the Assembly had begun work. Adult franchise was adopted despite some murmurs. The mammoth task of preparing electoral rolls on this basis was accomplished rather smoothly.[72] With Partition, the option of separate or communal electorates for minorities was simply ruled out and replaced by joint electorates. The only remaining question was whether there would be reserved seats for minorities. Initially, the Draft Constitution of India, finalised in 1948, did make provision for reserved seats. However, by 1949, the mood had changed. Amidst considerable behind-the-scenes political activity, except for the Scheduled Tribes and Scheduled Castes, no other community was granted reserved seats. The Anglo-Indians were granted representation through the provision of the President and the Governors of some states nominating the representatives of the community to the lower house of Parliament and the lower houses of the provincial legislatures respectively.[73] The Constituent Assembly, after considerable debate, also decided that some provinces would have bi-cameral legislatures.

Thus, the architecture of the Indian electoral system was set in place. Two pieces of legislation, both titled 'The Representation of the Peoples Act', the first passed in 1950 and the second in 1951, filled in the details. The second prohibited cumulative voting in multi-member constituencies. The Election Commission, another body set up by the Constitution, was entrusted with the task of delimitation of the constituencies as per the provisions of the first Act. The Commission was to be advised by provincial Parliamentary Advisory Committees in finalising the delimitation proposals. These proposals, or Delimitation Orders, were laid before the Provisional Parliament, the nomenclature that the Constituent Assembly had adopted for itself once its task of framing a constitution was over. These orders were debated and amended in Parliament and then notified.

The first general elections in India were held in late 1951 and early 1952. Most of the constituencies were single-member ones. The overwhelming majority of the constituencies, where provision was made for reservations for the Scheduled Castes, were double-member seats. This system of some two-member constituencies lasted till the 1960s with the passage of the Two-Members Constituencies (Abolition) Act, 1961, which in turn was repealed in 2001. Therefore, while the Constitution prohibits separate or communal electorates, it certainly does not prohibit multi-members seats and/or proportional representation by means of a Single Transferable Vote. Thus, the way to re-imagine the institutional design of the electoral system, and by extension, that of legislative institutions and thus of political representation in India is open.

4

Claims to Political Representation

The process of the development of representative institutions in India was marked by claims of varying intensity made by diverse communities and sectional interests for political representation. Communities and interests, through their spokespersons, deployed a wide range of arguments and reasons to justify their demands, which in turn evoked counterclaims. The colonial regime accepted some and rejected some demands for representation on a variety of grounds. This chapter seeks to examine and analyse these very arguments and reasons. The very acceptance of the claim of any group logically necessitated a working and, in some instances, a legal definition of what constituted a particular group. The very act of granting political representation led to the drawing of sharp group boundaries. The present chapter also seeks to trace the process of group definition in these cases. Only those demands which were strongly and sometimes vehemently made as well as those whom the Raj regarded as worthy of consideration have been discussed here.

The colonial regime was the ultimate arbiter of these claims, whose acceptance or rejection was more often than not governed by political exigencies. The assumption that underlay the debates generated by these claims was that India was not a homogenous society but a motley assemblage of castes, religious communities, tribes and other groups whose interests were supposed to be conflicting rather than complementary. If these interests, however defined, were conflicting, it then became necessary that they be represented. But this assumption did not emerge instantaneously but seems to have been a product of a long drawn process. While it is true that the Raj encouraged or in some cases gave a fillip to claims of political representation based on religion and caste, in certain other cases it denied those on the basis of sects within religious communities by assuming homogeneity of these communities. Thus, the regime laid itself open to the charges of practising a policy of divide and rule or, to put it more politely, a 'policy of counterpoise and concession',[1] yet one could also grant the colonial regime in some measure the benefit of doubt. It can be plausibly argued that caste, in the case of the Hindus, and religious identity in the case of the broader Indian society were the easiest categories that were then available on which a system of electoral representation could be constructed or based. That the Raj could have chosen not to do so assumes that this would have been proved acceptable to many vocal sections of Indian society and that it was blind to the obvious advantageous possibilities of divide and rule. It has been further argued that since the British did not regard representation as a substantive activity, they chose to emphasise the need for the representatives to be 'typical of the represented'. The Raj was more interested in who the representative was rather than what he did.[2]

But this is a partial argument. The authenticity and legitimacy of the acts of the representative, in any case, would have depended on his or her sharing the social attributes—whether of caste or religion, of those who he was representing or claiming to represent. Any arguments, demands or claims made by an individual who did not share the characteristics of those whom he was representing or claiming to represent could be dismissed on these very grounds. Even if the representation was thought to be a substantive activity, what could be described as the mirror theory of representation would still have been valid. Furthermore, many castes and religious communities did make claims for political representation explicitly on the grounds that those who did not share their social attributes could not possibly represent them in the sense of protecting and advocating their interests, material or otherwise. This argument, in fact, was at the heart of the claims made by diverse sections of Indian society.

The communities and interests whose claims to political representation would be examined here are the Muslims, the Sikhs, the non-Brahmins of the Madras and the Bombay Presidencies, the Depressed Classes (also known during the period under discussion as the Scheduled Castes), the aborigines/Scheduled Tribes and the

Anglo-Indians (earlier referred to as the Eurasians). Of course, there were some other communities which made specific claims, such as the Europeans settled in India and the Parsis but their demands rarely influenced the course of Indian politics beyond a point. The common factor among many of the demands that these groups made was that their claims were couched in terms of being a minority—for instance, those made by the Muslims and the Sikhs. Hence, this chapter also explores how the term 'minority' came to be defined, and the manner in which its meaning was sought to be extended beyond the numerical. Demands were also made for 'weighted representation', which meant that the quantum of representation that a particular community was to secure would be more than what was warranted by its numbers. The justification was offered more often than not for the claim that minorities deserved excessive representation. Similarly, claims to representation were also made in terms of 'backwardness' in the case of the Muslims of the Punjab and Bengal as well as the non-Brahmins of Madras and Bombay Presidencies. Political representation was seen not merely as a protective device. Access to power was seen as a path that led out of the very same condition of 'backwardness'. Broadly speaking, all these demands and claims reflected the assumption that communities qua communities, defined either in terms of religion or caste, had common interests, material and otherwise, and that political representation was essential to further and protect them.

The first clear statement on the part of the Raj as to whose representation was considered to be essential came in the 1888 report of a committee appointed by the then Viceroy, Lord Dufferin, to consider the expansion of the existing provincial councils. The committee identified the classes which required representation. The term 'class' was used in a dual sense—to denote specific economically defined groups as well as religiously defined communities, both of which possessed certain interests. The interests that it identified were the following—the hereditary nobility and the landed classes; trading, professional and agricultural classes; the planting and the commercial European community; and lastly and curiously, the interests of stable and effective administration. The last mentioned, obviously, meant something that needed to be preserved and safeguarded. The committee also talked of minorities that required representation, and specifically mentioned the Parsis in Bombay and the Muslims of Madras. It also referred to the Hindus and the Muslims as the 'two great classes' into which the bulk of the population was divided.[3] Clamour for political representation increased as political consciousness spread among various sections of Indian society so much so that formal memoranda, presented during the Indian tour of Edwin Montagu and Lord Chelmsford, making such demands were compiled to be published as an official parliamentary Command Paper.[4]

Yet, the very validity of such claims did not go unchallenged. In a sense, at stake were competing visions of what constituted Indian society. While the British assumptions that India was a mere conglomerate of castes and communities who had very little in common were shared by many representatives of minor religious groups and non-elite Hindu castes, the nationalist leadership articulated the vision of Indian society constituting a political community, albeit one which had not been formed fully. For instance, Gandhi, at the second Round Table Conference, while claiming that his fellow delegates either represented no one but themselves or at the most sectional interests, also claimed that he as the leader of the Indian National Congress represented all Indians. Such attempts did not deny the internal social heterogeneity of Indian society but rather denied that this fact prevented the constitution of a homogenous political community.

The Muslims

Though the first extended articulation of the demand of the Muslims came in 1906 with what was known as the Simla Address that preceded the establishment of the All-India Muslim League, the community had begun to demand separate political representation for itself much earlier. In the late nineteenth century, fears were expressed that since the Muslims were a numerical minority, any electoral system that lacked safeguarding provisions for the community would lead to it being swamped by the majority community (i.e. the Hindus). There are also arguments that representation in proportion to numbers would ignore the prominent position of the community in India.[5] Thus, apart from the feeling of distinctiveness, there existed a fear of political marginalisation of a community that had enjoyed political power for long, which were articulated, among others, by Sir Syed Ahmed Khan. These claims, of course, did not go unchallenged and were sought to be refuted by those Muslims closely associated with the Indian National Congress. But by 1896, demands were being made for separate electorates.[6]

The Simla Address, submitted to the then Viceroy, Lord Minto, on the eve of the Morley–Minto reforms made these arguments in demanding political representation for the Muslims. While conceding that the community did share many common interests with other religious communities, mainly the Hindus, the address stressed the distinctive interests of the Muslim community. It further rehearsed a familiar argument that any electoral system that created an electorate on a non-confessional basis would necessarily lead to Hindu domination and thus Muslim marginalisation. The address also demanded that the quantum of representation be over and above that the community would secure on the basis of its numbers, since it deserved so on grounds of its 'political importance' and their contribution to the defence of the British Empire. It asked that this share at all levels and in all spheres of decision-making should be officially stipulated not only for the Muslims but for the Hindus as well. This was to be determined by the 'numerical strength, social status, local influence and special requirements of either community'.[7] The Raj concurred with this argument of the Muslims when it conceded that the community had not secured representation 'commensurate with its numbers and political and historical importance'.[8] Moreover, the Government of India in its despatch to the Secretary of State for India acknowledged the distinctiveness of the Muslims.[9]

The demands made by the Muslims evoked a wide range of reactions. The Bombay Presidency Association pointed out that there were many Muslims who were converted descendants of Hindus and that their 'habits and modes of thought' hardly differed from the Hindus.[10]

Presumably, this nullified the claim of the Muslims that they were a distinct community with separate interests and, by extension, their claims towards separate representation. The claims that the Muslims were not a homogenous entity and had sectarian differences among them[11] and that the minorities per se had no interests distinctive from the wider Indian society[12] were made to deny the demands for separate representation for the community. It was hardly surprising that the Muslims whose opinions were elicited during the reforms process welcomed separate representation.

The demand of the Muslims for separate representation also had provincial angles to it. This was so because while the Muslims were an all-India minority, they constituted a majority of the population in Eastern Bengal and Assam, and the Punjab. Similar was the case with the community in the Bombay Presidency where it was a minority in the province as a whole but a majority in Sindh. In the Punjab, opposition to separate representation for the Muslims came not only from the Hindus and the Sikhs but also from many European government officials. The last argued that it would anger other communities and generate strife.[13] One official, A. Meredith, the Commissioner of Delhi Division, was blunt and opposed these demands saying it was 'unnecessary to flatter Muhammadan susceptibilities'.[14] These officials, of course, did not envisage a situation where the Muslims would be absent from or marginalised the legislative councils but proposed that nominations be used to redress any imbalance.

As far as the Punjab was concerned, it was also argued by a Hindu government official that since the Hindus and the Muslims were equal in political strength there was hardly any reason for the Muslims to be granted special concessions.[15] Some non-official Hindus, like Raja Narendra Nath (later to emerge as a prominent leader of the Hindus of the Punjab), claimed that since the Muslims were a majority in the province there was simply no need for any such provision.[16] It was also denied that the Muslims in the province were backward which necessitated separate representation.[17] The Muslims could not wish away their majority in the Punjab but it was argued that given the community's general backwardness it could not hold its own against the others and hence separate representation was necessary. The usual arguments of the historical and political importance of the community were also repeated. It was also claimed that the Muslims and the Hindus had different interests, and that the Hindu elected members of the provincial council had not represented Muslim interests.[18]

The Morley–Minto reforms for the first time explicitly recognised the Muslims as a distinct political entity for the purposes of representation through elections. The community was the only one that was granted recognition in this manner and that predictably drew strong criticism from the Indian National Congress, which denounced separate electorates in its annual sessions of 1909, 1910 and 1911. But by 1912, the organisation had changed its position and accepted separate electorates as a matter of expediency, while demanding that such a concession be extended to the Hindus in Sindh and the Punjab where they were a minority.[19] Opposition to communal electorates was reiterated at the 1913 session, and in 1914, it modified its stance by merely stating that it deprecated such a system and urged that it should not be extended to the local bodies. At the 1915 session, no such opposition was expressed and finally by the Lucknow Pact of 1916, the Congress finally accepted communal electorates for the Muslims.

The Report on Indian Constitutional Reforms, known as the Montagu–Chelmsford Report, granted separate representation to the Muslims without any reasoned discussion. It merely noted that such a concession had been granted during the Morley–Minto reforms, and hence was to be continued. It added the community regarded it as an essential safeguard and that any attempt to abolish it would lead to political difficulties, namely a probable straining of the community's loyalty to the Raj. But the Report clarified that this was to be done only where the Muslims were not a majority of the voters.[20] This meant that once again provincial considerations became significant. It is worth noting that the Lucknow Pact had granted communal electorates to the community in the Muslim majority provinces of the Punjab and the Bengal, as well as in the Bombay Presidency as a whole.

But this principle adopted by the Report was contested by the provincial governments of the Muslim majority provinces. The Bengal government claimed that any move to withdraw concessions granted to the community would be resented. It added that it adhered to the Muslim arguments that in Bengal despite a numerical majority in many districts their interests there would not be safeguarded due to the predominance of Hindu landlords and money-lenders.[21] The Punjab government did not protest vocally but noted that in a system of joint electorates that excluded the Sikhs, the Muslims and the Hindus would be elected in equal numbers. This would mean that those Muslims elected qua Muslims would be a minority as compared to the elected non-Muslims. This, the Punjab government noted, would not please the Muslims, and did not fail to remind all concerned that the Lucknow Pact had conceded separate electorates to the community in the province. Neither did it fail to report its opinion that communal electorates would solve the vexed question of settling claims for political representation.[22]

The Franchise Committee or the Southborough Committee appointed to translate the Montagu–Chelmsford reforms into reality worked within the framework of the reforms scheme. It toured the entire country holding discussions with the provincial government and examining witnesses. There was consensus in the submission made by the provincial governments to the Committee as to the necessity of providing for separate representation for the Muslims. The two provincial governments of the Muslim majority provinces raised the spectre of Hindu domination and consequent political marginalisation of the Muslims to support separate representation for the community in their respective provinces. If the Bengal government pointed out that except for a few districts, the Muslims were a minority in the electorate and the Punjab government declaring, even assuming, a best-case scenario for the community in mixed electorates would secure far less seats than its share in the population warranted, thus defeating the very purpose of reforms by leaving it dissatisfied.[23]

The committee justified communal representation for Muslims in the Punjab and Bengal on grounds that while the community constituted a majority of the population, in view of the proposed franchise qualifications, it would a minority of the electorate.[24] Thus, the yardstick of what constituted a minority was the strength in the electorate, and not the population at large. An overview of the evidence tendered to the Southborough Committee does not reveal any strong opposition to the Muslim demand for separate representation. However, the Central Provinces and Berar government reiterated its opposition so far as the province was concerned on the grounds that the Muslims constituted merely four per cent of the population in the province and hence it was almost impossible to constitute suitable communal electorates.[25] Opposition to separate representation for Muslims came from Assam. K.C. Das opposed such a provision for the Muslims of Surma Valley on grounds that the community there was neither in a minority nor backward.[26] Support for the position that where Muslims were a majority of the voters the community did not require separate electorates came from Aminur Rahman of Bengal. He stated that as far as Bengal was concerned, such a provision was patently unfair. He suggested that the principle of communal electorates for the minority be applied at the constituency level and not at the provincial level.[27]

The theme that many Muslims in India were descendants of converts from Hinduism recurred during the Montagu–Chelmsford reforms, albeit only once. Raja Kishori Lal Goswami made the same point as far as Bengal was concerned in order to deny communal electorates for the community.[28] This argument was repeated by Sir John Rees during the examination of witnesses by the Joint Select Committee on the Government of India Bill, 1919, which was sharply contested by Sir James Meston who gave evidence on behalf of the Government of India.[29] Objection to the Muslims of Bengal being granted separate representation came from Sir William Meyer, a senior ICS officer. He claimed that doing so for a community that was in a majority was a 'mockery'.[30]

In the end, the proportion of Muslim representation for the Punjab and Bengal as stipulated in the Lucknow Pact was incorporated in the Government of India Act, 1919. However, in the 1920s, there were voices asking for the Muslims of Bengal to be given a majority of the seats in the local council on the grounds that they were a majority in the population. On the other hand, the Nehru Report rejected these demands on the very same grounds. It argued that since the community was in a majority in these two provinces, it could easily secure a majority in the local legislature—more so since the report had recommended adult franchise. It added that even if the Muslims did not do so in the Punjab, they were bound to be a powerful minority, which no one could ignore. The report further argued that the fears of the Muslims that their numbers would be outweighed by the educational and economic strength of other communities leading to them securing a minority of the seats in any system on joint electorates were imaginary.[31] The question of separate representation for Muslims in the Punjab and Bengal figured before the Simon Commission. There was opposition to communal electorates for the community in the Punjab on grounds of it being in a majority.

An elaborate defence of separate representation for the Muslims was launched in terms of the 'rights of the minorities' by Shafaat Ahmed Khan in the 1920s. Acknowledging that the system of communal electorates was transitional, he added that it was necessary for the time being, given that the Muslims were economically and educationally backward and that there existed a lack of confidence between the two major communities of the country.[32] He also argued that separate electorates would lead to effective representation for the community.

The Muslim claims to representation through separate electorates were reiterated during the Round Table Conferences. During the first conference, Muslims leaders like Fazl-ul Haq and Raja Sher Muhammad Khan among others talked of how the Muslims had once been rulers of India, their military contribution to the British war-effort and their rights as a distinct community, all in the same breath. The claim that the Muslims could not be said to have distinct interests qua Muslims since the bulk of the community consisted of converts from Hinduism re-emerged during the first Round Table Conference. Dr B.S. Moonje, the leader of the Hindu Mahasabha, dismissed the issue of historical importance by making this claim.[33] A general overview of the Muslim demands shows that for the Muslim leadership, effective Muslim representation meant that not only should the representative be Muslim but that he should be elected only by the Muslims as well.

There were, of course, dissenting voices from within the Muslim community in this context. There were denials that the community as such possessed any distinct interests, apart from those of the wider Indian society, which necessitated separate representation. It was also argued that even if the Muslims were electorally marginalised in joint electorates, it should not be a matter for concern, since any attempts by the Hindus to dominate the community would rebound on them.[34] However, these were straws in the wind. The very notion of a homogenous 'Muslim interest' was questioned by a mention of the existence of 'untouchables' among the community.[35] There were also voices that claimed that the Muslim demand for separate representation emanated from their consciousness as a distinct community and the 'memories of past domination' that were fresh.[36]

In the Constituent Assembly, there were demands for ensuring Muslim representation. But after Partition, the Congress was in no mood to entertain these demands which were rejected but not before the notion of the Muslims constituting a homogenous political community were questioned. Tajamul Hussain, a member of the Assembly, reminded his fellow members that he was a Shia and that his community had constantly stood against separate electorates.[37]

The Sikhs

Demands had been made by the Sikhs for political representation during the making of the Morley–Minto scheme. But these were largely ignored. The Punjab government in its proposals for an enlarged provincial council had provided for separate Sikh representation, albeit by nomination.[38] There were also claims by both Muslims and the Hindus that there did not exist much of a difference between the Hindus and the Sikhs. Both argued on these lines to prevent the emergence of a potential claimant for separate representation. The Sikhs, whose opinions about the proposed reforms were invited by the Punjab government, naturally supported the demand for separate representation for their community. It was argued that the Sikhs were more backward than the Muslims of the province[39] and that they were an important community worthy of consideration.[40] The most articulate advocacy of the Sikh claims came from Sardar Sundar Singh Majithia. He argued that if backwardness were to be a criterion for granting separate representation to the Muslims, then the Sikhs surely deserved it. At the same time, he evoked historical memories by pointing out that the British had conquered Punjab from the Sikhs and were the last to be defeated by the Raj. The usual themes of military service and loyalty were also evoked.[41] The Sikh leaders also pointed out that if the Muslims were a minority, then so was their community. There were almost no official opinions in favour of the Sikh demands.

The First World War, however, was to change the outlook of the Raj. The Montagu–Chelmsford Report was brutally honest when it granted communal electorates to the Sikhs in the Punjab. Noting that the community in the Punjab was a 'distinct and important' and that it was presently unrepresented, it added that the Sikhs 'supply a gallant and important element' to the Indian Army.[42] Thus, clearly contribution to the war effort was the reason for this concession. The Punjab government but naturally supported the Report's recommendation. The case of the Sikhs makes it clear that there was no clear yardstick by which claims to representation were accepted or rejected. It was pragmatism, pure and simple, that determined outcomes.

The Punjab government reiterated its support for separate Sikh representation in its submission to the Southborough Committee. It claimed that the role that the community had played in the province's history, the revenue it paid, and its heavy presence in the Indian Army warranted such a provision. It used a familiar argument when it claimed that the community was a minority in all districts and thus would fail to secure adequate representation in any scheme of mixed electorates.[43] It also conceded that there existed a problem in defining who exactly a Sikh was, thus indicating a problem of definitional certainty. It stipulated that anyone who claimed to be a Sikh and could be prima facie considered one would considered a Sikh for electoral purposes, since it wished to avoid what it termed 'an inquisition' on the issue.[44] The Punjab government at one stroke prevented itself from wading into the choppy waters of defining who exactly was a Sikh or what constituted the parameters of being one by simply sidestepping the issue. The Southborough Committee naturally recommended communal representation for the Sikhs but not before noting that as regards certain sections of the Punjab society, a clear-cut distinction could not be made between Sikhs and Hindus. It merely followed the Punjab government's solution when it suggested that a simple declaration before the official in charge of preparing the electoral role by a voter that he was a Sikh would suffice. The official was, of course, to be entitled to reject the claim if he doubted that the declaration was being made in good faith.[45]

The themes of contribution to the armed forces, significant position in land ownership, higher literacy rates as compared to other communities and the fact that the community had once ruled the Punjab figured in the Sikh claims for separate representation. However, the problem of definition figured in the evidence taken by the Southborough Committee. The claims of the Hindu witnesses, like Duni Chand who not only stated that it was difficult to distinguish between the two communities but that he himself was a Sikh,[46] were not difficult to understand. Separate representation, and that too one in excess of their share in population, for the Sikhs would naturally cut into the seats available for the Hindus. Not surprisingly, the Sikh witnesses denied that there could be difficulties in defining who a Sikh was. Barkat Ali, representing the Punjab Congress Committee, stated there was no point in granting separate representation to the Sikhs since they and the Hindus were practically the same in religious terms and also as far as social customs were concerned. He added that it was not in the 'national interest' to separate the two and that the there was no real demand from the Sikhs in this context.[47] Surprisingly, support for separate representation for the community came from R.N. Mudholkar, a former President of the Congress.[48]

The issue of Sikh representation was also discussed by the Joint Select Committee on the Government of India Bill, 1919. Sardar Thaker Singh, the only Sikh witness to appear before the committee, argued for separate representation on grounds of no member of the community ever being elected in the general constituencies.[49] The issue of definitions also cropped up, for Singh claimed that while Sahajdari Sikhs were judicially defined as Sikhs they had not been included during the census enumeration, thus leading to the Sikh numbers being less than what they actually were.[50] Interestingly, opposition to separate representation for the Sikhs came from Annie Besant. In a memorandum submitted to the committee, she claimed that no such provision for the community is required since its interests were the same as the Hindus.[51] This was, of course, a reiteration of the old claim that the Sikhs were a part of the wider Hindu fold. The Government of India Act 1919, of course, granted Sikhs separate electorates. However, in the later period, the Sikhs were always ready to give up their claims to separate representation provided all other communities did so.

The denial of a separate Sikh identity came from a surprising source. Sir Muhammad Shafi, the principal spokesperson of the Muslim League, in his evidence to the Simon Commission, argued that there was no real distinction between the Sikhs and the Hindus, and whatever difference did exist was analogous to that between the Shias and the Sunnis. He claimed that this distinction was being made for mere political purposes.[52] This was a clear attempt to minimise the claims of weightage for the non-Muslims in the Punjab. The Sikh witnesses naturally opposed these attempts to deny their separate existence.

The question of separate representation for the Sikhs arose once again in the wake of Partition. The Sikh demand for communal electorates and weightage was rejected in favour of reserved seats coupled with the right to contest non-reserved seats. As sentiments against reserved seats for minorities hardened, the Sikh leaders gave up this provision in return for the inclusion of the 'Scheduled Castes' among the community in the broader category of 'Scheduled Castes'.

The Indian Christians

During the Morley–Minto reforms, there were hardly any discussions on the need for representation for the Indian Christians, though the

Madras government in one of its proposals for the provincial council did suggest communal electorates for the community. However, the proposal did not go far. During the Montagu–Chelmsford reforms, there were demands for separate representation for the community but the Montagu–Chelmsford report did not concede the demand for elected representation for the Indian Christians. However, the Madras Government in its response to the report made a strong case for separate electorates to be granted to the community. Numbers, high levels of education, homogeneity and general advancement were cited along with the usual claim that no member of the community would be elected in mixed electorates.[53] The Bengal government and the Chief Commissioner of Assam, Sir Nicholas Beatson Bell, supported this position.[54]

In its submission to the Southborough Committee, the Madras government repeated its assertions about the community.[55] The Southborough Committee seems to have agreed with the assertions of the Madras government, for it was only in this province that the Indian Christians were granted separate representation.[56] It also made a broader argument on behalf of the community when it stated that such a provision was necessary to enable it to take its share in the 'rapidly developing political life of India'.[57] Perhaps the committee was indicating that conversion to a religion identified with the colonial regime had alienated the community from the wider Indian society. The electoral representation for the community also received support from many witnesses who gave evidence to the Southborough Committee. The issue of electoral representation for the community did not figure prominently during the proceedings of the Joint Select Committee on the 1919 Act. While giving evidence to the committee, Lord Southborough stated that in Madras the Indian Christians had been granted separate representations not on the basis of numbers but on that of 'quality',[58] thus echoing what the Madras government had stated earlier. The opposition to the demands of the community now came from Annie Besant. She stated that the Indian Christians were a 'favoured community' and implying that it did not need any institutional protection. She added that its inclusion in the general electorate would be desirable and she appealed to it to 'unite politically with their fellow-countrymen'.[59] While there seems to have been a consensus among the representatives of the community who appeared before the two committees about separate representation per se, there was none about the method. What were displayed were sectarian divisions. The community could not speak with a single voice.

These divisions were also evident during the proceedings before the Simon Commission. Discrimination internal to the Christian community on the basis of caste emerged, perhaps for the first time in the political arena. A delegation of the Christian Depressed Classes appeared before the Commission to ask for the community to be merged into the general (i.e. Hindu electorate). It claimed that the community was marginalised in the Indian Christian communal electorate and that those elected from these constituencies represented only the upper caste Christians.[60] The church leaders who gave evidence to the Commission, of course, denied the severity of caste discrimination within the Indian Christian community.

The Christian representatives to the first Round Table Conference found themselves divided on the issue of separate representation. One claimed that if other communities were to be granted separate representation, then the Indian Christians too should receive the same privilege, while another made a strong plea for communal electorates. The question remerged before the Lothian Committee, which also saw discussions over sectarian divisions as well as the prevalence of caste discrimination among the Indian Christians. Here, the general leaning of the representatives of the community was in favour of communal electorates, albeit on different grounds. George Joseph, who was long associated with the Congress, actually advocated communal electorate on purely pragmatic grounds. He claimed that as long as stronger minorities were granted communal electorates, there was no reason why the Indian Christians should be denied the same.[61] Joseph, of course, had no objection if communal electorates were abolished as a part of a general political settlement.

The Indian Christian spokespersons also sought to downplay sectarian and caste divisions within the community. When asked about the representation of 'Depressed Class' Christians in the communal electorates for the community, M.S. Sreshtha, a member of the Madras Provincial Council, claimed that a convention could be arrived at whereby this section would secure some seats. He further claimed that the non-'Depressed Class' Christians were safeguarding the interests of their 'untouchable' co-religionists,[62] thus refuting probable demands for a quota within a quota. However, support for such a demand came from a surprising direction, P. Khalifullah Sahib Bahadur, a leading Muslim Leaguer from Madras. In his response to a question asked by Sunder Singh Majithia about Sikh and Muslim 'Depressed Classes' being granted the same political concessions as their Hindu counterparts, he concurred.[63] Khalifullah added that any scheme to combine all 'Depressed Class' voters, irrespective of religion, into a common electorate would not work.

The Indian Christians ultimately were granted communal electorates in the Government of India Act, 1935. In the wake of independence, Indian Christians were initially granted reserved seats only in the provinces of Bombay and Madras. This provision was rejected when reserved seats for all minority communities were abolished. However, caste discrimination within the Christian community was mentioned only once in the Constituent Assembly, when T.J.M. Wilson from Madras made a strong plea to consider the plight of his community whom he termed 'Harijan Christians'.[64]

The Non-Brahmins

The claim for the representation for the non-Brahmins first emerged in the Madras Presidency. The driving force behind these demands, strongly articulated primarily in Madras and Bombay, was the desire to restrict the Brahmin domination of public life in both the provinces just as the fear of Hindu domination fuelled Muslim demands for political representation. A desire to prevent this predominance of the Brahmins was reflected in the Madras government's proposal for an expanded provincial council made in the run-up to the Morley–Minto reforms.

It proposed a communal electorate restricted to the Brahmins, along with ones for Muslims, Christians and what was described as 'all other persons'.[65] The last category presumably entailed the non-Brahmins. This attempt to provide caste-based representation, albeit in a small measure, generated strong criticism. It was not surprising that Brahmins objected to it but many ICS officers and non-Brahmins too criticised it for different reasons. Furthermore, the fact of Brahmin domination was sought to be justified. V. Krishnaswami Aiyar described the scheme as a 'forced plan to minimise the natural influence which culture and intellectual leadership and hereditary attachment' had given to the Brahmins.[66] It was also claimed that the Brahmins per se had no special interest to serve,[67] which meant that the community served the interests of the general public a position many would have found hard to accept. The most astounding claim was that these days it was difficult to 'say who comes under the definition of a Brahmin'.[68] Another non-Brahmin dismissed the need for both caste and religion-based representation, arguing that the legislative council was not 'a religious or social conference that ought to embrace representatives of all castes and religions'.[69] Alexander Cardew, a senior officer in the Madras government, was critical of the attempt to restrict Brahmin numbers in the local council, as it would give 'inadequate representation to the ablest and best educated class in the country'.[70] This was ironical since in the 1920s, Cardew was to be one of the most strident supporters of the non-Brahmin cause. Supporters of this scheme were rare, and it was put onto the backburner.

In the Bombay Presidency, despite the fact that as early as 1906, the provincial government had decried the preponderance of the Brahmins whose interests it claimed were 'not identical with those of the mass of the Marathas and the other castes',[71] the official scheme did not propose caste-based representation. There were, of course, some demands from the non-Brahmin communities, namely the Lingayats, for separate representation on the grounds the community contributed large amounts by way of land revenue and income tax to the exchequer.[72] A general demand for the representation of the backward castes was made.[73] There was no official enthusiasm for caste-based representation either. The joint report of the Divisional Commissioners noted that while it would be difficult to ignore the interests of the backward communities, caste-based communal electorates would deprive the voters of their right to elect a representative of their choice and that there was no evidence that the members of the professional classes (this seems to be a short-hand for Brahmins, at least as far as the Marathi speaking areas of the province were concerned) had failed to articulate the needs of the people at large. They added that it would not be advisable to sharpen caste differences.[74]

The Montagu–Chelmsford Report had noted the Madras non-Brahmin demands for communal electorates but had rejected them stating that it would be unwise to extend this principle any further.[75] The Madras government did not make any strong response to this rejection. However, in its submission to the Southborough Committee, it strongly demanded separate representation for the non-Brahmins, preferably through communal electorates. It argued that though the non-Brahmins were in a majority, the Brahmins who would deploy their educational superiority and social pre-eminence to sweep the elections would outmanoeuvre them. It cited the results of the previous elections to the local council to buttress its assertions.[76] A detailed note by Cardew accompanied the submission, wherein a bleak picture of Brahmin domination was painted.[77] In the discussions with the Committee, the Madras government remained firm on its support for the non-Brahmin demands.

The Bombay government equivocated on the issue. It merely set out the three different viewpoints on the question of non-Brahmin representation in the provinces, an indication perhaps that it was divided on the issue. But it did introduce for the edification of the committee, the census category of Maratha and the Allied Castes accompanied by detailed population statistics. These Allied Castes did not intermarry with the Marathas but could interdine.[78]

The South Indian Liberal Federation, the political vehicle of the Madras non-Brahmins, stressed the theme of the Brahmin stranglehold over the province. The Brahmins were declared to be incapable of articulating or protecting the interests of the non-Brahmins.

Apprehension was expressed that the non-Brahmins voters, despite being in a majority, would be swayed by Brahmin influences. But the fact that the Federation essentially represented the landed non-Brahmin castes was revealed when the statement clarified that heterogeneity of the community did not matter, since particular regions of Madras were dominated by particular castes, thus ensuring all castes under the broad category of 'non-Brahmin' would be elected and thus would secure representation.[79] On the other hand, spokespersons of the Bombay non-Brahmins stressed, along with the spectre of Brahmin domination, the backwardness of the non-Brahmin castes. The general argument in Bombay was that the non-Brahmins were 'helpless' when faced with Brahmin influence.[80]

The veteran Congressman, P. Kesava Pillai, a non-Brahmin himself, questioned the theme of Brahmin dominance of political, social and administrative spheres in the Madras Presidency. Drawing upon his experience derived from a long stint on the Madras legislative council, Pillai in fact claimed that his Brahmin colleagues 'had never done harm to anybody', adding that they had joined him in the fight for the rights of all sections of society. He further claimed that in some parts of the province, Brahmins were more sympathetic to the cause of the 'untouchables' than some of the non-Brahmins, and that in the past 'Brahmin ascendancy had been to the good of the people'.[81]

The Madras government, a strong supporter of the non-Brahmin demands, was reminded by the Southborough Committee that it had opposed caste-based representation during the Morley–Minto reforms. When asked about this shift of position, H.G. Stokes, the Acting Secretary to the Government, evaded the issue by saying he did not know about it.[82] The Bombay government persisted in its equivocation on granting separate representation to the non-Brahmins of its province. The reason might be that while in Madras the non-Brahmin issue was spread almost throughout the province, in Bombay it was confined to the Marathi-speaking areas. Hence, the Bombay government could probably afford to do so. Furthermore, unlike in Madras, the non-Brahmin movement in Bombay was dominated by a single caste-group—the Maratha community. Hence, in Bombay the demands of the non-Brahmins were often couched and referred to in terms of those of the Marathas. Furthermore, the non-Brahmin movement had a long legacy of principled opposition to the dominant position enjoyed by the Maharashtrian Brahmins in the local society derived from Mahatma Jyotirao Phule. L.C. Crump who appeared before the Southborough Committee as the representative of the Bombay Government noted that it was difficult to define who a Maratha was[83] but did submit a detailed statistical chart of the population of the Marathas and the allied castes. This definitional problem was questioned by Bhaskarrao Jadhav, a leading light of the non-Brahmin movement who argued that it would be 'easier to define a Maratha than to define a Brahmin'.[84]

An acknowledgement of the internal homogeneity and stratification within the category 'non-Brahmin' can be seen in the evidence of K.R. Koregawkar, representing the Maratha Aikyechhu Sabha, who mentioned that the real division among the Hindus was between the advanced and the backward castes rather than the Brahmins and the non-Brahmins[85] but A.B. Latthe claimed that the terms Backward Castes and non-Brahmins were synonymous and that he preferred the second term for it was easy to define.[86]

There appears to be a distinct difference of approach on part of the Brahmin leaders of Madras, on one hand, and those from Bombay on the other, towards the non-Brahmin demands for separate representation. The Madras leaders were stridently opposed to communal electorates for the non-Brahmins. They rehearsed the old arguments of non-Brahmins being in a majority. But they were willing to consider some form of reserved seats. However, almost all, in particular Govinda Raghava Aiyar, C.P. Ramaswami Aiyar and K. Srinivasa Ayyangar, challenged the validity of the category of 'non-Brahmin'.[87]

The Bombay leaders' acknowledgement, albeit grudging, of the non-Brahmin claims had a precedent. Gopal Krishna Gokhale's scheme for post-war political reform prepared in 1915 had made provision for representation of the Lingayats.[88] Most of the schemes for the Bombay council proposed by the Brahmin leaders from the province suggested reserved seats for the non-Brahmins. But they did not allow non-Brahmin claims to go uncontested. R.P. Paranjpye presciently predicted the development of differences among the non-Brahmins and denied that the non-Brahmins would be electorally marginalised due to the influence of the Brahmins.[89]

Interestingly, the Madras Presidency Muslim League also opposed communal electorates for the non-Brahmins. An examination of its submission reveals that this might be because of its fear that a similar demand might emerge on sectarian lines within the Muslim community.[90] Two non-Brahmin witnesses, the Raja of Kollengode and the Raja of Ramnad, supported these positions. The former claimed that the non-Brahmins were a majority of the voters and hence not entitled to separate electorates, while the Raja of Ramnad stated that there existed a division between the advanced sections and the backward sections within the category of non-Brahmins. Kollengode was a Malabar landowner and he defined himself as a Kshatriya, thus obviously not a Brahmin, but one more allied to the Brahmins than the non-Brahmins. His statement that the non-Brahmins of Malabar were well-educated indicates a confidence to hold their own against the Brahmins.[91] Opposition to the non-Brahmin demands in Bombay came from a most surprising quarter—Dr B.R. Ambedkar in what was his first formal foray into public life. He pointed out that the non-Brahmins as such had no common interests that required protection and hence did not deserve communal electorates.[92]

The committee did take note of the strident demands made by the non-Brahmins of the Madras and the Bombay Presidencies for separate representation, only to reject them. It noted the community constituted an overwhelming majority among the population and that under any probable franchise qualifications, it would still be a majority. For this reason, the non-Brahmin demands were not accepted.[93] The Committee instead advised the non-Brahmins to organise themselves politically so as to resist Brahmin influence. This opinion of the Committee was strongly countered by the Government of India, at least as far as Madras was concerned. As it argued, the Raj could not expect any 'co-operation and goodwill' from the non-Brahmins if no measures were taken to placate them. But it took a detached and procrastinating stand in the case of Bombay, when it noted that the 'Maratha problem was not as acute as the non-Brahmin question'.[94] Clearly, a community's nuisance value counted for its demands to be granted. These views of the Government of India were echoed by the Joint Select Committee on the Government of India, 1919. It recommended reserved seats for the non-Brahmins of Madras and Bombay.[95]

The demands of the non-Brahmins received renewed attention when the Joint Select Committee on the Government of India Bill, 1919, examined witnesses on the issue. The Brahmin witnesses rehearsed their objections to the demand for communal representation by denying the validity of the category of 'non-Brahmin' and by explaining away Brahmin predominance in the local legislature. Yet, they were also willing to accept reserved seats as compromise. C.P. Ramaswamy Aiyar claimed the Brahmin dominance of the local council was due to the fact that many seats went uncontested. He added that the category 'non-Brahmin' was far from being united or homogenous.[96] These positions were supported from others, such as Annie Besant and the Aga Khan.[97] Sir John Rees, a member of the committee, a former ICS officer who had served in Madras, accused the Government of India of creating a caste divide in south India, where it did not exist by supporting the non-Brahmin demands.[98] Lord Southborough reiterated his opinion that instead of asking for institutional safeguards, it would be better if the non-Brahmins organised themselves, again a Processualist argument.[99]

The non-Brahmin witnesses from Madras rehearsed their previous arguments. K.V. Reddi Naidu, in fact, declared his willingness to be included in joint electorate with anyone but the Brahmins. He claimed that the Brahmins were so powerful, that the non-Brahmins, notwithstanding their numbers would never prevail over them. He added that the statistics which showed Brahmins to be a minority of the voters were deceptive, for they masked what he described as the community's 'religious, educational and official influence'.[100] It was also argued by one witness that such provisions would be transitional in nature.[101] Presumably this meant that communal representation would not be necessary once the non-Brahmins became strong enough to withstand Brahmin influence. The fear of Brahmin dominance also found support from Sir Alexander Cardew, who argued that separate representation was necessary to protect the non-Brahmins from the Brahmins. He also forestalled the question of internal tensions among the non-Brahmins by acknowledging them but claiming that their intensity was much less than the antagonism between the Brahmins and the non-Brahmins.[102] He did admit the difficulties in including a wide variety of castes under a common appellation but defended it that this was what the non-Brahmins themselves wanted.[103] Sir Chettur Sankaran Nair, admittedly the most successful non-Brahmin lawyer of his province and times, supported the non-Brahmin demands for separate representation largely on pragmatic grounds saying that it would be safer to grant the same.[104]

The Bombay non-Brahmins were represented before the committee only by Bhaskarrao Jadhav. He sought not communal electorates but reserved seats for the non-Brahmins on the grounds of their educational backwardness.[105] Jadhav's arguments were the same as the one he presented to the Southborough Committee. It was the Deccan Ryots Association that raised the spectre of the Bombay non-Brahmin joining hands with the Extremists if they were denied separate electorates,[106] a clear use of threat to secure political representation. Finally, the non-Brahmins of Madras and Bombay secured separate representation not in the form of communal electorates but through reserved seats. A settlement was imposed by the Raj in the absence of any broad consensus about the quantum of reservation.

But the rules framed under the Government of India Act, 1919, demonstrate that the Raj made a distinction between these two provinces when it came to providing institutional safeguards for the non-Brahmins. In Madras, the non-Brahmins were given the privilege of reserved seats. This term was not explicitly defined, and thus did include the 'Depressed Classes' as well. However, in Bombay, it was the 'Mahrattas' who were granted reserved seats and the category was to include a list of castes, referred to as the 'Allied Castes', that was named in these rules. It was but obvious why the category 'non-Brahmin' was not deployed in Bombay. The strident non-Brahmin demands originated primarily in the Marathi-speaking areas, and secondarily in the Kannada-speaking areas of the province. Any use of the category would have meant that even the non-Brahmin castes of Gujarat would secure reserved seats, something that they had not even demanded. But more importantly, the provincial government was empowered to include any caste it wished in the category of 'Mahratta', which it did in the early 1920s.[107] Thus, what was presented to the Southborough Committee as a census category, derived from sociological reality, turned into a political one, which was to be changed to suit the exigencies of the times.

The period of dyarchy gave the non-Brahmins a share of political power at the provincial level. There does not seem to have been much debate about the merits of system of reserved seats, though non-Brahmin leaders continued to stress the necessity of such a system. The Bombay non-Brahmins continued to couch their demands for political protection in terms of their educational backwardness, and resisted attempts to question the homogeneity of the category 'non-Brahmin'. The differing political trajectories of the non-Brahmin movement in Madras and Bombay had an impact on their demand for political representation. The Indian Statutory Commission, or the Simon Commission, noted that while the Madras non-Brahmins had been politically successful, their Bombay counterparts were rather disorganised.[108] The logical outcome of this political reality was reflected in the recommendations of the commission. It suggested that since the Madras non-Brahmins had won more seats than those reserved for them, they were in no further need of reservations, while the Bombay non-Brahmins often could elect their representatives because a given seat was reserved and hence reservations should continue.[109] Thus, what the Commission was arguing was that if electoral process did lead to a desired outcome, then Institutionalist arrangements were not necessary. The Madras Provincial Committee, dominated by the non-Brahmins, recommended the abolition of reservations, since the representatives of the community found it unnecessary.[110] The Bombay Provincial Committee, however, recommended continuing of reservations for the community since there was no evidence to suggest that it would hold its own in the absence of such a safeguard.[111] The most eloquent defence of the continuation of reservations came from Dr Ambedkar. He claimed that though the non-Brahmins were in a majority, they lacked political consciousness and hence required such concessions.[112]

The Madras Government, in its report to the Simon Commission, further reiterated that the non-Brahmins of the provinces were no longer in need of reservations.[113] The Bombay Government, however, was more circumspect when it concluded that reservations should be discontinued where the community had been able to secure seats but not otherwise.[114] The issue of whether the Bombay non-Brahmins had been successful in non-reserved seats also figured in the proceedings before the Commission. The entire non-Brahmin question almost disappeared from the constitutional debates of the 1930s. The only reference to the retention of reserved seats for the Marathas and Allied Castes came from Bhaskarrao Jadhav at the first and the second Round Table Conferences.

Yet, there seems to have been widespread agreement that while the Madras non-Brahmins no longer required reservations, the status quo had to be maintained in the case of the Bombay non-Brahmins. The Lothian Committee concurred with recommendations of the Bombay government and the Bombay Provincial Franchise Committee that reservations for the non-Brahmins should continue.[115] However, Rao Bahadur R.R. Kale penned a note of dissent, once again arguing that the non-Brahmins were in a majority and hence, in no need or any Institutional safeguards. However, the Bombay non-Brahmin witnesses before the Committee were somewhat divided over the need for reservations. Though the spectre of being dominated by the 'advanced classes' was raised by all and hence the need for reservations, Bhaskarrao Jadhav claimed that if single-member constituencies were granted then there would be no need for reservations.[116] The logic of this position is difficult to understand.

The Depressed Classes or the Scheduled Castes

The need for representation for the 'Depressed Classes' hardly found a mention during the Morley–Minto reforms. But by the First World

War, political consciousness among the community had risen and a section of the nationalist leadership had started taking active interest in its problems. Addresses or submissions had been presented to Edwin Montagu and Lord Chelmsford when they toured India. It was noted that of the total Addresses presented to them, eight related to claims of the 'Depressed Classes'.[117] The Depressed Classes Mission Society at a meeting held in Bombay had already demanded that the community have the right to elect its own representatives in proportion to the population.[118]

The Madras government was the first to draw attention to the need to secure representation for the 'untouchable' communities then referred to as the 'Depressed Classes'. In its response to the Montagu–Chelmsford Report,[119] as well as in its submission to the Southborough Committee where it noted that given the high levels of the probable franchise qualifications no member of the community would be elected in any scheme of non-communal electorates,[120] it stressed the need, though on both occasions it preferred nominations. The Central Provinces and Berar government also stressed of the need for the representation of these communities.[121] The Bombay government, however, noted that it was difficult to precisely define the term 'Depressed Classes'.[122]

Reasons for denying the 'Depressed Classes' representations through elections were varied. Sachchidananda Sinha from Bihar claimed that since there was hardly any political activity among the community there was no reason to grant them this kind of representation.[123] Pandit Motilal Nehru representing the United Provinces Congress, in fact, claimed that in his province 'the depressed classes problem did not exist as elsewhere',[124] thus denying the very visible fact of untouchability. N.K. Kelkar of the Central Provinces even went further when he claimed that the interests of the community would not suffer due to lack of representation.[125] The Raja of Ramnad argued that the problems faced by the community were not as acute as in Malabar. He made the astounding claim that the disabilities faced by the 'Panchamas', as the community was referred to in the Madras Presidency, was more due to their professions and that members of the community who were white-collared professionals or employees would not face any discrimination.[126]

But many did recommend nominations. A Muslim witness from Bihar, Saiyid Nurul Hasan, claimed that without representation the circumstances of the community would not be improved.[127] Many upper caste Hindu witnesses from Bengal, such as Dr Pramatha Nath Banerjee, Ambica Charan Muzumdar, the former Congress president, Sir Rajendranath Mookerjee, the leading businessman, and Dr S.P. Sarbadhikari, did speak of considering these demands sympathetically and generally recommended nominations.[128] There also seems to be awareness that access to power was a solution to the demeaning treatment meted out to the community. Banerjee specifically cited the instance of the Namasudras, whose disabilities according to him were more social than political but that in view of these it would be 'fair' to grant the community representation. Some submissions of political organisations and evidence tendered by caste Hindu witnesses did support, albeit conditionally, separate electorates for the community. The community even found support from a European witness—H.M.P. Rae of the Madras Branch of the European Association.[129]

Not surprisingly, the witnesses from the 'Depressed Classes' made short shrift of all these opposing arguments. G.A. Gavai defined the community as 'the classes untouched by the Hindu community'.[130] Dr B.R. Ambedkar in his first formal foray into public life also questioned this difficulty of definition. In fact, he pointed out that no one who did not belong to the 'Depressed Classes' would want claim to be one for the sake of political convenience.[131] The theme of loyalty and past service to the Raj figured in the claims to representation made by the community. The Madras Adi Dravida Jana Sabha[132] stressed these factors which did not figure in the evidence of other witnesses from the community. This was, perhaps, the last time this theme was deployed to demand political representation for the community. The other Dalit witnesses, notably Ambedkar, demanded representation as a matter of right. Ambedkar particularly seems to have conceived access to political power or participation in decision-making as a means to dealing with the social and religious disabilities, which in turn led to denial of educational and employment opportunities to the community, a point he was to explicitly make during the first Round Table Conference.[133]

The Southborough Committee recommended nominations for the community, a view shared by the Government of India. The only point of dispute was the number of seats allotted to the community. The introduction of elections for the 'Depressed Classes' had to await the next round of constitutional reforms. The only redeeming feature of the Montagu–Chelmsford reforms, as far as the community was concerned, was that the rule made under the Government of India Act, 1919, stipulated that five members be nominated to the Madras council to represent five specified communities, all of whom were regarded as belonging to the 'Depressed Classes'. The need for representation for the community was, however, not strongly felt by any section of the nationalist movement, even in the 1920s.

The issue of definitions came to the fore in the 1920s and 1930s as the 'Depressed Classes' became a political force to be acknowledged. The Simon Commission noted that this definitional quandary was not uniform throughout the country, for in Madras, Bombay and the Central Provinces, it was clear who the 'Depressed Classes' were, while in Bengal, the United Provinces, and Bihar and Orissa it was not.[134] The commission reiterated its feeling that the term 'Depressed Classes' required precise definition,[135] an opinion shared by the Government of India's 1930 proposals of constitutional reforms.[136] In Bombay, by 1930, the 'Depressed Classes' had already been defined by restricting the term to include only those castes regarded as being 'untouchable'.[137]

Dr Ambedkar once again made a strong plea for the representation of the 'Depressed Classes' and argued that political power would enable the community to deal with its social disabilities.[138] Dr Ambedkar in his evidence to the Commission based his demand for separate representation for the 'Depressed Classes' not on grounds of past loyalty to the Raj but on the grounds that it was a distinct minority community separate from the wider Hindu community, and that its social situation warranted far greater protection than other minorities,[139] a point he reiterated during the first and the second Round Table Conference.

At the former, Dr Moonje seemed to be inclined to agree with Ambedkar, for which he was criticised by Sir A.P. Patro.

There were attempts to minimise the gravity of the social situation of the community and thus deflate demands for separate representation. The Punjab Government in its memorandum submitted to the Simon Commission claimed that the phenomenon of untouchability in the Punjab was mild.[140] The issue of terminology and definitions also cropped up before the Simon Commission. Babu Rama Charana from the United Provinces pointed out that the term 'depressed' had come to be associated with the notion of 'untouchability' and hence many castes, even those regarded as being untouchable, hesitated to describe themselves as so. He suggested that the term 'Hindu backward classes' be adopted to describe the 'untouchable' castes.[141] The All-India Jatava Mahasabha asked that the term 'depressed' be confined only to those castes regarded as 'untouchable'.[142] The All-India Namasudra Association, however, equated the terms 'Depressed Classes' and 'backward classes' while primarily defining them as those backward in education.[143]

The problem of heterogeneity of the category 'Depressed Classes' and that of caste distinctions within the community were raised before the commission. Clement Attlee, then a second-rung figure in the Labour Party, and P. Khalifullah Sahib Bahadur, a member of the Madras committee, both questioned the representatives of the community from Madras on this point. While it was not denied that such distinctions existed, they were stated as not being of such marked importance. It was also claimed that the difference between the caste Hindus and the community was much sharper than the one within it.[144] This issue was raised by Raja Narendra Nath during the second Round Table Conference. He stressed the internal stratification within the category 'Depressed Classes' and argued that there were castes within the category which were regarded as 'untouchables' by other castes belonging to the same category. Given this, he added, how someone belonging to a caste within the category could represent the same as a whole.[145] Furthermore, claims were made that in Bengal the problem of the 'Depressed Classes' was not severe and that many communities who were not 'untouchable' were seeking entry into the category to derive political advantage.[146]

Again, it was Dr Ambedkar who tackled the issue of nomenclature and definition, this time at the second Round Table Conference. He now objected to the very term 'Depressed Classes' terming it 'degrading and contemptuous' and suggested 'Non-Caste Hindus', 'Protestant Hindus' or 'Non-Conformist Hindus' as the alternatives. He also stressed that the category 'Depressed Classes' should be statutorily defined not at an all-India level but at the provincial level, and should include all those who suffered from the practice of untouchability as it was practised in a given province.[147] This was perhaps a tacit acknowledgement that the manner in which 'untouchability' was practised was not uniform throughout the country.

The question of definitions was raised before the Lothian Committee which saw wide-ranging debates and discussions of definitions, and the actual numbers of the community. It was obvious that numbers depended on the precise definition adopted. After reviewing the attempts at defining the category 'Depressed Classes', the Committee at its fourth meeting held on 4 February 1932 in Delhi adopted the criterion of 'untouchability' to define the same. It added that 'untouchability' would encompass denial of access to the interior of Hindu temples, and the causing of pollution by either touch or coming within a certain distance.[148] Dr Ambedkar submitted an extensive note discussing the issues of definition as well as nomenclature. He pointed out that only those who suffered from untouchability should be considered as the 'Depressed Classes' and that it was precisely this bearing the brunt of social discrimination that led to common consciousness, thus leading the community to constitute a distinct political category. He acknowledged that while the manner in which untouchability was practised might differ across the country, this in no way led to any significant variations in the social conditions of the community.[149] Ambedkar also suggested that the term 'Hindu exterior castes' first proposed by C.S. Mullan, the Census Superintendent for Assam, be adopted. He claimed that this term was more accurate than 'Depressed Classes' which he described as vague and offensive.[150]

However, the very idea of 'permanent untouchability' was contested by E.A.H. Blunt, a senior ICS officer from the United Provinces. He claimed that the phenomenon of 'untouchability' was no longer a caste attribute but more a personal one. He explained that if members of those castes that were regarded as 'untouchables' had abandoned those professions considered socially inferior and degrading, then they were no longer regarded as being 'untouchable'.[151]

Blunt's definition would have excluded many members of the community from the category of 'Depressed Classes' thus reducing their numbers, and consequently affecting the claim to a certain quantum of representation. Hence, Dr Ambedkar strongly contested this opinion of Blunt in the note referred to above and criticised the United Provinces Government's attempts to apply Blunt's criteria to determine the number of 'Depressed Classes' in the Provinces. Ambedkar made a distinction between 'untouchability' in its literal sense and in its notional sense. He argued that individuals who belonged to castes regarded as 'untouchables' but who no longer practise occupations that would have led them to be regarded as so might not cause pollution per se (i.e. are not any longer 'untouchable' in the literal sense) but would still be regarded as being ' impure' (i.e. 'untouchable' in the notional sense).[152]

This definitional certainty was not agreeable to all members of the committee. Three members, R.R. Bakhle, C.Y. Chintamani and S.B. Tambe, all Brahmins, submitted a long dissenting note where they dealt with issue of 'Depressed Classes'. They claimed that the community constituted a distinct one only in Bombay, the Central Provinces and Madras, and not in other provinces. The trio claimed that untouchability was more an attribute of the profession followed rather than the caste background. They also acknowledged that while 'untouchability' existed among the Muslims, the Sikhs and the Indian Christians, only the figures for Hindu 'untouchables' should be considered in order to determine the number of the 'Depressed Classes'.[153] Heterogeneity among the 'Depressed Classes' was once again used to question the feasibility of separate representation. Rao Bahadur Kale claimed that in Bombay it was difficult to draw a line between the 'touchables' and the 'untouchables'. He added that there existed untouchability within the 'Depressed Classes'.

The Government of Bengal adopted an equivocal attitude over the entire issue of definition. It reported to the Lothian Committee that it had not decided who exactly were the 'Depressed Classes.[154] It went even further when it claimed that if the Lothian Committee's definition were to be applied, there was only one caste that could be considered 'Depressed' in Bengal.[155] This denial was, of course, contested by Mukunda Behari Mullick, a leading political leader of the community. Conceding that it was difficult to have a 'cut and dried' definition of who the 'Depressed Classes' were, Mullick did offer a set of criteria. Apart from causing pollution by touch or approach as well as denial of access to temples, he argued that denial of entry into hotels or eating houses run by caste Hindus, unwillingness of Brahmin priests to officiate at household ceremonies and denial of service by caste Hindu barbers would also count as defining characteristics of 'untouchability'. He further admitted that the phenomenon of 'untouchability' as it existed in many parts of the country did not exist in Bengal.[156]

A majority of the Punjab Franchise Committee also claimed that, strictly speaking, there were no 'Depressed Classes' in the Punjab.[157] Two members, however, claimed that while no such category could be said to exist among the Muslims, it certainly did among the Sikhs and the Hindus.[158] Later, the same majority did concede that two castes in the province could be described as being 'untouchable'.[159] The provincial government, however, submitted a list of castes who it felt fell within the category of 'Depressed Classes'.[160] Yet, as far as the Punjab was concerned, it was Chaudhuri Chhotu Ram who discussed the issue in a detailed note. He made a distinction between castes who could be regarded as 'depressed' whom he described as 'Dalit' and those regarded as 'untouchable' whom he regarded as '*achhut*'. Ram added that the former did not suffer from any social disabilities or discrimination unlike the second group of castes. He pointed out that the practice of untouchability was prevalent even among the 'untouchable' castes and cited instances. Yet, he claimed that the problems faced by the 'Depressed Classes' in the province were not as severe to justify separate representation.[161] Similarly, the Bihar and Orissa Government while acknowledging the existence of 'untouchable' castes in the province claimed that the problems faced by them were not so acute so as to justify separate representation.[162]

In Assam, Kanak Lal Barua, a minister, argued that a desirable process by which 'untouchable' castes' had been rising in their social status and thus being admitted into the fold of 'caste' Hindus could be observed in the province. He claimed that separate representation had to be rejected, for it would put a stop to this process and perpetuate social divisions. Yet, he suggested that the members of these castes should be give an option of being either included in the general (i.e. Hindu) electorate or in a separate communal electorate for themselves.[163] A majority of the local Franchise Committee like its counterparts in other provinces also stated that going by the yardsticks prevalent in the rest of the country there were hardly any 'Depressed Classes' in Assam, yet suggested a list of castes to be included in the category. A minority, in fact, claimed that there were no 'Depressed Classes' in the province at all.[164] Ambedkar might have supported the nomenclature proposed by Mullan, but Mullan himself was not comfortable with the task of identifying the 'Depressed Classes', for his province. He explained why he abandoned the term 'Depressed Classes'. He claimed that no caste in Assam suffered from the kind of severe social discrimination as practised in Madras and could not be called 'depressed'. He added that he had invented the term 'Hindu exterior castes' in view of the permission granted by the Census Commissioner of India to use any term suitable in light of provincial considerations. Mullan also clarified that he was not pleased with this invention of his but could do no better in view of lack of suitable alternatives. He added that the process mentioned by Barua was a reality in Assam. Finally, he claimed that the whole issue was so nebulous that it would be difficult to decide with certainty who exactly the 'Hindu exterior castes' were while citing instances of social discrimination being practised among this category.[165] It was only the Governments of Bombay, Madras, the Central Provinces and Berar, and their Franchise Committees did not raise any difficulties about definitions and supported separate representation for the 'Depressed Classes'.

The evidence tendered before the Lothian Committee once again revealed that the category 'Depressed Classes' was still a political artefact and had not yet achieved enough cohesiveness to enable it to acquire more than a modicum of social reality. The All-India Arundhateeya Sabha, which despite its name, was an organisation based in the Madras Presidency, called for, if possible, separate electorates for individual 'untouchable' castes or at least reserved seats, with the communal electorates for the 'Depressed Classes'.[166] The internal heterogeneity of the category was, of course, not denied. What was denied was the claim that this heterogeneity invalidated the reality of the category itself. As Dr P.G. Solanki, a close associate of Ambedkar, told the Lothian Committee that while 'untouchable' castes did not inter-marry or inter-dine that did not mean that 'they were hostile to each other'.[167] Yet Solanki, after strong questioning, first acknowledged that 'untouchability' was practised within the 'Depressed Classes' as well and that he had no objection to reserving seats within the quota for the community for those castes regarded as 'untouchable' even by the 'untouchables'.[168]

There were also demands that the category 'Depressed Classes' be restricted only to those castes regarded as 'untouchable'. The Depressed Classes and Aboriginal Tribes Committee appointed by the Bombay Government in the late 1920s had noted that the term 'Depressed Classes' had come to include the 'untouchables', the tribals as well as some backward castes and as mentioned previously had recommended that it be restricted to include and thus denote only the 'untouchable' castes.[169] While apprehensions were expressed that some communities might want to sneak into it to secure political influence,[170] it was argued that a more flexible definition would lead to those groups who do not require Institutionalist safeguards securing them. Thus once again the debate raged on how the category was to be defined. Separate representation for the community was sought to be denied on the grounds that if the 'Depressed' among the Muslims did not have communal electorates why those among the Hindus should be granted the same.[171] There was also a mention of numerically weaker castes within the category being granted Institutional safeguards.

Though many witnesses opined that 'Depressed' meant 'untouchable', arguments about definitional uncertainty persisted. J.H. Darwin, a senior ICS officer from United Provinces, talked of 'degrees of untouchability'.[172] Some argued that 'Depressed' did not just mean 'untouchable' but that it included educationally and socially backward Hindu castes as well. There was even talk of the 'Depressed Classes' among the Sikhs, the Muslims and the Christians. Even a witness like Rasik Lal Biswas from Bengal who belonged to the community acknowledged this definitional difficulty.[173] However, a large delegation of the leaders of the community with M.C. Rajah at its head rejected this alleged ambiguity. Rajah explicitly stated 'untouchability' was the defining test of being a member of the 'Depressed Classes.[174] Furthermore, Ambedkar's increasing insistence that the 'Depressed Classes' must be treated as a distinct entity and not as a part of the wider Hindu society found an echo in the Punjab. The Ad-Dharmi Mandal, in its submission to the committee, explicitly stated that they were not Hindus while making a strong demand for communal electorates.[175]

Ultimately, the entire issue of definitions and terminologies was largely resolved by the constitutional proposals of the Indian Government, known as the White Paper of 1933, which appended a province-wise list of 'Scheduled Castes', as the 'Depressed Classes' were now known,[176] but not before the developments that led to the Poona Pact, which is discussed in the next chapter. But not all regarded the question as closed. The memorandum of the Hindu Mahasabha submitted to the Joint Committee on Indian Constitution Reform denied that there were hardly any 'untouchables' in Bengal while the category did not even exist in the Punjab.[177] There was an underlying logic to these persistent denials. The Hindus were a minority in these two provinces. Acknowledging the existence of the 'Depressed Classes' would have meant that the community would have received political representation, which would have been carved out of the share allotted to the Hindus. Thus, the caste-Hindu leaders of the two provinces were, of course, loath to share what had come their way with anyone else.

The question of representation for the community was revived in the early days of the Constituent Assembly. P.R. Thakur from West Bengal, speaking on the resolution on the resolution on Aims and Objectives, or the Objectives Resolution, called for representation to be given to the community on a population basis. He further argued that if any other community was to be given weightage, then the 'Scheduled Castes' should also receive the same concession. His claim to representation was now couched in entirely different terms. Thakur now argued that representation was a right since his community were the original inhabitants of India and had not entered it as invaders, a category in which he bracketed both caste Hindus and the Muslims.[178] This was a theme that was to recur.

While the question of the definition was largely settled by the time the Constituent Assembly convened, the issue of whether the Scheduled Castes were a distinct political entity, and thus whether the community was an integral part of the broader Hindu society was not decided. If Thakur asserted that the community was a political minority, H.J. Khandekar from the Central Provinces emphasised that the Scheduled Castes 'are Hindus, will remain Hindus and will secure our rights as Hindus'. But this did not prevent him from asking for representation on a population basis.[179] After some debate, the Scheduled Castes were granted reserved seats for the Lok Sabha and provincial legislative assemblies in the Constitution of India.

Concerns were also expressed that in the absence of reservations, the community might not find adequate representation in the Council of States and the provincial upper chambers. There were also attempts in the Assembly to once again question the validity of the category 'Scheduled Castes'. Mahavir Tyagi claimed that this was an artificial and fictional construct and castes with varying social status had been cobbled together to form this category.[180] There were demands that the Constitution explicitly define the Scheduled Castes as a part of the 'great Hindu community'. There was also mention of the fact that there was opposition from the Scheduled Castes to the inclusion of the castes among the Sikhs that had been regarded as 'untouchable' within the category of Scheduled Castes.[181] It was left to Sardar Patel to clarify this point. The Scheduled Castes leaders apparently had taken the position that the Sikh 'untouchables' were either Sikhs or Scheduled Castes and could not be both. However, they were convinced to agree to the inclusion, as Patel put it, for the 'sake of peace'.[182] This was a clear case of political considerations leading to a re-definition of the category 'Scheduled Castes'. There was, of course, grumbling in the Assembly that reservation to the Sikh Scheduled Castes was eating into the share of the Hindu Scheduled Castes and that the share granted to the former should have been carved out of the general (i.e. non-reserved) seats rather than that of the Hindu Scheduled Castes. This was again contested by some Sikh members.

The problem of definition of the Scheduled Castes re-emerged during the debate in early 1951 on a bill seeking to amend the Representation of the People Act, 1950, so as to provide reserved seats for the community as well as the Scheduled Tribes in the Part C States. Dr Punjabrao Deshmukh raised the issue by informing the Provisional Parliament that he had received many representations that many communities listed as 'Scheduled Castes' in the Orders in Council issued under the 1935 Act had been excluded in the list issued by the Government of India.[183] He was joined by R. Velayudhan from Madras, who claimed that this had been done deliberately, for if all the communities listed as 'Scheduled Castes' as per the 1935 Act had been included in the post-independence list, then the number of reserved seats would have been larger.[184] To this, Dr Ambedkar clarified that no community had been excluded but that two communities from Bombay had been included.[185] He reminded his fellow members that the term 'Depressed Classes' had been an imprecise term and had included even those communities who were educationally backward. He added that it was he who had been largely responsible for defining the 'Scheduled Castes' as comprising those castes regarded as 'untouchable'.[186] This seems to have settled the matter, for no further issues were raised, though later Dr Ambedkar conceded there were some who were pretending to be 'Scheduled Castes' in order to obtain the concessions given to the community.[187]

The Tribals

The tribals (or the aborigines as they were referred to then) of India did not figure anywhere in the early days of the discussions on political representation in India. The Montagu–Chelmsford report and the First Despatch, the Government of India's response to the report, either did not mention them at all or made a cursory mention. The only provincial governments which had something to say about the community were the three with large tribal populations, namely Bihar and Orissa, the Central Provinces and Berar, and Assam. There was, of course, no talk of elections but all three suggested nominations, which was accepted by the Southborough Committee. The community did not figure much during the deliberations of the 1919 Joint Select Committee or under the rules made under the Government of India Act, 1919, and neither did the constitutions framed by the nationalist movement during the 1920s take note of the community. The Simon Commission, however, ruefully noted that in Bihar and Orissa the majority of those elected from the tribal-dominated seats were, in fact, non-tribals[188] but refrained from making any concrete recommendations.

The question of tribal representation received a mention in the evidence tendered to the Simon Commission. Again, the issue of whether non-tribals could be considered representatives of the community and that of whether conversion to Christianity divided it came to the fore. The distinguished anthropologist Sarat Chandra Roy was elected to the Bihar and Orissa council from a predominantly tribal constituency. He was described by J.A. Hubback, the Special Officer, Reforms of the local government, as being a tribal representative 'because he commands the respect of the tribals', while Roy himself deprecated the fact that both members nominated to represent the 'aborigines' were Christian missionaries when in fact the non-Christian element of the community was numerically stronger than its Christian counterpart.[189] However, the question did not even figure in the official submission of the Government of Bihar and Orissa to the commission. The Lothian Committee also did not consider the question of political representation of the tribals but rather left it to the provincial governments to decide.

Again, it was Roy who made a strong plea for tribal representation on the grounds of their general backwardness.[190] Of the witnesses before the Lothian Committee, there were very few who made it a point to mention the representation of the tribals.

Once again, the issue did not figure prominently during the proceedings of the Joint Committee on Indian Constitutional Reform. The notion that tribals could not represent themselves seemed common. Only Colonel Josiah Wedgwood, a leading Labour MP, raised the issue but suggested that in the all-India legislature, the tribals could be represented by English anthropologists,[191] while Sir Henry Gidney, the Anglo-Indian leader, opined that Christian missionaries could represent them.[192] But opinions were also expressed that the community did not even need representation. Wing Commander A.W.H. James, an MP, who had widely travelled among the tribals advocated that all tribal-dominated areas be termed 'Excluded' (i.e. removed from the purview of reforms) and later termed tribal representation as 'valueless'[193]. Dr J.H. Hutton, the Census Commissioner of India, repeated his preference for the nomination. This indifference to the representation of tribals was spread far and wide. Even Dr Ambedkar was dismissive on the issue but for different reasons. He claimed that the community then lacked 'political sense to make the best use of their political opportunities' and thus this made them vulnerable to the machinations of the others. Thus, Ambedkar argued that representation would not generate any benefits to the tribals. He suggested that the tribal-dominated areas continue to be designated as 'Excluded Areas' and be administered by a Statutory Commission.[194]

This neglect of tribal interests was, of course, to change by the time the Constituent Assembly convened. The community now had found a doughty spokesperson in the person of Jaipal Singh. In his first speech in the Assembly, Singh asked for a higher quantum of representation for his community and reminded his audience that the tribals were not only the original inhabitants of India but had been on the receiving end of what he called the racialism of the Hindus for thousands of years.[195] There was some resentment in the Constituent Assembly that the report on Minority Rights had not listed the Scheduled Tribes as being one of the communities that were being granted reservations. Sardar Patel assured the members that a separate committee was to deal with the issue. The Assembly appointed two sub-committees, the first one chaired by Gopinath Bordoloi, the Premier of Assam, which dealt with the Assam tribals, and the second, chaired by the veteran social worker A.V. Thakkar (also known as Thakkar Bappa), to address the issues of the tribals in the rest of the country. The Bordoloi Sub-Committee did not favour reservations for the tribals of the hill districts of Assam since the community was in a majority in the area.[196] The Thakkar Sub-Committee strongly recommended reserved seats both in the provincial and the national legislatures, failing which the tribals would not secure representation in the legislatures.[197] However, there were demands, notably made by Singh, that tribals were being underrepresented in the membership of the Assembly as compared to their share in the population.

Hitherto, the validity of the category 'tribals' or 'Scheduled Tribes' had not been questioned. L.N. Sahu from Orissa reminded his fellow members that two tribes from his provinces were politically advanced and thus no longer qualified for inclusion in the category. His argument seemed to be that high levels of political consciousness meant that institutional safeguards in the form of reservations were no longer required and hence the two could be safely excluded. Sahu also noted that a gradual process of Hinduisation of the tribals was taking place, a prospect that seemed to have pleased him, for he recommended that the pace of these developments not be forced and they be allowed to work at their usual speed.[198] K.M. Munshi refuted Singh's attempts to construct the tribals into a single entity when he pointed out that there was hardly any commonality between the various tribes that constituted the category 'Scheduled Tribes'.[199] The Assembly also saw a debate on how the term 'Scheduled Tribes' should be translated into Hindi. Singh supported the use of 'Adivasi' over any other. Beyond this, there was not much debate on the issue.

Europeans and Anglo-Indians

During the Morley–Minto reforms, the European commercial interests reiterated their demand for representation, which they had enjoyed since 1861 through the European dominated commercial organisations. There do not seem to have been any demands from the Eurasian community, as the 'Anglo-Indians' were known then. In any case, the Eastern Bengal and Assam government dismissed any such demands arguing that the numbers of the community did not warrant separate representation.[200]

It was expected that the reforms proposed after the First World War would continue representation to the European commercial interests and extend the right to the Anglo-Indians. The question was whether the Europeans qua Europeans were to be granted representation. The Montagu–Chelmsford report was not very clear on this though it mentioned the need for the representation of the 'general European community'.[201] It had been proposed that these two communities be represented by nominations. But the Bengal government in its response opined that recourse to such a method was unjustified and suggested elections. While it did not advance any reasons for asking for elections for the Anglo-Indians, in the case of the Europeans it claimed that the community had a 'vested right' to elect one of their own and that it could form a suitable electorate.[202] Given that Calcutta was the centre of European commercial interests in India and possessed a numerically significant European community, the provincial government's stance was not surprising. A similar demand was made by the Assam Government.[203]

The Bombay Government in its submission to the Southborough Committee made a strong case for the political representation of the Europeans whose interests it described as being important. It noted that the community was politically advanced but would be unrepresented in mixed electorates. Addressing the possible objection to European representation qua Europeans that the European commercial organisations already elected their representatives to the local council, the Bombay government claimed that the interests of the community were not exclusively commercial.[204] Thus, it was being suggested that representatives of European commerce could no longer serve as spokespersons for the community's wider concerns and that this necessitated a general non-commercial European representation.

Many Indian witnesses found it galling that Europeans were to have representation through both commercial bodies and communal electorates. While the visibility and significance of European commercial interests could hardly be denied, the opposition to communal electorates centred on claims by Indian witnesses that there were hardly any Europeans in India who were employed outside the business world.[205] It was naturally countered by European witnesses like Colonel A.J. Pugh and T.E. Welby.[206] The Bombay Chamber of Commerce went a step further in justifying communal electorates for Europeans. It stated that the community was 'best qualified by hereditary and education for taking an intelligent part in political developments',[207] a self-revealing and self-explanatory statement.

The Southborough Committee separately granted these two communities communal electorates but not in all provinces. It asserted that such a provision was made wherever the 'strength and importance' of the communities justified it.[208] The committee took it for granted that the Europeans qua Europeans must be given separate representation for reasons of 'history and existing facts'. Anticipating the criticism that would be levelled against separate representation for the Europeans given that European-dominated commercial bodies were electing members of the community to the various councils, it noted that there were many Europeans, not all of whom were engaged in commercial activity, who could not be represented by 'members selected primarily on behalf of the capital concerned in commercial and industrial activities'.[209] In the case of the Anglo-Indians, the committee advanced the same arguments as it had done for the Indian Christians, an acknowledgement of its deliberate distancing from the broader Indian society.[210]

But in the case of the two communities, the committee was confronted with the question of definition. The appellation 'Anglo-Indian' was itself of recent vintage having been conferred in 1911 on the community who desired to abandon the earlier term used to describe it namely 'Eurasian'.[211] This issue figured in the submissions made by the provincial governments as well as the discussions that the committee had with them. It resolved the problem by providing definitions of its own, after considering suggestions received from provincial governments and the representatives of the organisations of the communities. Judging by the text of these, first or second generation 'pure' Europeans were defined as 'Europeans', while those long settled in India were clubbed with those of mixed ancestry, albeit only those of patrilineal European descent, as 'Anglo-Indians'.[212] Thus clearly, the committee did not wish Europeans of a recent vintage to be compelled for political purposes to be associated with 'the country-born'. However, it seems to have been aware of the tenuous nature of its definition, for it recommended, like in the case of the Sikhs, that the official in charge of preparing the electoral roll should accept claims of a given voter to be included either in the European or the Anglo-Indian electorate unless there were good grounds for suspicion.[213] The distinction made by the committee between recent European migrants and those of an earlier era seem to have been derived from the European Association of Calcutta, which argued for a distinction to be made on grounds that older immigrants were 'unlikely to have any share in the communal life of Europeans'.[214]

The issue of definitions emerged during the evidence of the Southborough Committee. J.H. Kerr, the Chief Secretary to the Bengal government, stated that it was difficult to define who exactly was an Anglo-Indian[215] but this difficulty was sought to be surmounted by J.W. Chippendale of the Anglo-Indian Association who defined an Anglo-Indian as being either a 'pure' European domiciled in India or one of mixed ancestry.[216] The same definition was offered by Lt.Col (later Sir) Henry Gidney representing the Bombay branch of the Anglo-Indian Empire League,[217] who later emerged as the leading spokesperson of the community. The themes of past services and loyalty to the Raj as well an insistence that the community was as Indian as any other, apart from the usual one of the necessity of protection of special interests, figured prominently in the claims being made by the representatives of the Anglo-Indian community.

There does not seem to have existed a very strong feeling against representation per se for these two communities. Schemes concerning the composition of the provincial councils submitted by many of those who appeared as witnesses before the Southborough Committee did make provisions in this regard. However, the opposition to electoral representation came from some Indian witnesses and that too largely on the grounds of small numbers or what was often described as their interests not being on sufficient importance. Pandit Madan Mohan Malaviya representing the United Provinces Congress claimed that the communities were too small and then that in mixed electorates the members of the community could get elected in a constituency like Cawnpore. His next comment was revealing. He opined that the two communities should 'work with the Indians' thus stating that reflected a desire to bridge the social gulf that existed between the two and the wider Indian public.[218] Dr Pramatha Nath Banerjee also claimed that the Europeans in Bengal could succeed in general electorates.[219] There also might have been selfish considerations at play for elected seats, for the two would have meant a concurrent reduction in the same available for the Indians. The non-official European witnesses in the United Provinces contested the claim that a member of the community could be elected in a mixed electorate in Cawnpore.[220] The hope that the absence of communal electorates would make the domiciled Europeans 'care for India' was dashed when the Punjab branch of the Anglo-Indian Empire League asserted the community 'cared for England more than India' and doing away with such electorates would not change the situation.[221] Some Indian witnesses, such as L.A. Govinda Raghava Aiyar of Madras, in fact suggested that the Anglo-Indians be included in a common Indian electorate so that feelings of separatism and aloofness would disappear[222]—thus indicating a desire to welcome the community into the mainstream of Indian society and perhaps to prevent from drifting into the political arms of the Raj.

There was not much discussion of the European and Anglo-Indian case before the Joint Select Committee on the Government of India Bill, 1919. Only Annie Besant opposed communal electorates for the two communities. She claimed that the Europeans were already well-represented through their commercial organisation, and hence required no representation qua Europeans, while she described Anglo-Indians as a 'favoured community'.[223] The definitional conundrum was resolved by the rules made under the 1919 Act, by which 'Europeans' were defined to include both 'pure' Europeans and those of mixed parentage but of a recent vintage, while 'Anglo-Indians' meant those of mixed-descent with roots in the Anglo-Saxon world.

As expected, the Indian Statutory Commission retained communal electorates for the Europeans as well as for the Anglo-Indians. However, the Indian Central Committee treated them on a different footing. The former were given separate electorates on the grounds that they could not speak the local language and hence could not possibly canvass a general electorate, while the Anglo-Indians were urged to look upon themselves as 'citizens of India having joint interests with the bulk of the inhabitants of the country' and hence were granted reserved seats, albeit wherever possible.[224] The question of definition came up before the Simon Commission. The Anglo-Indians coupled with the Domiciled Europeans offered their definition of 'Anglo-Indian', which included those of mixed ancestry and those 'pure' Europeans long settled in India.[225] Once again, the theme of loyalty to the Raj was evoked. The same arguments were repeated during the first Round Table Conference. Sir Henry Gidney, by now the acknowledged leader and spokesperson of the community, represented it at the conference. He now emphasised the fact that the Anglo-Indians were as Indians as any other community, albeit one with deep-rooted connections with England or as he put it, 'If India is our Motherland, Britain is our Fatherland'. Hence, he argued that the protection of the community was the joint responsibility of both India and England. He also stressed the contribution that the community had made in welding India together through their service in the railways and the telegraph department, thus claiming that their stake in the future of India was more than what appeared or what was warranted by their mere numbers while painting a picture of a community facing economic distress. Yet, the theme of past military service and present-day assistance in maintaining law and order in the face of 'India seething with civil disobedience and revolution' was also evoked.[226]

The proceedings before the Lothian Committee once saw renewed demands for the representations of the Europeans qua Europeans. The question had acquired sharper resonance since the official bloc, which had consisted mainly of British ICS officials was to disappear from the local councils. The European representatives argued before the Lothian Committee that they required representation as a community so as to represent 'the British point of view'. It was also argued that European commercial bodies generally elected older individuals and hence communal representation was required so as to secure representation for the younger generation of Europeans.[227]

The European community of India reiterated its demands for the continuation of communal representation for itself before the Joint Committee on Indian Constitutional Reform, now not in terms of the usual argument of a stake in the country but on pragmatic grounds. Its memorandum argued that Europeans were neutral in communal matters, regarded parliamentary practice as a valued tradition and possessed administrative skills and thus a significant European element in the Indian legislature would positively contribute to the development of democratic institutions.[228] Presumably, the Indians did not possess these characteristics. The Anglo-Indians, represented by their indefatigable spokesperson Gidney, renewed their demands for separate representation before the committee. The theme of loyalty to the Raj and the claim that the community as being rooted in the country and thus possessing a stake in its future were reiterated. But now the fear of being abandoned by the Raj also came to the fore.[229]

The definitional uncertainty re-emerged. Gidney expressed his dissatisfaction at the definitions framed by the 1919 Act and claimed that those had enabled many Anglo-Indians to pass off as Europeans and thus had reduced the community's numbers. He added that the term 'Anglo-Indian' should encompass proper Anglo-Indians and Domiciled Europeans. Gidney defined the former as those of mixed European and non-European descent but with European ancestry in the male line, and the 'Domiciled Europeans' as 'pure' Europeans who were long-standing permanent settlers in India. The nomenclature 'European' was restricted to those 'pure' Europeans who were in India for temporary purposes.[230]

The Government of India Act, 1935, however, did away with racial definitions or those dependent on ancestry. Instead, it adopted the criteria of whether an individual was permanently settled in India or not. Clause 26 (1) defined the Europeans as those with European ancestry in the male line but not 'natives of India', while the Anglo-Indians were those with European ancestry in the male line but who were 'natives of India'. Thus, now the category of 'Europeans' could theoretically include those of mixed descent. With this definition, the term 'Domiciled European' became irrelevant.[231]

As independence approached, the Anglo-Indians were naturally anxious about their future and were accommodated in the Constituent Assembly. The community was initially granted reserved seats and later, as with other communities, reservations were abolished. However, the Indian Constitution provided for the representatives of the community to be nominated to the Lok Sabha and the legislative assemblies of certain states if it failed to secure representation through the electoral process.

What is a Minority?

The general theme underlying the debates on political representation was to see to it that minorities were not electorally or politically marginalised. Nominations were seen as a compensatory device for providing representation to those who had been left out of the electoral process. But the real question was how this notion of a 'minority' was going to be defined. The first and foremost criteria, the one most easily available, were religion, and then came caste. But this was not always acceptable. During the Morley–Minto reforms, one prominent Congress leader, C.Vijayraghavachariar, posed the rhetorical question as to whether a minority could be defined on a religious basis,[232] while during the Montagu–Chelmsford reforms, R.P. Paranjpye noted that minorities need not be defined in religious or caste terms. He argued that as political activity picked pace and political consciousness spread, political opinions and ideologies would form the basis of defining a minority.[233]

The Madras non-Brahmins offered their own definition of a minority, which they claimed could not be defined merely in numerical terms.

They claimed that a numerical majority should be treated as a minority if it was politically disorganised or had low levels of political consciousness and subject to the influence of outsiders. This was echoed by G.H. Hidayatullah of Sindh who described the Muslims of his region as an 'illusory majority', thus implying that they should be treated as minorities for political purposes.[234] A rhetorical definition of a minority came during the evidence given by N.K. Kelkar to the Reforms Enquiry Committee. He claimed that all communities in India were in a minority.[235] But this was a mere ploy to deny the logic of communal electorates to any community. Dr Ambedkar in his evidence to the Simon Commission offered his own definition of a minority. For him, mere small numbers did not make a minority, which was to secure political concessions. Only a minority that was oppressed or whose rights were being denied by the majority could be defined as such for political purposes.[236] Despite its deceptive simplicity and appeal, this was a clear attempt to portray the 'Depressed Classes' as a community requiring special protection.

The question of who exactly were the communities that were to be considered as minorities for the purposes of political representation cropped up during first Round Table Conference. The issue at stake was minority representation in the provincial executive. The Nawab of Chhattari demanded that the Instruments of Instruction to the British provincial Governors should stipulate that they should ensure the presence of minorities in their Cabinets. To this Lord Zetland, a former Governor of Bengal, asked 'All minorities?', and the response was 'Important minorities'. Dr Ambedkar joined in by asking 'What is an important minority?' to which Chhattari's response was whosoever the provincial Governor considers important.[237] This left the question unresolved.

The theme of rights of minorities and the protection which had been evoked largely by the non-Hindu communities, notably the Muslims[238] and even by 'Depressed Classes', was now stressed by the Hindus of the Punjab. Raja Narendra Nath made a strong plea at the first Round Table Conference for the recognition of the Punjabi Hindus as a minority in the province. His main grouse seemed to be that his community was under-weighted as regards the quantum of representation. As in many cases, Dr Ambedkar hit the constitutional nail on its head at the first Conference, when he declared that the crux of the Indian problem was the minority question and that its resolution would lead to that of the country as well.

The second Round Table Conference, as is well known, was marked by the presence of Mahatma Gandhi. It was also at this conference that the attempt to resolve the 'minorities' question collapsed. The overall posture adopted by Gandhi seemed to be that only the Muslims and the Sikhs were to be considered as the minority communities to be taken into account for the purposes of a constitutional settlement.[239] In fact, during the proceedings of the Minorities Sub-Committee, Gandhi explicitly denied the 'Depressed Classes' the right to separate representation.[240] This was contested by Ambedkar, Gidney and even Dr Moonje, who talked of the Hindus of the Punjab and Bengal as minorities. The entire exercise culminated in the Minorities Memorandum signed by the leaders of almost all minority communities, which demanded that these communities should receive separate representation which in turn should not be less than their share in the population. The memorandum also stipulated that in no province should a majority community be reduced to a legislative minority. Furthermore, the Congress also circulated its own scheme for a constitutional settlement. According to this scheme, the Hindus in Sind, the Muslims in Assam, the Sikhs in the Punjab and the Frontier, as well as the Hindus and the Muslims in any province where they constituted less than 25 per cent of the population were to secure separate representation.[241] Thus, for the Congress, the Hindus of the Punjab and Bengal were not minorities, nor were communities like the 'Depressed Classes', Indian Christians or the Anglo-Indians.

The issue of who could be considered a minority once again came to the fore during the proceedings of the Joint Committee on Indian Constitutional Reform. The occasion was how were the tribals to be regarded and this led, perhaps by chance, to an authoritative statement from the Raj as to who should be regarded as a minority. Lord Zetland, a former Governor of Bengal, asked Hoare as to whether the tribals should be regarded as a minority. To which, Hoare responded that only religiously defined communities could be recognised as minorities adding that 'there is considerable practical difficulty when you get away from that conception'.[242] Hoare was being disingenuous. The Raj had recognised the 'Depressed Classes' as a minority despite being Hindus (at least till then). If religion was to be the criteria then all the three Christian communities, namely the Europeans, the Anglo-Indians and the Indian Christians, should have been combined in a single electorate, which was not done. Hoare's explanation apart, the term 'minority' was something that was applied as per the political convenience of the Raj.

The overall thrust of Ambedkar's politics at least since the 1930s was to obtain the recognition of the 'Scheduled Castes' as a distinct social and hence a political minority community so as to be considered for separate political representation. This can be clearly seen in his address to the Scheduled Caste Federation in 1945, which was later published and is known as 'The Communal Deadlock and the Way to Solve It' and his 1947 work 'States and Minorities'. It was in the second work that Ambedkar discussed the basis on which he regarded the 'Scheduled Castes' as a separate minority community. He did not quite refute the claim that the 'Scheduled Castes' were Hindus, something that was being deployed to deny the community the status of a minority. Ambedkar argued that not just religion but social discrimination faced by a community determined whether it was a minority or not.[243]

His efforts seemed to have borne fruit for Sir Stafford Cripps during his mission to India acknowledged that the community should be regarded as a minority, along with other communities, which would secure all the requisite constitutional protections.[244] Later, he assured Ambedkar and M.C. Rajah that the community came within the definition of racial and religious minorities.[245] However, it was realised that unlike the Muslims, the 'Scheduled Castes' were not geographically concentrated in any part of the country and that the Raj could do nothing to safeguard the community's interests. Yet, in the run-up to the process of constitution making in India, Jagjivan Ram and other 'Scheduled Caste' leaders asserted that the community was a minority.[246]

The debates in the early days of the Constituent Assembly reveal a concern about dealing with the issue of minorities. The resolution on Aims and Objectives, popularly known as the Objectives Resolution, moved by Pandit Jawaharlal Nehru in the Assembly on 13 December 1946 talked of adequate safeguards for the minorities. Moreover, there were discussions in these pre-Partition days of who exactly should be regarded as a minority. Dr S.P. Mookerjee reminded the Assembly that the Hindus were a minority in four of the British Indian provinces and that were thus entitled to all the safeguards stipulated for the minorities.[247] The demands of the Sikhs were also couched in terms of the community being a minority by Sardar Ujjal Singh.[248] A similar demand was made by P.R. Thakur who explicitly asked for the 'Scheduled Castes' to be regarded as a minority. But significantly, Thakur denied that his community was a racial or religious minority but asked that it be recognised as a distinct political entity, a political minority.[249] Minorities were also sought to be defined in non-communal or non-religious terms. Interestingly, Jaipal Singh denied that the tribals were a minority without explaining the reasons for his assertion.[250]

The mind of the Government and by extension of the Congress was revealed in the Interim Report on Fundamental Rights. Clause 18, which encompassed cultural and educational rights, talked of minorities based on 'religion, community or language'.[251] The first and the last were self-explanatory. It was the second which was the odd man out. Was it a concession to the Scheduled Castes whose constant demand had been for the community to be regarded as a distinct political entity? If they were considered as a part of the Hindu community, then they were not a religious minority, and, in any case, could by no stretch of imagination be described as a linguistic minority. The only way out was to define them in terms of caste. Perhaps that was felt to be rather explicit and hence the euphemism of 'community' was resorted to.

However, this discrepancy was sought to be ironed out by the time the report on Minority Rights was tabled in the Assembly. K.M. Munshi moved an officially approved amendment seeking to make explicit the mention of the Scheduled Castes as a community that was to be granted reservations. Munshi clarified the necessity of this amendment on the grounds that since minorities were generally considered to be religious, racial and linguistic, and that since the Scheduled Castes did not fall into any of these three categories, there was need to have a specific mention of the community. Yet, he claimed that since the Constitution was going to abolish all social disabilities faced by the community, any recognition and thus any granting of safeguards for it would be 'illogical' and 'prevent their complete absorption in the Hindu fold'.[252] Clearly, the Congress was reluctant to accept the Scheduled Castes as a distinct political entity.

In general, three broad positions regarding minorities can be discerned. The first which while acknowledging the existence of minority communities desired and hoped that these communities would soon integrate with the rest of Indian society to form 'one corporate nation, a homogenous nation' as Minoo Masani, who described himself as a member of the 'tiniest of all national minorities'.[253] A similar sentiment was expressed by Mahavir Tyagi who wished 'to dissolve minorities into the majority'.[254] However, he went even further when he claimed that minorities were 'a mere fiction having no existence'.[255] Dr S. Radhakrishnan was even blunter when he described minorities as a 'disruptive element' who should not be 'perpetuated'.[256] Even Dr Ambedkar, while reiterating his previous stand that the majority in India was communal and not political, hoped while presenting the Draft Constitution to the Assembly that it would soon be possible for 'majorities and minorities to merge someday into one'. Of course, this objective was to be secured by the majority ensuring that the minorities are not discriminated against. Once this discrimination ceased, as Ambedkar put it, 'the minorities have no ground to exist. They will vanish.'[257] One Muslim member, Tajamul Hussain, claimed that the term 'minority' was a British creation and now no such thing existed in India.[258]

The second position again acknowledging the existence of such communities hoped that a *modus vivendi* would be worked out by which the minorities would retain their distinct identities and be granted certain rights without any adverse political consequences, either for themselves or for the country as a whole. This seemed to have been the stance taken by many Assembly members who belonged to the minority communities like Father Jerome D'Souza, Sardar Harnam Singh and Sardar B.S. Mann.[259]

The third emphasised these distinctive identities and sought institutional arrangements for the same. This was seen in the repeated demands made by some Muslim members of the Assembly for separate electorates, even after August 1947. Overall, the third position lost ground with Partition and the first became the dominant one.

The minority question came up for discussion during the meetings of the Minority Sub-Committee of the Advisory Committee of the Constituent Assembly. In its meeting on 24 July (i.e. after the Partition Plan had been announced), the committee drew up the following list of minorities—Anglo-Indians, Parsis, Plains tribesmen of Assam, Indian Christians, Sikhs, Muslims and the Scheduled Castes.[260] The claims of the Scheduled Tribes were once again overlooked but not for long. The Thakkar Sub-Committee emphatically recommended that the tribes be regarded as a minority,[261] perhaps in order to bolster the case for its recommendation that the community be granted reserved seats.

Despite the abolition of separate electorates and even reserved seats for the minorities, the issue of who exactly were the minority communities remained alive. It was revived when on 26 August 1949 Dr Ambedkar moved an amendment to the Draft Constitution providing for the appointment of a Special Officer for the welfare of the minorities. This sparked off a debate on who should be treated as the minorities and ultimately a discussion on the issue was postponed. However, this debate does not seem to have taken place.

Logic of Weightage

Another issue that bedevilled the debate on representation was that of 'weightage'. Generally, the assumption was that any group or section of society demanding separate representation should secure it in proportion to its numbers. However, it was claimed that some groups, for a variety of reasons, should secure a quantum of representation in excess of what would have been due to it in terms of its share in the population. This was what was meant by 'weightage'. However, there does not seem to be any reasoned discussion or justification for the logic of weightage. The Morley–Minto reforms scheme introduced weightage for the Muslims. A command paper submitted to the British parliament suggested that this quantum of this weightage separately in each province was based on the 'status, character, and educational attainments' of the Muslims in that province.[262] Though the Congress opposed weightage for the Muslims in 1909, ultimately in 1916 by the Lucknow Pact, it conceded the principle of weightage to the Muslims in those provinces where they were a minority but in those provinces where they were a majority, the community actually received a share of representation below what was warranted by their share in the populace.

The Southborough Committee broadly accepted the Lucknow Pact in fixing the proportion of Muslims representation in the provincial councils. There were murmurs of protest from the higher echelons of the Raj on this excess of representation but the Government of India while expressing its dismay at the quantum of weightage granted to the Muslims accepted it as a *fait accompli*.[263] However, it is not clear whether the Government of India was objecting to the principle of weightage or its quantum though it did note that had it been writing on a clean slate the representation granted to the Muslims would have been close to the community's share in the population. Sir William Vincent, a member of the Viceroy's Executive Council, in his note of dissent while protesting the adoption of the Lucknow Pact, laid down certain conditions for granting of weightage to the Muslims. He said weightage should be calculated on a sliding scale, which meant that the lesser the proportion of the Muslims in the population of a province the higher should be its quantum of representation in excess of this proportion.[264] Thus, weightage was clearly seen as a compensatory device for the numerical and hence political weakness of a community. However, in the case of the Sikhs, the Punjab government was clear that weightage was due to them for a host of reasons, mainly their contribution to the war and their historical position in the province,[265] a sentiment shared by the Sikh witnesses who appeared before the Southborough Committee as well as the Joint Select Committee of 1919. Objections to the weightage granted to the Muslims came from the Bombay province where Ambedkar and Latthe registered strong objections to it. Their argument was that the grant of any excess share to any single community would deprive other needy communities even a share in proportion to their population.[266]

The complexities of granting weightage to minorities where the majority community enjoyed a tenuous majority came to the fore in the case of the Punjab and Bengal. However, a principle that sought to balance the two came to the fore in the 1920s when Shafaat Ahmed Khan from the United Provinces talked of minorities being given effective representation while majorities should not be turned into legislative minorities.[267] This perhaps could be interpreted as a sign that the Muslims of the provinces where the community was a majority were no longer prepared to whittle down their due legislative share to accommodate their co-religionists from the minority provinces.

Furthermore, the Nehru Report entirely rejected the idea of weightages. It argued with reference to primarily the Muslims, that since the minorities were being granted reserved seats in proportion to their population and an additional right to contest non-reserved seats, weightage simply could not be conceded.[268] Thus, the additional right was seen as a substitute for weightage. Furthermore, the Simon Commission noted the problem created by granting of weightage to any one or more than one community. It pointed out that weightage for some necessarily meant the reduction of representation in the proportion of the population to others.[269] Despite this, it did recommend weightage for the Sikhs in the Punjab arguing that the community's influence at the all-India level depended on its political strength at the provincial level.[270]

Curiously, the Commission recommended that the 'Depressed Classes' be under-weighed. The percentage of seats reserved for the community from among the general seats (i.e. Hindu) should be three-quarters of its share in the Hindu population. The commission's argument was that given the 'poverty and want of education' among the community it would simply be difficult to find suitable candidates. It justified its recommendations by stating that the community would be served better by a smaller number of 'qualified spokesmen rather than by a larger number of ineffectives'.[271] The Commission sought to maintain the status quo as far as the quantum of Muslim representation was concerned pointing that granting the Muslims representation in terms of their share in population in the Punjab and Bengal without doing the same in the Muslim-minority provinces was not possible without an inter-communal agreement.[272] The Indian Central Committee had its own take on weightage. It suggested either that the quantum of representation for minorities be determined by a share in population or by voting strength, whichever was favourable.[273]

The most elaborate discussion of the logic of weightage came from Dr Ambedkar in his separate report attached to that of the Bombay Provincial Committee. He first concentrated his fire on the weightage granted to the Muslims. He argued that the Muslims demanded weightage primarily out of a feeling that they were once rulers of the country and hence their importance should be not be determined by mere numbers. However, Ambedkar did not dismiss the principle of weightage per se. As he put it, 'unless the representation of minorities is intended to provide political fun' weightage must be adopted to ensure adequate representation for the minority communities. He also cautioned that this must not lead to a situation where the minorities overwhelm the majority. But he also provided a benchmark of how this weightage was to be calculated. Ambedkar stated that the quantum of representation for each minority should be calculated by multiplying its share in population by a factor somewhere between one and two. However, the factor for each community was to be different and this, in turn, was to be determined by the needs of a given community. The higher the levels of educational attainments and economic standing, the lower would be the factor. It was on this basis that Ambedkar reduced the Muslim share while enhancing that of the 'Depressed Classes'.[274]Ambedkar reiterated this argument of his in the evidence tendered to the Simon Commission and during the first Round Table Conference.[275] The issue that Muslim weightage blocked the demand for the same for the 'Depressed Classes', first flagged by Ambedkar, recurred before the Lothian Committee.

The question of weightage of minorities bedevilled the Punjab where the Muslims were in a bare majority. The Punjab Provincial Committee, while declaring its desire to grant the Hindu and Sikh minorities due weightage, expressed its inability to do so since that would have meant the Muslims becoming a legislative minority. Yet, it also promised the Sikhs weightage to the fullest possible extent. Ultimately, it proposed two schemes for the constitution of the local Council which would give the Muslims a majority of one member.[276] This led to strong criticism from the two Hindu members of the committee, Raja Narendra Nath and Dr Gokal Chand Narang. The duo stated that ideally they preferred joint electorates, and demanded that the Hindus and the Sikhs be given due weightage. They claimed that there was no reason for the two communities to be deprived of their due just because the Muslims were not in an overwhelming majority in the Punjab.[277]

The Muslim League in its submission to the Simon Commission demanded weightage for the community in the Muslim-minority provinces citing the old arguments of political and historical importance as well as economic and educational backwardness. It extended the same concessions to non-Muslims wherever they were in a small minority but without reducing the quantum of representation for the Muslims of the Punjab and Bengal below their share in the population.[278] The Hindus of Bengal and the Hindus and the Sikhs of the Punjab were denied weightage by the League's principal spokesperson, Sir Muhammad Shafi, on two grounds. Firstly, weightage would reduce the Muslims to a minority in the local councils and secondly, since the non-Muslims constituted almost 45 per cent of the population they could hardly be described as minorities in need of any additional protection.[279] At the first Round Table Conference, he added that if the Hindus were democratically entitled to their majorities in the Muslim minority provinces, then the Muslims had the same right where they were the majority.[280] The collapse of the attempts to resolve this problem ultimately caused the failure of the second Round Table Conference.

The question of weightage naturally figured during the first Round Table Conference where the Sikh representatives demanded it in the Punjab on grounds of not past service but contributions to the treasury,[281] which was reiterated in the second Round Table Conference. At the First Round Table Conference, Dr Ambedkar and his colleague, R. Srinivasan, made a strong plea to the first Conference for weightage to the 'Depressed Classes' of Bombay and Madras as a means to resolving the problems faced by them.[282]

The principle of 'weightage' was conceded in the Government of India Act, 1935. However, in the run-up to independence, the question was reopened. Once again, it was Ambedkar who provided a theoretical justification for the principle of 'weightage'. He argued that since the majority in India was a communal one and not a political one, there was no chance for the minorities to have access to or obtain a share in power. Hence, he devised an elaborate scheme, known as 'The Communal Deadlock' scheme, which provided for weightages. According to Ambedkar, the minorities should receive weightage in inverse proportion to 'their social standing, economic position and educational conditions'.[283] The theoretical position underpinning this scheme was that the majority community, the Hindus should not be in a position to form the government without the co-operation of any of the larger minority communities, namely either the Muslims or the 'Scheduled Castes'. This would, of course, have proved to be politically unacceptable. Ambedkar provided a similar scheme of weightage in early 1947 with similar arguments about the nature of the majority in India.[284] He further argued that weightage was necessary for minorities in order to give them effective representation.[285] Ambedkar knew well enough that no amount of weightage could reduce the majority community to a legislative minority. This state of the affairs he attributed to the insistence of what he called the 'Communal Majority' to maintain its political majority. Perhaps, this was the reason he argued that the effectiveness of representation depended not only on its quality but on its the quantum as well. For Ambedkar, weightage was essential in order to prevent the minority from developing a feeling of being overwhelmed by the majority. However, the Constituent Assembly did away with 'weightage' and thus an issue that had bedevilled Indian politics faded into irrelevance.

5

Methods of Political Representation

The diverse claims for political representation made by various sections of Indian society had to be translated into practice and it was this necessity that began the debate on the methods of representation. The legislative bodies that were established and then expanded from the nineteenth century onwards had to be representative, broadly speaking of these very sections, and thus, this debate focussed on the issue of which institutional arrangements would best secure this objective. In the initial period, the discussions revolved around whether the best method was electoral or non-electoral, and later, once the former had become the dominant mode of representation, around how an electoral system should be framed, given the goal of securing legislatures that were representative in character.

The first issue in the context of methods was that of the relative merits of nominations, a non-electoral method of political representation versus elections. The principle that representatives should be elected became acceptable much later, in the early twentieth century. But in the late nineteenth century, nomination was regarded, in the Indian context, as a method superior to elections. Apart from the usual argument that the backwardness of India meant that it was not eligible for self-government, let alone elections, it was argued that there was no marked enthusiasm for elections in India, and that given the strongly hierarchical nature of Indian society, the elites would not deign to canvass their social inferiors for votes and thus stay away from elections,[1] and by extension the legislative bodies. Underpinning this worry was the belief that these elites constituted the 'natural leaders' of Indian society and that their collaboration was essential for both the stability, and the legitimisation in Indian eyes of the colonial regime. The newly established legislatures were seen as institutionalised mechanisms of this collaboration, and hence the absence of these very elites from them would weaken the Raj. This, along with the assumption that the colonial rulers knew what was best for the 'natives', made nominations preferable to the electoral principle.

Around the turn of the century when adoption of the principle of elections was regarded as being inevitable sooner rather than later, nominations were posed as an alternative to elections where the latter were not feasible. Moreover, nominations were also regarded as being supplementary devices to ensure representativeness of the legislative bodies in case elections resulted in the dominance of a particular section of society. Much later, nomination was seen as an arrangement by which certain social groups whose representation was seen as desirable but could not be ensured by election were to be represented. This was driven by the perception that elections were majoritarian and exclusionary in character, and hence could not by themselves ensure the representativeness of the legislatures. This was reflected in the provisions of the 1919 and the 1935 Acts that empowered the provincial Governors to nominate a specified number of individuals belonging to communities or interests, who had not secured representation through elections to their local legislatures.

The all-India and the provincial governments nominated the first Indian members of the Legislative Councils established by the Act of 1861. It is only with the coming of the 1892 Act that the electoral principle was introduced through the backdoor when certain institutions were given the right to recommend to the government who their representative should be, with the proviso that the government had the right to reject the individual so nominated. It was only during the period of the Morley–Minto reforms that the issue of nominations versus elections came to the fore. The general approach of the Raj, as discerned in the proposal for an enlarged all-India legislative council as formulated by the Government of India, seemed to be that those interests that deserved representation should be represented by nominees rather than through elections if they could not be constituted into suitable electorates, while adding that elections were 'the ultimate objective to be secured'.[2] Furthermore, many individuals, both Indian and European, who made submissions to the government on the question of the expansion of the councils argued for nominations being used as supplementary to the electoral principle.[3] Yet, there were others, both British and Indian, who regarded nominations as being preferable since that India was politically backward.[4]

But overall, it seems that the supporters of nominations were on the defensive. Yet no strong defence of elections as the best means to secure representation was mounted, though some took the opportunity to point out that the probability that elected bodies and representatives would enjoy a larger measure of public confidence.[5] The electoral principle became more of a preferred option during the Montagu–Chelmsford reforms. This preference was perhaps again driven by the necessity to secure the collaboration of important sections of Indian society who now desired to choose their representatives for themselves. Elections were now seen as a legitimising device, both by the Raj and the vocal sections of Indian society. Thus, the period between the Morley–Minto reforms and the Montagu–Chelmsford reforms is crucial in the journey from nominations to elections.

The rise in claims of political representation by numerous sections of Indian society meant that it was necessary to decide how these claims, if acknowledged, were to be translated into reality. This gave a fillip to the debate between elections and nominations. While the Montagu–Chelmsford Report proclaimed the virtues of elections, the limitations of the very scheme of reforms ensured that the system of nominations would continue to exist. The Report declared that in order to prevent an excessive number of elected members, it would prefer certain sections to be represented by nomination. It mentioned nominations as being both supplementary and alternatives to elections and that they were superior to communal electorates since they could be easily abolished.[6] The Southborough Committee also cited political education as an advantage of the electoral principle.

The debate between elections and nominations resumed with the underlying issue being that of electoral feasibility. If a certain community or interest could constitute a suitable electorate, it could be represented through elections and if not through nominations. This issue became sharper particularly about the 'Depressed

Classes' or the Dalits. While there was widespread support to the representation of the community per se for it was acknowledged that it had significant interests that required political representation, there was, however, significant opposition to the community being represented through elections and there also was broad agreement on the necessity of nominations. The arguments against elections ranged from the impracticality of constituting a substantially large electorate given that the qualifications for enfranchisement, based on income or ownership of property were so stringent, that most of the 'Depressed Classes' would not qualify as voters in the first place, to the alleged lack of education among the community. These arguments obviously meant that the community could be best represented through nominations.

It was, of course, but natural that the only two Dalit witnesses, who gave evidence before the Southborough Committee, supported elections. It must be noted that in this entire process, the Dalits were the only community for whom nominations were seen as being desirable as also preferable to elections. Indeed, there were proposals that the 'Depressed Classes' could be represented by Hindu upper-caste social reformers, European officials or Christian missionaries. In fact, the Joint Select Committee on the Government of India Bill, 1919, seems to have assumed that the 'Depressed Classes' would have to be represented by non-members, for it directed the Government of India to ensure that persons nominated to represented the community should, as far as possible, not be civil servants.[7]

This was astonishing since the Southborough Committee recommended representation through elections to numerically smaller communities like the Europeans, the Anglo-Indians and the Indian Christians. Elections for the last two were advocated on the grounds that it would provide an 'opportunity for political education'.[8] Similarly, the difficulty in determining who exactly was an 'Anglo-Indian' did not prevent the committee from recommending communal electorates for the community, albeit not in all provinces. The criteria used to determine the provinces where the electoral principle was granted was the 'strength and importance' of the communities concerned.[9] In the rest of the provinces, the committee made it a point to recommend representation by nominations.

The Southborough Committee in its detailed proposals for each provincial council specified the communities and economic interests that were to be represented to nominations arguing that such an arrangement was being made for those who could not be represented through elections.[10] Furthermore, the rules regarding political representation made under the Government of India Act, 1919, specified the economic interests that would be represented through nomination. Thus, for example, the cotton trade and the working classes were to have representatives in the local council in Bombay. Thus, some communities and interests were important enough to be granted representation qua communities and interests respectively but not important enough for them to have their representatives elected.

Furthermore, nominations were also seen at this stage as being supplementary in nature for the Southborough Committee recommended them to correct any imbalance caused by the electoral dominance of a particular community.[11] Furthermore, the rules also permitted the provincial governments of Madras and Assam to select nominees from among those persons selected by those interests and communities that were to be represented by nomination, a change proposed by the Joint Select Committee.[12] Thus, an element of the electoral principle was introduced within the system of nominations, albeit one that was not mandatory.

If the principle of elections found favour, it led to the question of direct versus indirect elections, an issue that cropped up during the Montagu-Chelmsford reforms. The Morley–Minto scheme had expanded the scope of the electoral principle but only in a limited sense. In the all-India legislative council as well as the provincial councils, the non-communal territorial constituencies elected their representatives through an indirect method. Only the special interests and the Muslims could directly elect their representatives. Since the Montagu–Chelmsford reforms envisaged substantial devolution of power to the provinces, it was clear that provincial councils with a large proportion of indirectly elected members would not be suitable. Hence the reforms proposed direct elections for the provincial councils on a franchise that would be as broad as possible.[13] There seems to be no extensive debate on this issue. It seems that there was widespread consensus on this count.

However, whether direct elections should be provided for the Indian Legislative Assembly and the Council of State, envisaged as the lower house and upper house respectively of the all-India legislature that was proposed in the new reforms, proved to be a matter of debate. The Council of State with a smaller proportion of the elective element as compared to the Legislative Assembly was proposed as some kind of a bulwark against nationalist passions. It was a chamber where the Government of India could ensure the passage of essential legislative measures that faced opposition in the lower house. The Montagu–Chelmsford Report proposed that the upper chamber be largely indirectly elected.[14] It preferred direct elections to the Assembly but acknowledged the difficulties of conducting them on the grounds that the country was large. But it entrusted the Franchise Committee to resolve the question.[15]

These difficulties stemmed from the logic of the reforms themselves. The emphasis of continuing the strong position of the Government of India in the all-India legislature entailed that the lower house could not be expanded beyond a certain point. If the lower house was expanded, then it was obvious that the proportion of Indian members, both elected and nominated, would have to be increased and then they would have had to be balanced by a significant number of official members so as to maintain the position of the executive. Sparing a large number of officials to act as ballast for the executive would have proved difficult. Hence, it was imperative from the imperial point of view to have a lower house of manageable proportions, a point acknowledged by the Government of India.[16] This naturally meant a fewer number of directly elected members, which in turn would have led to geographically huge constituencies with a large number of voters, a prospect the colonial regime found fraught with administrative difficulties.

The Southborough Committee endorsed the views of the Report. It did explore the option of direct elections to the Assembly with a higher level of franchise qualifications, only to reject it on the somewhat specious grounds that the landed element would dominate in such a situation, and that it was illogical in view of a broad franchise for the provincial councils.[17] Evidently, it only considered income or property as the best qualifications for granting the vote. The possibility feared by the committee could have been easily obviated with the introduction of education as an additional qualification for voting. But this was rejected as being unsuitable.[18] Many Indian witnesses did support direct elections to the Assembly. It was obvious that the submissions made to the committee would support direct elections to the provincial councils.

Interestingly, it was the Government of India that opposed indirect elections for the Council of State and was divided on the same issue with reference to the lower house. In the case of the former, the government claimed that it envisaged the upper chamber as where elder statesmen would gather and hence advocated that its elected element be elected directly on a high franchise qualification. For the lower house, the government found itself divided and suggested the formulation of a scheme for direct elections in the near future.[19] Interestingly, it was the Joint Select Committee on the Government of India Bill, 1919, who directed the Government of India to frame a scheme for direct elections to the Legislative Assembly.[20] This was perhaps due to the Government of India's change of heart over the issue. However, the committee acceded to the Indian government's pleas for direct elections to the Council of State.

If it was thought that direct elections had won the day, the Simon Commission reopened the debate by recommending indirect elections to the Indian Legislative Assembly. The provincial councils were to elect representatives to this body, now proposed to be renamed as the Federal Assembly.[21] It claimed that direct elections would entail geographically large and thus unwieldy constituencies, which in turn would lead to administrative difficulties in conducting elections and would also make it difficult for the voters and the representatives to keep in touch with each other. The Commission's arguments were entirely specious, for it had not only recommended an expansion in the quantum of elected membership of the Assembly but also the franchise. This would no doubt mean an increase in the number of voters but at the same time would mean geographically smaller constituencies. If 'huge' constituencies, albeit with a limited franchise, under the Montagu–Chelmsford reforms had not posed administrative difficulties, it is hard to imagine smaller ones doing so. A widening of the franchise would no doubt have meant a larger number of voters in these smaller constituencies but the fact that now the election in a given constituency would be conducted over a much reduced area would have meant administrative convenience. The Simon Commission simply seems to not have applied its mind to the issue.

The debate over direct or indirect elections took place in the context of the proposed new bi-cameral Federal legislature. This resolution of this debate was contingent on the nature of the federal structure that was to be devised for India and the powers that were to be granted to the two chambers of the legislature. The participants in the first Round Table Conference seemed to be divided on racial lines over this question since the British delegates largely favoured indirect elections while the Indian ones supported direct elections. The British participants preferred indirect elections on grounds of convenience. The general position of the Conference was that the Upper House was to act as a revising chamber so as to prevent the Lower House from pushing through radical legislation. Arguments for an indirectly elected upper chamber were of the usual kind, for they claimed that such an arrangement would provide representation to the provinces per se and would safeguard the federal character of the constitution. However, it was Sir Tej Bahadur Sapru who emphasised a point that had been missed. He objected to direct elections for the Upper House since then it would be difficult to deny that body a voice in financial matters. He added that if this body was conceived as one that would act as a 'brake' on 'hasty' legislation, it should be preferably indirect. Yet at the same time, he conceded the difficulty in undoing what the Montagu–Chelmsford reforms had granted.[22] The Federal Structure

Sub-Committee that dealt with this issue finally plumped for the norm practised in federal political systems and recommended a directly elected lower house and an indirectly elected upper house. This upper house was to be elected by the provincial councils using PR-STV (Proportional Representation-Single Tranferable Vote).[23]

The issue of nomination cropped up in the discussion of the Provincial Constitution Sub-Committee. The question was how should those communities who had failed to secure representation through elections be represented in the provincial councils. Sir Chimanlal Setalvad suggested co-option which was strongly objected to by Dr Ambedkar. He pointed out that such co-opted representatives might turn out to be 'subservient to and willing to play into the hands of the majority'.[24] This was a reiteration of his insistence on 'authentic representation'. But the alternative to co-option was nomination by the provincial Governor. Dr Ambedkar did not clarify how this would have ensured the 'non-subservient' representatives of these communities.

At the second Round Table Conference, the idea of indirect elections and co-option converged in Mahatma Gandhi's scheme for an electoral system. He proposed a system of indirect election at all levels except the lowest administrative unit that would be coupled with adult franchise. Those interests or communities who failed to secure representation would have their representatives co-opted by the elected members.[25] The whole question was tentatively resolved with the Federal Structure Committee recommending in its Third Report that the Federal Upper House be indirectly elected with the provincial councils being the electorate and that the Lower House be either indirectly elected, similar to the second chamber or be directly elected.

The Lothian Committee that had been appointed as per the decision taken in the first Round Table Conference reiterated the recommendations regarding the Federal legislature but not before exploring some options. It listed the alternatives, which included indirect elections combined with adult franchise, and direct elections with adult franchise in select areas, only to reject them on grounds of administrative difficulties. It plumped for the expected solution, which was direct elections with a restricted franchise. The issue of nominations also figured in the debate on the issue of the representation of the 'Depressed Classes'. The United Provinces Franchise Committee proposed that the representatives of the community be nominated to the provincial council after their names had been suggested by representatives associations of the 'Depressed Classes'.[26] A note by Maurice Hallett, an ICS officer serving in Bihar and Orissa, submitted to the provincial Franchise Committee, argued that nomination or co-option was the best method of providing representation to the 'Depressed Classes' since no viable system of reservations or separate electorates could be devised as the community was widely spread in the province.[27] Similar was the case with the tribals. Both the Central Provinces Government and the Franchise Committee recommended that the tribals be represented through nominations, for no suitable electorates could be devised for the community.[28]

Among the witnesses who appeared before the organisations that made submissions to the Lothian Committee, those who supported nominations were few and far between. The All-India Arundhateeya Sabha wanted what it called a system of 'quasi-nomination' for the 'Depressed Classes'. It argued that despite the lowering of the franchise, members of the community would not qualify as voters in numbers large enough to ensure the election of a significant number of its members, and hence it supported nominations.[29]

The White Paper of 1933 that formed the basis for the Government of India Act, 1935, recommended that the Council of State be indirectly elected by the provincial legislature, whether uni-cameral or bi-cameral.[30] The Federal Assembly was to be directly elected.[31] The provincial Legislative Assemblies too were to be directly elected.[32] In the three provinces where provincial upper houses, the Legislative Councils, were to be established, a mixed system was proposed. Some members were to be nominated by the Governor in his discretion, some elected by the lower house and the rest directly elected on a restricted franchise.[33] Thus the principle of nomination was reintroduced. This seems to have been regarded as a substitute for the official bloc that was now to be abolished. The question of nomination emerged during the proceedings of the Joint Committee on Indian Constitutional Reforms that was appointed to draft the bill that would translate the White Paper into an Act when Dr J.H. Hutton, the Census Commissioner, opined that the tribals would be best represented by nominations.[34]

This entire question was reopened during proceedings of the Joint Committee on Indian Constitutional Reform appointed to draft what was to become the Government of India Act, 1935. The general opinion seems to have leaned towards indirect elections. A memorandum by Sir Samuel Hoare, the Secretary of State for India, discussed the relative merits of the two alternative means of elections and preferred the indirect method. Hoare argued on familiar lines when he claimed that direct elections would entail a large body, thus making it unwieldy and that such a method would pose administrative and logistical difficulties.[35] Another memorandum by three senior Conservative leaders, Lords Derby and Zetland and Sir Austen Chamberlain, who were members of the committee, supported an indirectly elected federal lower house, albeit by STV, on the grounds that it obviated the need for communal electorates at the federal level and make for a numerically smaller and hence manageable body.[36] Attlee argued that given the nature of the proposed federation, it was preferable that the legislature represented the federal units rather than what he described as 'blocks of population'.[37] Apparently, he believed that this would counteract possible centrifugal tendencies. Evidently, Attlee was more concerned with safeguarding the federal character of the proposed new constitutional arrangements than the representativeness of the federal legislature.

Ultimately, the Joint Committee defying all political logic recommended that both the chambers of Federal Legislature be indirectly elected. It suggested that the lower house, the Federal Assembly be elected by the provincial lower houses, the Legislative Assemblies, while the upper house, the Council of State, was to be elected by the provincial upper houses, the Legislative Councils, where they existed and by ad-hoc electoral colleges where they did not.[38] A nominated element was retained in the Legislative Councils to redress inequalities of representation and to secure the representation of women.[39] This retention was supported by entirely specious grounds.

Since almost all communities, except for the Parsis, had been granted communal electorates and nearly all special interests had been granted separate representation, there was hardly anybody left unrepresented. Furthermore, special seats were also to be granted to women. Thus, what purpose was the nominated element in the provincial upper houses supposed to serve remains unclear. Their numerical strength was so meagre that they could not have possibly restrained the possible excesses of a popularly elected government.

The Government of India Act, 1935, finally decided upon these matters. The Council of State, the upper chamber of the Federal Legislature, was to be partly directly elected. There were to be general (i.e. non-communal Hindu dominated), Muslim and Sikh territorial constituencies. The Anglo-Indians, the Indian Christians and the European representatives in the Council of State were to be elected by the members of the provincial Legislative Councils, the upper houses of the provincial legislatures, and, where they did not exist, the Legislative Assemblies, the lower houses, who belonged to the respective communities. A similar provision was made as regards the seats reserved for women. The women members of the provincial legislatures were to constitute the electorate for the same. Six seats were to be filled in the Council of State, by the Governor-General in his discretion.

The Federal Assembly, the lower house of the Federal Legislature, was to be largely indirectly elected by the members of the Legislative Assemblies. Here, the members belonging to the Muslim and the Sikhs as well as those elected from general constituencies were to separately constitute electorates. Thus communal electorates were introduced even in indirect elections. The women members of the Legislative Assemblies were to constitute the electorate for the seats reserved for women. A similar provision was made for the three minor communities mentioned above. The representatives of the Indian States were to be appointed by the Rulers. This meant that they could be nominated with or without any form of elections. This provision left open the possibility that these representatives might be elected in the future.

In the case of the provincial legislatures, the Legislative Assemblies were to be directly elected. Provision was made for a nominated element in the Legislative Councils where they were established. The rest of the members were to be directly elected, except in Bengal and Bihar where a certain number was to be indirectly elected by the members of the respective Assemblies. The question of direct versus indirect election in the case of the tribals had been left open by the 1935 Act by not specifying the method. Five seats had been allotted to the tribals in the Orissa Legislative Assembly by the Act. The Indian Delimitation Committee, known as the Hammond Committee after its Chairman, Sir Laurie Hammond, a former Governor of Assam, adhering to the local government's proposals recommended that four of the five seats be filled through nomination.[40]

The bulk of the constitutional schemes, including the ones formulated by the Sapru Committee and Ambedkar, being devised in the 1940s to settle the communal problem largely supported direct elections. However, M.N. Roy proposed an elaborate scheme that was characterised as 'Organised Democracy' and which combined both direct and indirect elections. He argued that this would be conducive to political education and obviate 'the difficulties of holding elections in a vast country' like India. Directly elected People's Committees were to be set up in each village and urban locality. These committees were to be tasked with nominating candidates for as well as conducting the elections to the federal and provincial legislatures. A directly elected electoral college to elect a representative was to be formed for each constituency at both the levels. The federal upper house, the Council of State, was to consist of members nominated by the provincial government from certain stipulated professions.[41] A similar elaborate scheme of indirect elections for India with the village as the basic unit was proposed by Shriman Narayan Agarwal and was described as Gandhian in inspiration. It was argued that since the members of the lower bodies would elect to the upper bodies, this scheme would eliminate malpractices and at the same time ensure accountability of the representatives.[42]

With the British demission of power imminent, the issue that needed to be settled was how the Constitution-Making Body proposed by the Cabinet Mission Plan was to be elected. The Mission itself commented that ideally such a body should be directly elected by adult franchise but that such a procedure would lead to a long delay and hence stated that it be indirectly elected with the provincial Legislative Assemblies as the electorate.[43] The elections to the Constituent Assembly were held in 1946 and it held its first meeting in late 1946. However, with the Muslim League boycotting the Assembly, its proceedings and those of its committees had an air of unreality about them. But this did not prevent wide-ranging debates on the future constitutional structure of the country.

The representation of the minorities was a key issue herein and nominations soon returned as an institutional measure to secure the representation of those minority communities who were numerically small. The question of the representation of the Anglo-Indians was settled after the representatives of the community withdrew their demand for reserved seats. A compromise was struck and it was stipulated the members of the community would be nominated to the legislatures if it was realised after the elections that it had not secured adequate representation.[44] Nominations also figured in the report of the Union Constitution Committee. It recommended that the Council of States should have 10 members to be nominated after due consultations with Universities and scientific bodies.[45] Thus, nominations were seen as a device to ensure the presence in the legislatures of those communities and persons who otherwise would be absent. In the former instance, nomination was an accommodative device, while there was more of a utilitarian purpose in the second. The nomination of experts was also a throwback to the colonial times when experts could be nominated to the legislatures to secure their viewpoint in the debates over technical issues or legislative measures.

These questions also cropped up in the replies to the questionnaire issued by the Provincial Constitution Committee. Despite the nationalist movement's commitment to adult franchise, some felt that it would be premature to introduce it in the first election and thus indirect elections once again came into the picture. Rajkumari Amrit Kaur proposed a system of indirect elections for the provincial legislature at least for the first two elections.[46] The issue of indirect elections cropped up in the early days of the Constituent Assembly with reference to how the representatives of the Indian States were to become members of the Assembly. However, after much wrangling, the Princes and the Committee came to a compromise, which was reported to the Assembly by Jawaharlal Nehru, that in those States where legislatures existed at least 50 per cent of the representatives of the given State should be elected by the elected members of its legislature. Where such legislatures did not exist, suitable electoral colleges were to be established for the same.[47]

The final recommendations of the Union and the Provincial Constitution Committees were embodied in the first draft of the Constitution prepared by Sir B.N. Rau, the Constitutional Advisor to the Constituent Assembly. The provisions regarding functional representation in the Council of States and the Legislative Councils (i.e. the upper chambers of the provincial legislatures) presumably entailed indirect elections, while nominations were absent except for the Anglo-Indians.[48] Indirect elections once again were introduced by the provision that one-third of the members of the Legislative Councils were to be elected by their respective Legislative Assemblies, the provincial lower chamber. The Governor of a province also was to nominate some members of these councils.[49]

Meanwhile, the Drafting Committee was set up by the Constituent Assembly in August 1947 and Dr Ambedkar was elected the chairman. The Draft Constitution as prepared by the Drafting Committee was submitted to the Assembly in February 1948. Indirect elections and nominations were to be used to constitute the Council of States, while the House of People was to be directly elected.[50] Furthermore, a similar arrangement was made for the state (earlier known as provincial) legislatures. The only difference was that functional representation was recommended to partly fill the Legislative Council, the provincial upper house.[51] The Parliament and the state legislatures were empowered to fill in the details regarding the electoral system for themselves. This power was later exclusively placed in the hands of the Parliament. Despite the decision that the lower house of both the Parliament and the state legislatures was to be elected directly, there was some talk of indirect elections. But the Drafting Committee did not give way and direct elections and adult suffrage were left undisturbed. Similarly, there was some talk of a system of indirect elections or nominations for the tribal areas. However, the sub-committee appointed by the Constituent Assembly to report on the issues relating to the tribals other than those living in Assam, chaired by A.V. Thakkar, dismissed this and recommended direct elections.[52]

The provision for nominations in the Council of States was hardly debated in the Constituent Assembly. Whatever little debate took place was about the professions or walks of life from amongst which nominations were to be made. There was even an amendment to the Draft Constitution moved by Dr Ambedkar himself which provided for the nomination of not more than three experts to the Council of States to advise the Parliament with regards to a particular bill. These experts were to have the right to participate in the proceedings but not the right to vote.[53] This was a throwback to the colonial times and Ambedkar defended it as a useful arrangement. However, the government was soon to change its mind and the amendment was withdrawn. Ambedkar later explained that the feeling now was that the provision of nominated members for the Council of States would serve the purpose of involving experts in the legislative process.[54]

Nominations once again made a comeback as a supplementary device. Sardar Hukum Singh moved an amendment stating that the President be empowered to nominate to the House of the People member of any minority community, which is not adequately represented in that chamber.[55] This amendment was opposed on the grounds that it militated against the Assembly's decision to abolish any institutional arrangements to ensure the representation of the minorities. With only two members participating in the debate, and both in opposition, the amendment was defeated.[56]

The second set of institutional arrangements that were discussed were those of communal or separate sectional electorates, on one hand, and joint electorates, with or without reservations, on the other. These three alternatives could be regarded as forming a continuum on the Institutionalist-Processual axis with communal electorates forming the former end and joint electorates forming the other end. Joint electorates with reservations, along with various schemes for proportional representation were seen as the via media, indeed at times measures to avoid communal electorates altogether. In the entire debate on political representation in India, these methods were seen as mutually exclusive. There was almost no viewpoint which argued for these to be used in conjunction with each other. Furthermore, scholarship on this issue has largely been dominated by the demands for communal electorates made by the Muslims, and more recently those made by the Dalits.

The demands for communal electorates were principally couched in terms of the notion of 'marginalisation' and the concept of 'authentic representation'. Ever since representative institutions were introduced in India, there were concerns that certain groups, either numerical majorities or dominant minorities, would predominate. If the Muslims feared that the Hindus would swamp them, the non-Brahmins in the Madras and the Bombay Presidency were apprehensive of Brahmins sweeping the elections, thus leading to a possible continuation of their social dominance. Those who felt that they would be excluded by the electoral process demanded communal electorates so as to guarantee minimum representation.

Another assumption underpinning this demand was that only an individual belonging to a specified group could represent it in the true sense. The possibility that a group could also be effectively represented, or that it would want to be represented, for some reason, by someone who did not belong to it was rarely considered, indeed institutionally foreclosed. Interestingly, this issue of 'authentic representation' was not applied during the Morley–Minto reforms to the tenant-farmers, the tribes and what were then described as the 'Depressed Classes'. They were to be represented by official members who were experts of matters of land revenue and other related matters. Evidently, some Indians were fit to be represented by one of their own while some others were best represented by outsiders.[57]

During the Morley–Minto reforms, the debates on separate representation revolved largely around the claims of the non-Brahmins in the Madras Presidency and those of the Muslims at the all-India level. The claim that the Hindus, being in a majority, would only elect their own to the exclusion of individuals belonging to all other communities was contested. Others pointing out the opposite countered those who cited evidence that Hindus had elected Muslims. But more importantly, the issue raised was whether a religiously defined minority had distinct political interests of its own qua a religious minority. At this juncture, the claims of the Muslims as a religious minority at the all-India level were under scrutiny. It was argued that if the Muslims were to be regarded as constituting a religious minority requiring separate representation then there were other communities who could be described as the same. This line of argument seemed to undermine the logic of separate representation by expanding it. Since granting separate representation to all minority communities was obviously not feasible, this was sought to be used as an argument against the same for the Muslims.

Furthermore, internal diversity among the Muslims was utilised as an argument against separate representation. It was argued that the granting of a few seats for the community would not enable the representation of minorities within it, and thus there was no point in conceding separate representation.[58] Any reopening of the question of communal representation for the Muslims was foreclosed during the Montagu–Chelmsford reforms. As the report formulating the reforms pointed out, the Muslims had been granted this concession during the Morley–Minto reforms and that it would not be possible to abolish it without adverse political consequences.[59] Evidence offered to Southborough Committee, however, saw a replay of the debate on the issue of communal representation.

The usual arguments of separate electorates being divisive, accentuating and perpetuating existing social divisions, and obstructing the creation of a common Indian identity were trotted out. If leading Congressmen articulated these opinions, there was also an odd British officer like H.J. Maynard, the Financial Commissioner of Punjab, who expressed similar views. There were also voices who argued that communal electorates were necessary as a transitional measure given the stage of political development that India found itself at. Given that the strongest demand for communal electorates came from the Muslims, it was hardly surprising that most witnesses belonging to the community, barring three—Mazhar-ul-Haq from Bihar and Mirza Ali Muhammad Khan and Sir Fazul Currimbhoy of Bombay—supported communal representation. Individuals belonging to other communities also put forth similar claims. But the most sophisticated defence of separate electorates came from Dr B.R. Ambedkar which turned around the notion of 'authentic representation', something that he described as 'personal representation'. For Ambedkar, the interests of individuals belonging to diverse communities seemed to be of two kinds—non-religious and religious. Non-religious interests of a given community could well be represented by someone who did not belong to it but religious interests would be truly represented only by a member. Since individuals in India would prioritise religious interests over their non-religious ones, they would vote for someone who belonged to their groups rather than a non-member who by virtue of sharing these non-religious interests could or would effectively represent them. This would render minimal the possibility of members of minority groups being elected to the councils, and hence the need for communal representation. Ambedkar further argued that communal electorates, by ensuring the representation of all social groups in the councils, would bring together individuals who otherwise would not interact socially into a common arena or what he called 'associated life'. This social interaction, Ambedkar further argued, would dissolve social divisions.[60]

This defence of Ambedkar's, though, was not without its ambiguities. He explicitly repudiated the non-Brahmin demand for communal electorates and neither did he display any singular enthusiasm for the Muslim demand for the same. He admitted that his argument was largely limited to the cause of separate electorates for the 'untouchable Hindus'.[61] Ambedkar naturally found support on this count from G.A. Gavai, the only other Dalit witness to appear before the Committee, but also from the same four witnesses who supported elections for Dalits, V.R. Shinde, N.M. Joshi and P.R. Chikodi from Bombay and B. Pattabhi Sitaramayya.[62]

The question of separate electorates was predicated on the assumption that minorities qua minorities required safeguards. No one could seriously dispute the assertion that there was a possibility that the interests of the minorities might be overlooked in any system of representation primarily based on elections and that hence they would require special consideration. Indeed, the Lucknow Pact of 1916 conceded not only separate electorates for the Muslims on the grounds that they were a minority community but also representation in excess of their share in population on the basis what was recognised as the principle of 'weightage'.[63] But not all spokespersons of minority communities supported communal electorates. K.T.Paul, representing the All-India Christian Conference, in his evidence to the Joint Select Committee on the Government of India Bill, 1919, in fact repudiated them on grounds that it would lead to the separation of this community from wider Indian society, and asked for reserved seats.[64]

However, no one seems to have given a thought to the fact that not all individuals belonging to a given community that had been granted separate electorates would actually want them or that voters in such electorates would want their choice of candidates to be restricted to members of their own communities. Two witnesses who appeared before the Southborough Committee, R.P. Paranjpye of Bombay and N.P. Asthana of the United Provinces, asked for the Muslims to be given an option as to whether they could like to be voters in communal electorates or not.[65] Yakub Hasan, a Muslim League leader from Madras, suggested that Hindus should be allowed to contest in the Muslim communal electorates.[66]

If separate electorates were regarded as one of the safeguards for minorities, this claim was contested by the Nehru Committee Report. The report departed from the usual practice of criticising communal electorates for being divisive or being obstacles in the process of formation of a nation. It resorted to what could be easily described as commonsensical arguments. It pointed out that minorities are in fact adversely affected by such a system of representation, for it ensures that a communal minority will always remain a political minority and moreover make it the target of a hostile majority.[67]

However, the key question was that of majorities who claimed that they equally required special treatment on the grounds that they would be marginalised by strong minorities. This issue largely arose due to the absence of adult franchise, which entailed that a community that constituted a numerical majority in the population might well be a numerical minority in the electoral arena. This knotty question remained unresolved till the Partition of the subcontinent but not before generating a debate on how majorities as well as minorities were to be defined.

The majority–minority problem during the Morley–Minto period was restricted to the Punjab and the province of Eastern Bengal and Assam, both where the Muslims constituted a numerical majority. Here the official argument of minority protection was turned on its head. The Muslims in Eastern Bengal and Assam were unorganised,[68] while those in the Punjab were backward.[69] This, of course, did not go unchallenged, for it was pointed out that it was the Hindus who were the minority in these provinces and hence required separate representation. The same problem bedevilled the Bombay Presidency with reference to Sindh, a Muslim majority region, in a non-Muslim majority province. The Bombay Presidency Association treated the issue of separate representation for Muslims as one pertaining to all minority communities, and hence asked for safeguards where the Muslims constituted a numerical majority.[70] The Morley–Minto reforms did not grant communal electorates to the Muslims in Punjab. But this was more because the elective element in the provincial council was kept minimal. In Eastern Bengal and Assam, however, the Muslims were granted separate electorates. Since the Muslims qualified to be voters could vote both in communal and non-communal electorates, separate representation in these two provinces was perceived as being an institutional measure to ensure minimum Muslim representation.

The majority problem was somewhat subdued in the Madras Presidency where the provincial government in its reform proposals sought to legally restrict the number of Brahmins that could be elected to the local councils. There was strong opposition to these proposals not only from Brahmins but also from British officials. But no one seems to have asked why if the non-Brahmins who were a majority needed protection from the Brahmins. This issue was to come to the fore a decade later with the Montagu–Chelmsford reforms.

The Montagu–Chelmsford Report tried to tackle the problem of the Muslim majority provinces by declaring itself against communal electorates for the community where it constituted a majority of the voters,[71] a crucial proviso. But in the absence of adult suffrage, it was evident that the exact level of franchise qualifications would determine the share that the various religious communities would obtain in the electorate. Thus, the Muslims could become a minority in the electorate of those provinces where they were a majority in the population.

However, the Lucknow Pact had already granted communal electorates to the Muslims in the two provinces, Punjab and Bengal, where the community constituted a majority of the population. But the Muslims were denied the right to vote in non-communal electorates, a privilege that had been granted to them by the Morley–Minto reforms. This trade-off, in a sense, resolved the issue. Furthermore, the Southborough Committee conceded communal electorates for the Muslims in Punjab and Bengal since it realised that the franchise qualifications that it proposed would leave the community in a minority in the electorate in both these provinces.[72] This possibility could have been obviated by lowering the franchise qualifications for the community, a course the committee declined to follow.[73] These views of the committee were endorsed by the Government of India and were embodied in the Government of India Act, 1919, and rule made thereunder.

The question of non-Brahmins in Madras and Bombay presidencies as well as that of the Muslims in Sindh revived the question of majorities seeking communal electorates, though there were significant differences between the two instances. This, particularly with reference to the non-Brahmins, was debated in terms of what could be called the notion of 'electoral autonomy'. If individual voters belonging to a majority community were in thrall of a powerful minority community leading to members of such a minority community being elected in numbers disproportionate to their strength, then the former evidently were not politically autonomous. Two related attitudes can be discerned in this context. Firstly, the phenomenon of non-Brahmins electing Brahmins was seen by the spokespersons of the former as somewhat anomalous. The notion seemed to be that Brahmins could not function as 'authentic' representatives of the non-Brahmins. Secondly, it was regarded as equally anomalous that a small minority like the Brahmins should dominate electoral politics.

The Madras Government was one of the strongest supporters of the non-Brahmin demand for communal electorates. It, of course, could not avoid the fact that the non-Brahmins constituted a majority of the Hindu voters under the Morley–Minto reforms scheme. But in an extensive statistical analysis, it demonstrated that the number of successful Brahmin candidates had increased with each successive provincial election, that of 1909, 1912 and 1916.[74] It argued that the high social status of the Brahmins coupled with their dominance in the administration and the professions ensured electoral success despite being a minority in the electorate, which thus necessitated safeguards for the non-Brahmins, thus pursuing an Institutionalist line of argument.

However, the Southborough Committee dismissed the non-Brahmin claims on the grounds that it would be illogical to grant communal electorates to a community that would evidently constitute a majority under the expanded franchise entailed by the reforms. It advised the non-Brahmins to politically organise themselves to neutralise 'the power and influence of the Brahmans'.[75] This was clearly a Processualist argument for the Committee was implying that the logic of electoral politics would neutralise the non-Brahmin grievances.

The scrutiny of the Indian testimonies before the Southborough Committee does not reveal any reasoned arguments on the issue. Most Brahmin witnesses preferred to dodge the issue of Brahmin domination and instead sought to refute non-Brahmin demands by arguing that a cohesive entity called 'Non-Brahmin' did not exist. They preferred to remain silent over the claims that Brahmins would dominate the electoral process, despite being a minority in the electorate. Those non-Brahmins who appeared before the committee did not display any enthusiasm for the demand for communal representation. The Raja of Kollengode claimed that this demand was being made only by the educated sections among the non-Brahmins in the Presidency except those in his home district of Malabar. He claimed that in Malabar, the educational position of the non-Brahmins was excellent. The Raja of Ramnad echoed Brahmin claims that there was no such entity called the 'non-Brahmin' and presciently pointed out that educational disparities among the various castes among the non-Brahmins would lead to 'the same feeling' between them 'as now existed between the Brahmans and the non-Brahmans'. P. Kesava Pilla, a non-Brahmin leader associated with the Congress, in fact argued that the 'ascendancy of the Brahmins' in the past had served the public good.[76]

The Bombay Government followed the Madras Government in raising the possibility of Brahmin electoral dominance but unlike its southern counterpart did not take any position on the issue of how the non-Brahmins were to be represented.[77] There does not seem to have been much resistance in the Bombay Presidency to non-Brahmin demands for representation per se on part of the Brahmin witnesses. It must be noted that these demands were primarily confined to the Marathi and Kannada speaking areas of the province. While Brahmin witnesses were opposed to communal electorates for the non-Brahmins, the representatives of the non-Brahmins were not uniformly insistent on the same. One witness accepted reserved seats as alternatives to communal electorates under protest.[78] They did consider the option of multi-member seats with reservations. However, the Deccan Ryots Association sought to bridge the Institutionalist-Processualist divide on this issue. While it advocated reserved seats, it suggested that their numbers should depend upon how well the non-Brahmins fare in the non-reserved seats. If the community succeeds significantly in the non-reserved seats, the quantum of the former should be reduced.[79] Interestingly, it was Ambedkar who opposed communal electorates for the non-Brahmins on the grounds that they did not constitute a common interest, though admitting that given their low numbers among the electorate, the Marathas might lack personal representation and hence required some institutional safeguards.[80]

The issue of institutional safeguards for the non-Brahmins of Madras was played out again before the Joint Select Committee on the Government of India Bill, 1919. The Brahmin witnesses had no option but to squarely face the fact that Brahmin candidates had dominated the elections to the provincial council. They argued that this happened because the seats were uncontested and that in many contests, non-Brahmin voters preferred to vote for Brahmin candidates rather than those from their own community. This was a Processualist argument since it implied that if the non-Brahmins wished to increase their representation all that they had to do was to organise themselves politically. On the other hand, for the representatives of the non-Brahmins, this was proof of the strength and influence of the Brahmins, and hence insisted on communal electorates for themselves.

So far as the Montagu–Chelmsford reforms were concerned, these related issues were largely resolved with the stand taken by the Government of India which supported reserved seats for the non-Brahmins in Madras and Bombay on grounds of political expediency[81] and its subsequent embodiment in the Government of India Act, 1919, and the rules made thereunder.

The Morley–Minto reforms had introduced the electoral principle but it was the Montagu–Chelmsford reforms that built upon it. Hence with the Montagu-Chelmsford reforms, came the question of whether the constituencies were to be single-member or multi-member. There seemed to have been very little reasoned debate on whether these two options were to be treated as mutually exclusive alternatives or whether a mixed system could be adopted. In general, all institutional electoral arrangements other than single member constituencies seemed to be advocated as alternatives to communal electorates. It was thought that such arrangements, by ensuring the representation of minorities, would obviate the need for separate electorates.

The Southborough Committee recommended a system of single member constituencies on the grounds that it was the simplest method available. It argued that since the proposed expansion of the franchise would mean the inclusion of a large number of politically inexperienced individuals on the electoral roll, it was necessary to have easily comprehensible electoral system. The committee, however, conceded that multi-member constituencies would have to be granted in Madras and Bombay provinces in view of their special circumstances, a clear reference to the non-Brahmin demands for communal electorates. It also allowed cumulative voting in Bombay city arguing that since the system had been in place for municipal elections, the voters were used to it.[82] With this, all non-majoritarian electoral systems were ruled out.

However, many of the submissions made to the committee explicitly supported proportional representation as an alternative to communal electorates arguing that it would naturally lead to the representation of minorities, thus obviating the need for institutional safeguards.[83] Thus, one set of institutional arrangements was being substituted for the other. But proportional representation was not seen as a non-majoritarian electoral system that would lead to a more representative legislative body per se but merely as an alternative to communal electorates.

R.P. Paranjpye's proposals extensively dealt with proportional representation. Since he admitted that he took separate electorates for Muslims as a 'settled fact', his proposals did not talk of it as an alternative to communal representation. But his proposals demonstrate an awareness of the non-majoritarian, indeed anti-majoritarian, character of proportional representation. He suggested a system of single transferable vote (STV) coupled with multi-member constituencies. For Paranjpye, the former would lead to adequate representation of minorities and the multi-member constituencies would settle the claims of the majorities apprehensive of a dominant minority. Since he hailed from Bombay, the suggestions were explicitly made in context on non-Brahmin claims. He was also conscious of the fact that the minority communities for whom communal electorates were being granted were not internally homogenous and hence he suggested proportional representation be implemented for the Muslims which would help the minorities among them. Paranjpye further argued that with political development, religious and caste minorities would be replaced by ideological ones and then proportional representation would serve to elect representatives of these as well.[84]

The usual argument that voters would find it difficult to understand any system of proportional representation was trotted out to oppose it. But the most serious, albeit a misplaced one, objection to proportional representation came from Ambedkar. He argued that it led to the representation of views and not groups.[85] By the former, he presumably meant material interests and ideological preferences. This was a gross misunderstanding on Ambedkar's part since proportional representation does lead to representation of groups, however defined and organised. Proportional representation per se would not have precluded 'authentic representation' of the minorities and also would have led to their representation in proportion to their share in the electorate. The Joint Select Committee on the Government of India Bill, 1919, however, recommended that a detailed exploration of the suitability of proportional representation in view of Indian conditions be undertaken.[86] No such study seems to have taken place and an opportunity was missed. However, rules made under the Government of India Act, 1919, permitted the provincial councils to approve of a resolution asking for proportional representation. But this resolution was not to be binding on the local government, another missed opportunity.

Ultimately, the rules made under the Government of India Act, 1919, adopted an electoral system where proportional representation was given some space. For the multi-member seats in the provincial councils, cumulative voting was permitted only in Bombay, while distributive voting was stipulated in other provinces. One multi-member European constituency was to elect its representatives through STV. For the all-India legislature, cumulative voting was allowed in Bombay, and STV in Madras.

But the most popular alternative to communal electorates during the Montagu–Chelmsford reforms was multi-members seats with reserved constituencies. This option was advocated or supported mainly by Brahmin witnesses principally in the Madras and Bombay provinces as a concrete alternative to non-Brahmin demands for communal representation[87] but also as an alternative to the demands of other minorities.[88] The Madras Congress Committee, a Brahmin-dominated organisation, supported proportional representation to secure non-Brahmin representation.[89] Cumulative voting in multi-member constituencies was another alternative proposed to communal representation for the non-Brahmins.[90] Furthermore, there were a few witnesses who advocated some form of proportional representation without making it clear that they regarded it as an alternative to communal electorates.

The system of reserved seats also found support from outside the Madras and Bombay provinces.[91] Interestingly, A.K. Fazl-ul-Haq of Bengal stated that he supported a system of reserved seats even for the Muslims but that a majority of his co-religionists wanted communal electorates.[92] The opposition to this alternative proceeded from the argument that there was no guarantee that a candidate elected from the seat reserved for a given community would be representative of that particular community. There was always the possibility in this system that such a candidate would be elected in a reserved seat by the votes of voters who were not members of the community for whom the seat has been reserved. Two similar options were proposed to answer this objection, both which could be described as the 'Two-Round' election. The first one, made with reference to the European community in Bengal, asked that for a candidate to be successfully elected from reserved seat, he should have secured a certain minimum number of votes from the members of the community for whom the seat had been reserved.[93] In the second one, suggested by an European missionary from Madras, members of the communities for whom seats were reserved were to elect candidates in a first round of voting and these successful candidates would face the voters in joint electorates with other candidates.[94]

The question of how exactly would candidates in multi-member constituencies be elected also emerged during the Montagu–Chelmsford reforms. An illustration would suffice to explain the issue. Assuming a two-member constituency with one seat reserved for the non-Brahmin (or for any other specified group) with two Brahmin and two non-Brahmin candidates contesting, there can be six possible ways of the candidates being ordered, pertinent to the issue under discussion, according to the number of votes secured. The first case would be a Brahmin secures the highest number of votes followed by the two non-Brahmins with the second Brahmin coming last. In the second one, a non-Brahmin would come first followed by two Brahmins and the second non-Brahmin coming last. The third case would be of a Brahmin standing first, followed by a non-Brahmin, then by a Brahmin and the second non-Brahmin coming last. In the fourth case, a non-Brahmin stood first, followed by Brahmins and non-Brahmins alternating with each other. The fifth situation would be where two Brahmins secured the first two positions with the two non-Brahmins coming last, while the sixth would be the exact opposite.

Apparently, the Madras non-Brahmins had demanded that the person securing the highest number of votes among all the candidates, irrespective of community affiliation, be first declared elected, and then the non-Brahmin candidate securing the highest number of votes be declared elected for the reserved seat. The Joint Select Committee rejected this and stipulated that the non-Brahmin candidate with the highest number of votes be declared elected first, and then the candidate, irrespective of community affiliation, with the highest number of votes among all the candidates be declared elected for the non-reserved seat.[95] What would have been the impact of these two alternatives in the hypothetical constituency envisaged above? If the Madras non-Brahmins' proposal was accepted, then both the successful candidates would be non-Brahmins in the three of the six possibilities cited above, while if the official proposals would be accepted, it was only in the sixth case that both the elected candidates would be non-Brahmins. Thus, the non-Brahmins of Madras desired an institutional arrangement that would maximise their success, while the British Raj wanted to restrict them to a guaranteed minimum.

The decade of the 1920s was characterised by many efforts made by Indian political forces to come to a constitutional settlement that would be widely accepted. Similarly, there were official enquiries into the entire constitutional structure as a precursor to further reforms. The system of elections was a crucial issue of negotiation and attempts were made to find alternatives to communal electorates, which remained a key stumbling block to the forging of such a settlement. Proportional representation was almost never suggested as an institutional alternative, except on few occasions. R.P. Paranjapye perhaps was the only one who continuously argued for proportional representation. In his opinion included in the minority report to the Reforms Enquiry Committee, also known as the Muddiman Committee, he argued for multi-member constituencies with either STV or cumulative voting on the grounds that that single-member ones leave the minorities unrepresented. He further claimed that only geographically extensive multi-member constituencies would make likely the 'reasonable representation' of all sections of society.[96] Though this was not posed as an explicit alternative to the communal problem, it could be seen a suggesting one.

The underlying tone and tenor of the constitutional proposals emanating from the mainstream of the nationalist movement in the 1920s was explicitly Processual. They rejected all Institutionalist alternatives where they actually mattered and proposed them where, in a sense, they did not. The Nehru Committee Report unwillingly proposed reserved seats as an alternative, albeit temporarily, to communal electorates.[97] Its preferred choice was, of course, joint electorates. Moreover, it also rejected proportional representation as not being suitable given the existing circumstances in India but not before refuting arguments against the system.[98] However, it recommended this system for the upper house of the national legislature whose members were to be elected by the provincial legislatures.[99] The Swaraj Constitution's preferred choice too was joint electorates but unlike the Nehru Report it was prepared to consider some form of proportional representation.[100] The underlying assumption seemed to be that there was no reason for candidates from minority communities not to be elected. There were, of course, some Muslim voices who supported joint electorates on the grounds that they blocked the path to communal unity and thus to self-government.[101] On the other hand, it was argued that while joint electorates were ideal the times were not yet ripe for the abolition of communal ones and that the existence of such communal electorates had in fact reduced the possibility of communal tensions. Furthermore, PR was dismissed as a mean of protection of minorities. It was claimed that for this to happen minorities required to be well-organised which was absent in India.[102]

The Simon Commission, on the other hand, adopted an Institutionalist Approach to political representation. It reluctantly endorsed separate electorates[103] on the entirely logical grounds that they could not be abolished without the consent of those communities, particularly the Muslims, who had been granted them. It took note of the fact that in the case of the Muslims, the members of the community if elected from reserved seats would not be 'regarded by their co-religionists as authoritative and satisfactory representatives', thus acknowledging the validity of the 'authenticity of representation' argument. For the 'Depressed Classes' the Commission recommended reserved seats[104] on grounds that it would be unwise to politically separate themselves from the Hindus. The reservation for the Bombay non-Brahmins was continued since the Commission found no evidence either way to prove that the community would secure representation in the absence of institutional safeguards. In the case of Madras, it recommended abolition of reservations arguing it had been proved that the community could stand its ground even without such arrangements.[105]

But it took note of the institutional alternatives to communal representation. It talked of the Two-Round elections[106] mentioned during the Montagu–Chelmsford reforms but dismissed proportional representation as impractical.[107] The submissions of the provincial government also did not display any electoral imagination. The provincial committees, consisting of the members of provincial councils, did not come up with significant institutional alternatives. They largely supported the continuation of communal electorates. But the evidence before and submissions to the Commission saw an additional reason being cited against separate electorates, that they prevented the formation of political groupings/parties on explicitly political lines and encouraged their formation on clearly communal lines. On the other hand, communal electorates were defended on the grounds that they prevented communal tensions by the simple expedient of eliminating the possibility of political competition between communities.

However, the Bombay provincial committee recommended multi-member constituencies with cumulative voting, not as an alternative to communal electorates per se but for the protection of 'important minorities within the main divisions of Muhammadans and non-Muhammadans'.[108] This was recognition that there were limits to the extent to which social diversity could be used to grant communal electorates. The real question was why such and similar other alternatives were not proposed to replace separate representation. The only case for proportional representation as an alternative system came from the Punjab but was not extensively argued.[109]

Interestingly, Dr Ambedkar, who had so strongly advocated communal electorates during the Montagu–Chelmsford reforms, now argued for reserved seats in his minute of dissent to the Bombay committee's report. He, of course, stressed the need for minorities to have a certain assured quantum of representation. But whereas earlier he had called for representatives to have the same social characteristics as those they represent, now he urged that the former should share the 'aims, purposes and motives' of those who were being represented. Similarly, if he had earlier argued that a system of communal electorates would bring into the representative assemblies those who would otherwise not socially interact, now he claimed that the same system sharpened social divisions. Dr Ambedkar supported joint electorates by arguing that they made candidates of the majority community dependent on the votes of the minorities, thus enhancing social interaction. He further argued that the former who got elected with the assistance of minorities would be 'if not a member of *the* minority, will certainly be a member for *the* minority'. This meant that an individual, who belonged to the majority community and in whose successful election the voters of the minority community had contributed significantly, would perforce advocate and protect the interests of the minority community despite being a non-member. It is in this sense that the representative would be 'for' though not being 'of the minority'. Ambedkar further claimed that fears that the majority community would elect such candidates from the minority who would be favourable to them rather than the minority thus leaving it in a sense unrepresented were unfounded.[110] But Dr Ambedkar did not explain what institutional arrangements were required to dispel these fears. For him, adult suffrage would have solved this entire set of vexed questions. An analysis of his submission seems to indicate that his support for reserved seats was limited with respect to the Muslims, for in his evidence to the Simon Commission he urged communal electorates for the Depressed Classes, albeit if adult franchise was not granted.[111]

Thus, Ambedkar's positions vis-à-vis communal electorates seem to a shifting one. The arguments that he advocated against separate electorates for the Muslims could well be used against the provision of the same for the 'Depressed Classes'. It is evident that Ambedkar looked at the question of political representation for the Muslims and his own community from different standpoints. One could argue that for Ambedkar the problems facing the two were essentially not the same and thus had to be treated differently, and hence perhaps he proposed separate solutions.

The issue of communal electorates for majorities was replayed out once again before the Simon Commission. It linked the demands of the Muslims in the Punjab and Bengal for a majority of the seats in the proposed council made on the grounds that they constituted a majority in these two provinces with the fact that the community had been granted weightage in the provinces where it was a minority. Firstly, it stated that even if Muslims accepted joint electorates in these two provinces thus doing away with a statutorily guaranteed quantum of representation, this would be no reason to do away with the weightages and separate electorates in the provinces where they were a minority.[112] Thus, the Commission was not willing to curtail the representation of the Muslims in those provinces where the community was a minority as a trade-off for the abandonment was what had been described as ' statutory majorities' (i.e. the Muslim majority in the legislature was to be statutorily guaranteed) for their co-religionists in the legislatures of the Punjab and Bengal. While rejecting these demands for such 'statutory majorities', it cited the need for not disturbing the Muslim position in the provinces where they were a minority. The Commission strongly ruled out a scheme whereby such majorities were to be combined with weightages, implying that the Muslims could not have the best of both the worlds.

All these issues became enmeshed together during the first Round Table Conference. A settlement of the communal question, which in turn rested on the satisfactory resolution of the demands of the minorities for institutional safeguards, was essential for building a consensus on the nature of the electoral system in any future Indian constitution. Much bargaining and haggling took place. The key issue was firstly, whether the Muslims in the Punjab and Bengal where they constituted a majority were to be granted communal electorates, and if they were to be granted reserved seats should they constitute a majority of the total seats in the local councils, and secondly, should the Hindus in Bengal and the Hindus and the Sikhs in the Punjab be given representation in excess of their share of population. If the second arrangement was conceded, then that might have entailed the Muslims in these two provinces becoming a minority in the legislature, for the community enjoyed a bare majority in the population and representation had to be granted to the Anglo-Indians, Indian Christians and the European commercial interests. Since those concerned could not arrive at a mutually agreeable solution, schemes devised to solve this vexed issue collapsed but not before some institutional alternatives were proposed.

Certain themes resonated once again at the Conference. The usual arguments were made against communal electorates. There were suggestions of differential franchise qualifications for various communities so that their strength in the electorate would be as close as possible to their shares in the population. Presumably, this was made to obviate the need for separate electorates. However, this was not considered seriously. At the Conference, the demand for separate electorates for Muslims reiterated and was couched by Sir Muhammad Shafi in terms of 'authentic representation'.[113] As he argued, only if members of the minorities (which naturally included the Muslims) were elected through separate electorates could they rightly be called the representatives of the community which in turn would ensure representative government.

Dr Ambedkar cut to the core of the issue by emphasising that the extent of franchise was the real issue, and the question of electorates was contingent on that. He stated that if adult franchise was granted, then the Depressed Classes would ask for separate electorates for a short period and then later reserved seats in joint electorates. But if adult suffrage was not granted, then they should receive separate electorates.[114] This argument of his is not difficult to understand. Adult franchise would mean that the voting strength of the Depressed Classes would more or less correspond to their proportion in the population. Reserved seats, with or without weightages, would ensure a minimum quantum of representation besides compensating for the adverse effects of social prejudice among non-Depressed Class voters and lack of political organisation among the community. In the absence of adult suffrage, the qualification for franchise would be either income or payment of taxes or both. Given the economic status of the community, very few would be eligible for voters which would mean negligible voting strength. This would lead to the community's political influence being rendered nugatory, and hence the need for separate electorates to ensure a minimum quantum of political representation. Thus now, Dr Ambedkar's position seemed have shifted slightly. He no longer made the argument of 'authentic representation' and now adopted a position of conditional rejection of separate electorates. In a slightly different setting, he extended his arguments to cover all minorities. While speaking in the Franchise Sub-Committee, he explained that adult franchise would enable minority communities to exert political influence in proportion to their strength in the population, thus obviating any need for any electoral safeguards.[115]

Maulana Muhammad Ali strongly criticised joint electorates with reserved seats. In rather picturesque language, he claimed that both Muslims and Hindus elected from reserved seats wherever their respective communities are in a minority would be 'merely *religiously* Hindu or Muslim but not *politically* so' for they would be elected on by the votes of the majority community[116] (Italics in the original). Thus, being an 'authentic representative' was no longer dependent on shared religious affiliations but on willingness to translate it into community-based political action. His alternative scheme combined some features of separate electorates with those of joint electorates-reserved seats. In this scheme, while all communities would vote together and seats would be reserved for minorities, the success of candidates from the minority communities was conditional. To be declared elected, they had to secure at least 40 per cent of the votes from their given community, and at least 5 per cent from the majority community.[117] He declared his scheme to be superior to proportional representation. This could have provided a basis to assuage the fears of minorities, provide some guarantee of 'authentic representation' and make candidates of a given community dependent on the votes of the other groups. But this was not seriously considered, another missed chance. The Conference closed resolving to continue to pursuit of an agreement.

The second Round Table Conference saw sharp divisions emerge on the perennially vexed question of communal electorates. Gandhi consistently adopted a Processualist position not only during the conference but also during a speech in London. At the Conference, Gandhi claimed that adult franchise would solve all problems.[118] In the discussion after his speech at the Royal Institute of International Affairs, Gandhi claimed that members of minority communities would get elected if they had a record of service to their countrymen and specifically cited the example of the Parsis.[119] Despite this, the Congress was alive to the concerns of the minorities, at least the larger ones. A note circulated by it that was presented as formula for a communal settlement recommended reserved seats for some minorities in some provinces.[120] The Hindu Mahasabha, as expected, rejected communal electorates.

On the other hand, there were strong demands for institutional safeguards from the representatives of the minority community. They came together to submit what is known as the Minorities Memorandum which strongly demanded separate electorates accompanied by weightages. It added that they should not be abolished unless a particular minority community asked for it. But there were attempts to find a middle ground. Dr S.K. Datta representing the Indian Christians proposed a single electorate for all minorities.[121]

There were suggestions of weighted votes for minorities and that those members of minority communities who wished to register themselves as voters in non-communal or general electorates should be allowed to do so. Multi-member constituencies were proposed to deal with the issue of the representation of minorities. However, these suggestions were not followed up. Neither was the idea of proportional representation seriously considered though it was mooted as a solution by Dr Datta to what he euphemistically described as 'Indian electoral problems'.[122] Interestingly, Dr Ambedkar supported PR as a method for the election to the Federal Upper House. He argued that this would make the chamber non-communal, for the members would have been elected not on the votes of a particular community and would enjoy broad-based support.[123] However, two objections could be raised against this claim. Firstly, the provincial councils that would elect the Federal Upper House would themselves have been elected on a communal basis. This would mean that members of any given community might vote for a candidate of their own community. This would negate the supposedly non-communal character of the chamber. Secondly, if PR per se was to lead to a non-communal representative body, then why restrict it to the Federal Upper House. It could easily be applied to all representative bodies and thus go some way in resolving the question of communal representation. However, these issues were not thought of.

The Lothian Franchise Committee was not empowered to make any recommendations regarding communal electorates or joint electorates with or without reserved seats per se, though it stated that reservations for the non-Brahmins in Madras were no longer required, while not stating its opinion about the same community in Bombay. But more importantly, it acknowledged that the fair representation of all sections of a given society depended upon the system of elections.[124] But this did not encourage the Committee to go beyond the prevailing electoral system. Wherever multi-member constituencies were to exist, cumulative voting was allowed.[125] It discussed the second ballot and the Alternative Vote only to respectively reject them as expensive and difficult for the average Indian voter to understand.[126] It suggested that if communal electorates were to be accepted, then they should be accompanied by single member constituencies but if joint electorate with reserved seats were granted then there had to be multi-member constituencies. It added that the second combination was necessary since it was difficult to have reserved seats in single member constituencies,[127] a somewhat of a commonsensical argument. However, it could have recommended a combination of multi-member constituencies for the communal electorates, thus acknowledging the existence of minorities within minorities. Thus, it can be reasonably argued that the very concept of communal electorates contributed to the political homogenisation of those communities who were granted such electorates.

With the issue of separate electorates for the various minority communities largely decided upon, the question of whether the 'Depressed Classes' should extended the same privilege became contentious. The issue turned upon whether the community should be regarded as one distinct from or as a part of the broader Hindu community. If the first was to be assumed, there could be little argument against the Depressed Classes' demand for communal electorates, and if the second was assumed then a system of reserved seats could easily be proposed. In this entire debate, the fact that reserved seats might not lead to the election of those whom the community regarded as their real representatives was acknowledged. With it the possibility of preventing the Depressed Classes from breaking away from the Hindus and yet devising a solution to their misgivings was sought to be explored. In many provinces, the local franchise committees, while acknowledging the existence of castes who could legitimately described as 'Depressed Classes', sought to argue that the social disabilities were not so severe as to warrant separate representation. It was also argued that any attempts to grant separate electorates would increase the problems faced by the community.

The Madras Franchise Committee frankly acknowledged that reserved seats would lead to the election of those who might not be the choice of the 'Depressed Classes'. Hence it proposed that the community be granted separate electorates and its members be permitted to vote in the general (i.e. Hindu) electorates to prevent what it described as 'communal separation'.[128] A dissenting note by two members acknowledged the drawbacks of reservations, as they existed, and hence proposed a scheme of reserved seats similar to the one suggested by Muhammad Ali during the first Round Table Conference. It is perhaps because of this, the Madras Committee ultimately reversed its position on the double vote. The Bombay Franchise Committee was badly divided like all other issues on the method of representation for the

'Depressed Classes'. It supported separate electorates for the community for a period of 20 years.[129] The Bombay Government supported this proposal by arguing that the community would not be able to elect someone of its own choice in a system of reserved seats.[130]

On this question, the Bengal Government and the Bengal Franchise Committee, it seems, were in agreement but with a difference of emphasis. The former pointed out that while in Bengal members of the 'Depressed Classes' had been elected to the provincial council from general constituencies[131] the community was a whole was badly divided politically to ensure electoral success.[132] The Bengal Franchise Committee opined that the members of the community were likely to be elected with the new proposed franchise.[133] These arguments implicitly seem to be making a case against separate electorates in this case. In the Punjab, Chaudhari Chhotu Ram submitted a long note arguing against separate electorates for the 'Depressed Classes'. He argued that communal representation would not serve any purpose and would in fact harm the community by dividing it from the wider Hindu community.[134] But he did not propose any concrete proposal for the representation of the community.

Witnesses before the Lothian Committee were divided on the question of separate electorates for the 'Depressed Classes'. Generally speaking, members of the community favoured communal electorates while caste Hindu witnesses advocated a system of reserved seats, and both rehearsed arguments made previously. Alternatives to separate electorates for the community were also presented to the Lothian Committee. G.K. Devadhar of the Servants of India Society suggested that the franchise qualifications be specially lowered for the community in order to obviate the need for such electorates.[135] A lower franchise qualification would have meant a higher number of voters belonging to the community and thus enabling it to elect a representative of its choice. But no witness from the community appears to have supported it and indeed the All-Bengal Namasudra Association in its submission to the committee explicitly rejected it.[136]

The witnesses belonging to the minority communities like the Anglo-Indians and the Indian Christians largely insisted on communal electorates for themselves. Their arguments too were familiar. They argued that any system of reserved seats would not lead to the election of 'true' representatives of the community. The question of the representation of the tribals did not lead to much discussion. Representatives of the community from Bihar and Orissa asked for reserved seats for themselves.[137] However, the Census Commission of India, Dr J.H. Hutton, with reference to the tribals in Bengal, suggested that the community be granted communal electorates.[138]

Opposition to separate electorates was couched in the usual nationalist terms. Maulvi Syed Nausher Ali of Bengal was the only Muslim witness to oppose such electorates not only for his community but for all others as well. He argued that communal electorates had indeed harmed the interests of his community. He made an exception only in the case of the 'Depressed Classes' and the Europeans.[139] Though the issue of communal electorates was settled upon, there were alternatives that were suggested to it. Rao Bahadur R.R. Kale, a member of the Bombay Franchise Committee, proposed the method of electoral colleges or group elections, which had been tentatively suggested by Lord Zetland at the First Round Table Conference. Groups of a specified number of all adult voters would be formed first and then these groups would elect their representatives who would then constitute electoral colleges. Kale argued that this would obviate the need for communal electorates, for this system would make the voting strength of the minority communities more or less in proportion to their share in the population. He added that this system should have multi-member constituencies wherever possible and should be implemented as a supplement to the communal electorates. But he also asserted that the best system to provide representation to the minorities was PR.[140]

The most interesting and promising alternative to the vexed question of communal electorates in the 1930s came from Assam. In a note submitted to the provincial Franchise Committee, Rai Bahadur Kanak Lal Barua, the Minister of Local Self-Government, proposed communal electorates for the Muslims as well as the Hindus in addition to what he called the non-communal electorates. All those who believed themselves to be non-communal would be allowed to enrol in this last mentioned electorate, which would include the members of the smaller minority communities as well. All voters who desired to enrol themselves in communal electorates would be allowed to do so after the submission of an application. Barua argued that this would ensure that non-communal voters would have a platform of their own besides introducing a system of joint electorates along with other benefits.[141] Evidently the Assam Government found this proposal to be worth considering, for it suggested to the Lothian Committee that the voters should be given a choice of whether they wished to belong to a communal or non-communal electorate.[142]

These proposals are striking, for they mark a departure from the prevalent practice of privileging group identities. The entire structure of political representation was underpinned by the assumption that individuals belong to groups and that their interests, material and non-material, could be articulated and assured only through the medium of these groups. On the other hand, these proposals in one sense chose to emphasise individual choice and agency. Apparently, for those who made these suggestions, individuals no doubts belonged to some group or the other but that not all would want their interest to be mediated through the groups that they belonged to. Thus, these persons probably wished to separate their social identities on the one hand, and their political identities on the other. But again like many other ones, this was a missed chance. Another proposal in this context was made by the United Provinces Liberal Association which proposed multi-member seats with cumulative voting. The Association claimed that its alternative was superior to proportional representation and that this would ease the ultimate transition to joint electorates.[143]

The debate on plural versus single-member constituencies revolved around the issue of minorities. The proponents of single-member seats argued in favour of administrative convenience and closer contact with the voters. Multi-member constituencies were advocated as a measure of protection of minorities. But yet there seemed to confusion about the relative merits of single- versus multi-member constituencies when it came to representation of communities who were numerically strong but were thought to be deficient in political consciousness. B.V. Jadhav who advocated the cause of the Maratha and the allied castes claimed reserved seats for the community if multi-member constituencies were granted but not if single member ones were decided upon.[144] Reserved seats were necessary because the community was subject to upper caste influence which meant that without such a provision voters belonging to this community would vote for candidates who did not belong to it. But this could easily happen in single-member constituencies as well. But Jadhav's entire plea was convoluted and confused.

Alternate voting systems were simply not considered here or were dismissed out of hand. The Bombay Government further ruled out proportional representation on the grounds that it required an electorate 'much more educated and intelligent' than what it was at that point of time.[145] However, those who advocated multi-member constituencies were explicit about they being a means for proportional representation and hence called for either distributive voting, limited votes or STV to ensure proportionality. Proportional representation in the form of a list system was proposed by only one witness, N.K. Kelkar from the Central Provinces.[146]

The Franchise Committee submitted its report in the middle of 1932 with the communal question yet unresolved. The second Round Table Conference had been inconclusive and the onus of reaching a settlement rested with the National Government under Ramsay MacDonald. In late 1932, the Government announced its decision which was officially described as the Communal Decision and popularly known as 'Communal Award'. It granted communal electorates for the Muslims, Sikhs, Europeans, Anglo-Indians and Indian Christians. Furthermore, it granted the 'Depressed Classes' not only separate electorates but also a right to vote in the Hindu-dominated general electorates as well. This political separation of the community from the wider Hindu community unleashed a political storm that culminated in the Poona Pact. This pact substituted communal electorates for the 'Depressed Classes' and a right to vote in the general constituencies with a scheme that combined a system of reserved seats in joint electorates with two-round elections. Reserved seats as an institutional safeguard for the community was not exactly a novel proposal. It formed the core of the Moonje–Rajah pact so known after its principal signatories, Dr B.S. Moonje, the leading light of the Hindu Mahasabha, and M.C. Rajah, a well-known leader of the community from Madras.

As per the Poona Pact, in all multi-member constituencies where a seat had been reserved for the 'Depressed Classes', all the voters belonging to the community to constitute an electorate were to elect a maximum of four candidates belonging to their community. This would be the first round of elections or the primary election. These candidates would then go on to contest, in a joint electorate, the seat reserved for the community. This would be the second round. The candidate who secured the highest number of votes in this second round from among these four would be declared elected for the reserved seat. This scheme was to be applicable to both the provincial councils and the all-India legislature.

The distinction between these two schemes must be discussed. Firstly, the Poona Pact increased the quantum of representation that had been granted to the 'Depressed Classes'. Secondly, the Communal Award stipulated that the voters belonging to the community would have a voice in the election of caste-Hindu representatives. In contrast, the Poona Pact stated that both the caste Hindus as well as the 'Depressed Classes' voters would have a say in the election of individuals belonging to each other. However for the caste Hindus the choice of who the representative belonging to the 'Depressed Classes' was to be limited to the four candidates elected in the primary election. On the other hand, the 'Depressed Class' voters could vote for any caste-Hindu candidate they preferred.

It would be worthwhile to recapitulate at length the range of arguments used during the debates surrounding the provisions of the Communal Award as regards the 'Depressed Classes' and which culminated in the Poona Pact. The principle at stake was whether the community should be regarded as a part of the Hindu community or one distinct and hence separate from it. The Communal Award pointed out that since the voters belonging to the 'Depressed Classes' would not be in a position to elect members of their own community in the 'general' seats, presumably because they would constitute a numerically insignificant section of the electorate, special provision in the form of separate electorates would have to be made to secure the community's representation in the new legislatures. It thus justified communal electorates and the underlying assumption was that the community was a distinct but not separate part of the Hindu society.[147] Gandhi's opposition to these provisions was clear. He was opposed to any decision that would de-link the 'Depressed Classes' from the Hindu fold.[148] For him, such provisions were a disruptive force that would divide Hindu society.[149] Evidently, Gandhi's concerns for the unity of the Hindu community were the driving force behind the chain of events that culminated in the Poona Pact.

But more importantly, the Communal Award also finalised the composition of the provincial councils. In the Punjab and Bengal, the Muslims though a majority in the population were not granted a majority but rather a plurality of the seats in the councils. The non-Brahmins of Bombay were also granted reserved seats in multi-member constituencies. These aspects of the Award as well as the Poona Pact were embodied in the White Paper of 1933 that formed the basis for the Government of India Act, 1935.

The fact that the principle of communal electorates was settled did not prevent the issue being debated in the proceedings of the Joint Committee. The Hindu Mahasabha, as expected, adopted a holier-than-thou nationalist position to signal its opposition to separate electorates as such. But that did not prevent it from conceding that they constituted an Institutional safeguard for the minorities. However, it was quick to argue that whether the minorities wanted to be represented through joint or separate electorates should be decided by them and not as per the wishes of the majority.[150] This was a clear reflection of the demands of the Hindu minority of the Punjab and Bengal. The logical extension of this argument was that the demand of the Muslims of the minority provinces for separate elections would be considered legitimate. Moreover, Dr Moonje, the leader of the Mahasabha delegation, was quick to add that his party would not mind proportional representation in joint electorates and indeed regarded it as the best solution to the communal conundrum.[151] The Muslim witnesses strongly advocated communal electorates and declined to budge.

The issue of whether majorities required communal electorates now cropped up in the case of Sind, which was now to be separated from Bombay. The Hindu witnesses from Sind opposed communal electorates for Muslims and demanded that the Hindus be granted the same.[152] This issue remerged in the Joint Committee mainly due to the intervention of Lord Zetland, who as Lord Ronaldshay had served as the Governor of Bengal. He strongly opposed the granting of communal electorates to the majority community. He claimed that the minorities, whether Muslims or Hindus, should be given the right to decided whether they desired to be represented through separate or joint electorates.[153] His amendments to that effect were rejected. Though Zetland's submission largely concerned itself with the Hindus of Bengal, his argument was similar to that of the Hindu Mahasabha.

The Committee lost an opportunity to present an alternative to communal electorates when it recommended that members of the provincial legislatures would be constituted into communal electorates for the elections to the federal legislature. It considered STV as a method to elect the federal legislature but not before admitting that the results of such an election would not differ from those of its recommendations. However, it rejected STV on the grounds that it would not command the confidence of the minorities.[154]

Concurrently, with the drafting of the Act and its parliamentary passage, the process of delimitation of constituencies was taken up. Provincial Delimitation Committees, advisory in nature, were appointed to frame proposals for the same. These committees started their work as the Act was being drafted and concluded it after the process of parliamentary approval was complete. The number of seats stipulated for the provincial legislatures and the communities and the economic interests that were granted separate representation had been largely decided upon in the Communal Award, as modified by the Poona Pact. The provincial committees and the provincial governments were now charged with the minutiae of representation.

The key question during this process was whether constituencies should be plural or single-member. In Bengal, the local committee unanimously recommended single-member seats for the rural Muslim constituencies while admitting that this might not be entirely practicable.[155] The General (i.e. Hindu) rural constituencies were to be multi-member but only where seats were to be reserved for the 'Depressed Classes'.[156] The implicit argument was that a single-member constituency would have deprived an electoral opportunity to the caste Hindus and hence the scheme. But since the committee had also unanimously decided that all such reserved seats would be located in the rural areas,[157] albeit with the approval of the leaders of the 'Depressed Classes', the political interests of the urban caste Hindus were safeguarded and those of the 'Depressed Classes' living in urban areas overlooked.

In Bombay, the provincial government strongly supported multi-member constituencies with cumulative voting for the Bombay Presidency proper but single-member ones for Sindh, which was soon going to be separated from the province. It is clear that political considerations determined the Bombay Government's views. In the case of Bombay province, the Government argued for plural constituencies on the grounds that seats were to be reserved for the 'Depressed Classes' as well as the Maratha and the Allied Castes. Furthermore, it claimed that important minorities existed in the province which made such constituencies coupled with cumulative voting imperative to ensure their representation. It further claimed that single-member constituencies led to representatives of an inferior character and of a parochial nature.[158] STV was rejected on the usual charge of being complicated. The concern for minorities was plausible in the case of Bombay city where the Parsis were regarded as an influential and numerically strong community whose representation was necessary. However, this was not the case in the rest of the province. It can be argued that the Bombay Government's insistence on plural constituencies had more to do with the emergence of the Non-Brahmin movement, the caste tensions within it as well as Brahmin fears of being politically swamped. Multi-member constituencies could assuage the concerns of all concerned that they would not be politically marginalised and would have a reasonable chance of getting elected.

The Government of India Act, meanwhile, constructed the broad outlines of the electoral system in British India. The Muslim and the Sikh members of the provincial Legislative Assemblies as well as those elected from general constituencies were to constitute separate electorates to elect their representatives to the federal lower house. Thus communal electorates were introduced even in the indirect election. Given that these elections were to take place by a system of proportional representation with STV, there was no need for elections on a communal basis. This provision appears even more curious given that some members of the Bengal and Bihar Legislative Councils were to be elected by the members of their respective assemblies by the same method on a non-communal basis. Thus communal electorates for the Federal Assembly defied all logic.

The Act also incorporated the Poona Pact in the elections to the Federal Assembly. A system of two-step elections, similar to that for the provincial lower houses, was stipulated. Furthermore, the Act provided for a separate electorate for the tribals of Assam by providing that any person who was a voter for the constituency reserved for the community could not become a voter in any other provincial constituency except the one for women. Despite these detailed provisions, many matters were left out and these were to be provided for by the Hammond Committee, in addition to its principal task, which was preparing a scheme of delimitation of constituencies.

The two issues that the Hammond Committee had to tackle were the nature of constituencies and the system of voting. While noting the pros and cons of single-member and plural constituencies for the provincial Legislative Assemblies, the Committee noted that the Government had informed that it generally preferred the former kind except in Bombay and Madras. In the former province, reservations for Scheduled Castes, as the 'Depressed Classes' were now known as, as well as the Maratha and the Allied Castes in addition to a significant minority like the Parsis necessitated multi-member constituencies.[159] As regards Madras, the Committee noted that its provincial counterpart favoured single-member ones by a majority though from the testimonies of the witnesses from the province indicated a strong feeling for plural member ones. It noted that fears were expressed that single-member constituencies would exacerbate caste feelings and deprived the minorities of representatives. These minorities were described as those being within the Hindu fold which implied numerically weaker castes, and perhaps even the Brahmins. However, the Government of Madras was explicit in its support for single-member ones. It claimed not without plausibility that single-member constituencies would lead to the formation of a strong party government and that it preferred to this outcome to the representation of the minorities.[160] In hindsight, the Madras Government's claim came true in the 1937 provincial elections. The Congress barely managed a majority in Bombay where there were no single-member general constituencies. But on the other hand, in Madras which had a predominantly single-member system, the Congress swept the polls. There might have been local political factors that led to this outcome but it is also likely that the nature of the electoral system played a part.

For the multi-member constituencies, the Hammond Committee dismissed STV as being complicated and discussed four other alternatives, the Single Non-Transferable Vote (SNTV), the optional Distributive System, the compulsory Distributive System, and the Cumulative Vote. It recommended that unless the local government decided otherwise, the last option should be selected whether there was a reserved seat or not. It also ruled out SNTV for constituencies with seats reserved for Scheduled Castes on grounds that this would be make possible communal voting by the back door and violate the principle of mutuality entailed by the Poona Pact. It instead opted for the optional Distributive System for the second round of elections in the Scheduled Caste reserved constituencies.[161]

As regards Bengal, the Committee agreed with the provincial Delimitation Committee that seats reserved for the Scheduled Castes should not be located in the urban areas after having ascertained that this was what the representatives of the community wanted.[162] More significantly for the elections in constituencies with reserved seats for Scheduled Castes, the Committee stipulated that if two candidates from the community, both of whom had been elected at the primary election, came first and second respectively in the second round, then the former should be declared elected for the reserved seat and the one who stood second should be declared elected for the unreserved one. That there was a possibility of this happening in Bengal given the numerical strength of the Scheduled Caste voters in some constituencies was obliquely indicated. However, the provision in principle had the potential of enhancing Scheduled Caste representation, however unlikely the possibility, something acknowledged by the community itself.[163]

However, it recommended, on grounds of exceptional circumstances, that in Bengal but not in other provinces, Scheduled Caste candidates should be prevented from holding an unreserved seat, unless they had been elected in the primary elections. The Committee explicitly stated that except for Bengal, Scheduled Caste candidates could contest unreserved seats without contesting the primary elections.[164] These circumstances were explained by the Committee. There were fears that given the strength of the Scheduled Castes in some constituencies it was possible for the community to capture both the reserved as well as the unreserved seat. The Committee did not want this to happen.[165] During this period there were fears among the caste Hindus that they were being politically and thus electorally squeezed, due to the Communal Award, on one hand by the Muslims, and on the other by the Scheduled Castes.[166] This provision came about perhaps because the Committee gave in to these fears. Thus, as far as Bengal was concerned, reservation for the Scheduled Castes was, like in other provinces, a guaranteed minimum but an upper limit as well.

But perhaps, this was also to prevent the election in an unreserved seat of a Scheduled Caste candidate who did not command the confidence of a significant section of his community and had been elected mainly due to caste Hindu votes. Were there fears that in Bengal but not in other provinces, caste Hindus would elect Scheduled Caste candidates and enable them to pose as the community's representatives to the disadvantage of those who had qualified as candidates in the second round after being successful in the primary election? The available evidence does not offer any clue to this conundrum. The rules framed under the 1935 Act embodied the Committee's recommendation.

In the case of the tribals, the 1935 Act, in the Fifth Schedule, had provided for reservation of seats as an option and had not ruled out separate electorates. The Hammond Committee provided for separate electorates for the tribals in Madras, the Central Provinces and Assam,[167] but reserved seats in Bombay, Bihar and Orissa.[168] The rationale behind this differential scheme seems to the level of development of the concerned tribal communities. Where they could easily stand their ground with the general (i.e. Hindu) voters, reserved seats (and joint electorates) were prescribed, and where this was not the case, separate electorates were stipulated.

In the case of the Indian Christian representation, the Hammond Committee missed a chance to deal with the vexed question of communal electorates. The community had been allotted nine seats in Madras, where it was numerically strong compared to other provinces. The Committee had two options before it, either to allocate the seats in such a manner that would cover the entire province or to delimit them so that they would cover only some parts of Madras, presumably where the population of the community was concentrated. The first option entailed that the constituencies would be geographically large, and the second meant that the Indian Christian voters outside the areas which had been included in the constituencies would be included in the electorate for the general constituencies. The Committee selected the first option, saying that it was undesirable to leave some members of the community to be voters in general constituencies where their influence would be negligible owing to their small numbers.[169] Had the Committee selected the second option, the Indian Christians in Madras would not have had their quantum of representation reduced, and by virtue of some members of the community voting in general electorates would have been able to exercise some political influence. Here was a possibility of the community having the best of both worlds, another missed opportunity.

In the case of the provincial Legislative Councils and the Council of State, single-member constituencies were recommended in general. However, in Bombay, multi-member constituencies were proposed for the general electorate, keeping in view the local government's views. A system combining both kinds of constituencies was adopted in Madras for a similar reason.[170] The Bombay Government seems to have made the proposal for the same reason that it cited when it asked for similar constituencies for the Legislative Assembly, namely the representation of important minorities.

The question of voting systems figured prominently in the evidence of the witnesses who appeared before the Hammond Committee. There were two key issues here, the first being which system was best placed to secure representation to the minorities (within the Hindu fold) and the second, which one would best fulfil both the letter and the spirit of the Poona Pact.

A. Ramaswamy Mudaliar, a leading non-Brahmin political leader from Madras, strongly supported multi-member constituencies with cumulative voting as being the best system for the representation of the minorities, in this case minor castes in the Madras Presidency. This system would have enabled a given voter to cast all his or her votes for a particular candidate. When asked whether or not this would encourage heightened appeals to caste feelings, Mudaliar argued that a candidate belonging to a given caste would necessarily have to appeal to voters of other castes to ensure his victory.[171] He was supported by J. Sivashanmugham Pillai, a leading Scheduled Caste political leader from the same province.[172]

As regards the system of voting in the second round for the constituencies with a seat reserved for the Scheduled Castes, the opinion was divided. Pillai supported cumulative voting as this would enable the Scheduled Caste voter to cast all his votes for the candidate who belonged to his community.[173] Both Rao Bahadur R. Srinivasan and the Central Provinces Depressed Classes Federation asked for SNTV for reserved seats.[174] Dr Ambedkar objected to the distributive method in reserved seats on the grounds that it was mechanical but had no objections to the cumulative method.[175] A.V. Thakkar argued that the rationale behind the joint electorate would be defeated by any system other than distributive voting.[176] A similar position was adopted by Rai Bahadur Sonadhar Das of Assam who claimed that since reciprocity was required, compulsory distributive voting was required.[177] As mentioned earlier, the Committee permitted the voter to cast all of his or her votes for a single candidate or to distribute them among the candidates.

Underlying these preferences lay the question as to whether the caste Hindus and the Scheduled Caste voters should have a role in electing a candidate belonging to the other group. Those who argued for distributive voting wanted the two groups to be institutionally made dependent on the voters of each other. The support for cumulative voting and SNTV implied that the second round of election was to be disguised form of elections in communal electorates. Both would have enabled the Scheduled Caste voter (and the caste Hindu voter as well) to cast all of his or her votes, in the case of the first system, and the sole one in the case of the second system, to the candidate belonging to his or her community. Ambedkar's support for cumulative voting demonstrates that he had not reconciled to the principle of mutuality that underlay the Poona Pact. But his position was a nuanced one. He supported SNTV if the caste Hindus wished to play a role in the election of the Scheduled Caste candidate.[178] His underlying position was that since it was unlikely that the caste Hindu voters in this situation would abandon their chance of electing a candidate from their community, and that the Scheduled Caste voters would in any case support candidates from their community, there was no harm in conceding SNTV. Presumably, for Ambedkar, the caste Hindu voters could demonstrate their commitment to the cause that he had been fighting for by abandoning the chance to vote for a candidate of their community to participate in the election of the Scheduled Caste candidate.

The key issue in these discussions about alternative electoral methods was what constituted representation. Those who asked for cumulative voting or SNTV seemed to be more concerned with the notion of 'authentic' representation. These two methods would have implied that a group within a diverse electorate could elect, if it was organised enough, someone from among itself whom it preferred. Moreover, these methods would not have led to a situation where an individual belonging to a certain specified social group would have been elected by the votes of non-members or would in fact have been opposed by that group yet would have been able to claim to represent that same group on the grounds that he belonged to it. In other words, a Scheduled Caste elected representative could legitimately claim to represent the Scheduled Castes only he had been elected by the voters of his community, and not by others. On the other hand, supporters of distributive voting questioned this notion of 'authenticity'. They desired that the caste Hindu as well as the Scheduled Caste representative be elected by the votes of both communities and not just by those of their respective ones. Underpinning this position seems to be the idea that a representative would represent all the voters, including those who did not vote for him or her, and even if that was not so at least all those who voted for him. Thus, a caste Hindu and a Scheduled Caste representative would represent members of both communities. But the fly in the ointment in this argument was that in many, if not most, constituencies, the Scheduled Caste voters were numerically weak. Hence, while it was possible for a caste Hindu to be elected solely on the basis of the votes of his community, the Scheduled Caste candidates had to look beyond their community. This also meant that with planning caste Hindus could elect a Scheduled Caste candidate who lacked any significant support from his community. Whom did such an individual then represent? Those who elected him or the community he was supposed to represent? This was a problem that supporters of distributive voting could not address.

Furthermore, in the 1940s when it became clear that the British were not going to stay long in India, multi-member seats with or without reservations were seen as the best solution to the question of communal electorates and a system which would secure adequate representation to the minorities. The Hindu Mahasabhaite constitution decreed that no constituency at the provincial level would be a single-member one, which coupled with adult franchise obviated the need for weightages and reservations.[179] The second option was opted for by the Sapru Committee. It refuted that idea the candidates belonging to the minorities elected in constituencies with reserved seats would not be the 'real' representatives of their respective communities.[180] Dr Ambedkar though he had doubts whether the Sapru Committee's proposals would be regarded by the minorities as leading to the election of those whom they would regard as their own[181] did propose multi-member constituencies without reservations. He suggested that minorities would have double votes and that for a candidate belonging to a minority community to be elected he or she should have secured a minimum percentage of votes from his community. This for him was a system of joint electorates, which would grant 'equal protection' to the minorities.[182] Similarly, PR was also seen as a mean to assuage the fears of the minorities.[183] Meanwhile, proportional representation made a comeback by the recommendations of the Cabinet Mission Plan. The British Indian representatives of the proposed Constitution Making Body, later to be transformed into the Constituent Assembly, were to be elected by the members of the provincial Legislative Assemblies on a communal basis by STV.[184]

As the making of the Indian Constitution proceeded apace, discussions on fundamental rights led to those on the rights of and safeguards for minorities which in turn sparked off debates on the electoral system. Once again, it was Dr Ambedkar who made a significant contribution though his memorandum, which presented a constitutional outline for the country, submitted to the Assembly, later published in early 1947 under the title 'States and Minorities'. The 'States' in the title denoted the princely States whose constitutional status was yet unclear. It must be noted that this work of Ambedkar's was published much before the 3 June Plan or the Mountbatten Plan that announced the Partition of British India. The memorandum denounced the Poona Pact and demanded that separate electorates for the Scheduled Castes be restored besides asking that the community secure representation in all legislatures in proportion to its share of population. It also asked for a system of cumulative voting. Mention was made of the procedure to abrogate the provisions relating to the Scheduled Castes, including the above mentioned ones.[185]

Dr Ambedkar demanded separate electorates for the Scheduled Castes on two main grounds. Firstly, he claimed that the community was a minority and thus entitled to all measures possible to protect it. Secondly, he claimed that the two-round elections were a heavy encumbrance the community could ill-afford. Furthermore, he argued that the candidates belonging to the community who had been elected to the reserved seats in the second round of elections had been successful due to caste Hindu votes and were in fact not the first choice of their fellow community members in the primary elections. Thus, they could not be described as being the true representatives of their community.[186] He further supported the principle of communal electorates per se saying that these were the best measure for securing what could be described as authentic representation for the minorities. The minorities were to be the best judge of how they would choose to be represented. These arguments of Ambedkar were in continuation of those made in 'Communal Deadlock'. His support for cumulative voting does not fit easily in his above-mentioned scheme. Did he envisage this system of voting within separate electorates? If so, did he then implicitly acknowledge the presence of a substantial section of the Scheduled Castes who preferred to support the Congress, something that he had alluded to in his evidence to the Hammond Committee? The explanatory notes to his constitutional scheme make no mention of this point.

Constituent Assembly and After

Meanwhile, the real debate about constitution making was taking place in the various committees and sub-committees of the Constituent Assembly. They were concerned among other issues laying down the framework for the electoral system for a free India. The crucial question was once again how the minorities were to be represented. Once again, the two broad positions about political representation in India, the Institutionalist and the Processualist, could be discerned. The second position was stronger because the Congress dominated the constitution making process and the Muslim League had boycotted the Assembly.

While there was no opposition per se to the political representation of the minorities, the overall trend was against the continuation of communal electorates. They were seen as divisive and anti-national, a long-standing viewpoint of those who adopted the Processualist position. Yet there was also concern about ensuring that those members of the minority communities who had succeeded at the elections should be considered as the 'real' representatives of their respective communities. This was the issue of 'authentic' representation, one which had been pursued with tenacity till date by the Institutionalists. It was this very concern that sparked off a vibrant discussion on proportional representation. Those who favoured PR took an explicit Institutionalist stance when they advocated it as a method that would secure for the minorities such representatives who truly represented them. But there was opposition to PR.

Curiously, this was not framed in terms of the Processualist viewpoint but rather in terms of logistical difficulties. It was claimed that it was difficult to operate and implement in the Indian conditions. The institutional alternative to PR was the system of reserved seats. This option was preferred, indeed recommended, by the Processualists, albeit only till mid-1947, i.e. up to the point in time when the Partition of the subcontinent had not became a reality. After Partition, even reservations were ruled out for the minorities. Despite this limited support for reservations, there seems to be a consistent undercurrent of hostility to any institutional measures that would have enabled minority communities to elect representatives of their choice from amongst themselves. There seemed an unstated consensus that there should be no method or arrangement or set of rules that would allow organised minorities to vote en bloc and determine only by themselves who would represent them. Hence even proposals that for candidates to be elected from seats reserved for a given minority community they would have to secure a minimum stipulated percentage of votes from that community were rejected. It seems that the underlying notion was that the majority play a decisive role in deciding who the representatives from the minority communities would be. The spectre of communal electorates and the separatism that it had engendered, particularly in the case of the Muslims which in turn led to the division of British India on religious lines, had clearly cast a long shadow on the debate of the structure of the electoral system. This hostile attitude significantly contributed to the final outcome of the process of constructing an electoral system for a country on the threshold of independence.

The signal feature of this system was that it overwhelmingly consisted of single-member constituencies.

The Processualists fought a losing battle and were finally defeated by the events of 1947. It is interesting to note that the Processualists-Institutionalist divide was not on religious lines. Many members belonging to the minority communities opposed any institutional measures to ensure the representation of their co-religionists, while some other were vehement advocates of such measures. Equally, there were caste Hindu members who advocated PR as well as cumulative voting.

The early days of the Constituent Assembly also saw a debate on the choice of electoral system. Proportional representation was indeed seen in the period as a middle road between separate electorates, on one hand and on the other, any system that might lead to a majoritarian outcome. Somnath Lahiri, the sole Communist member of the Assembly, explicitly advocated PR so as to ensure that all parties, communal or otherwise, would secure representation in accordance with the votes that they had secured.[187] Sir H.S. Gour went a step further. He advocated reserved seats for the Muslims, which naturally entailed joint electorates. His scheme laid down that in such seats, a Muslim candidate would not be deemed to have been elected unless he or she secured a certain stipulated percentage of votes from Muslim voters.[188]

The decision to partition British India entirely changed the contours of the debate. In July 1947, the Minorities Sub-Committee of the Advisory Committee on Fundamental Rights overwhelmingly voted for abolition of separate electorates, thus solving the vexed question that had bedevilled Indian politics for almost half a century. This was hardly surprising since the mainstream of the nationalist movement had always looked upon these electorates as being inherently divisive and a British stratagem to 'divide and rule'. It also recommended reserved seats with the stipulation that they would be reconsidered after a decade.[189] The Sub-Committee in its report of July 1947 noted that the option of cumulative voting had been rejected. The demand that a candidate from a minority community to be elected should have secured a certain minimum percentage of votes from his community was referred back to the Advisory Committee. Dr Ambedkar's suggestion that candidates of the majority community to be elected should secure at least a certain minimum number of voters from other communities was rejected with only him voting for it.[190]

The matter was now taken up by the Advisory Committee. A perusal of the proceedings of this committee demonstrates that while separate electorates had been ruled out, reservations for the minorities were still the preferred option. At its meeting in July 1947, K.M. Munshi's resolution abolishing separate electorates was overwhelmingly carried. His other resolutions calling for reserved seats and their reconsideration after 10 years were similarly approved. Reserved seats presumably implied multi-member constituencies. Minoo Masani's amendment calling for PR, preferably cumulative voting in multi-member constituencies, was defeated.[191] Moreover, Munshi later moved a resolution explicitly stating that cumulative voting was not permissible. Masani's amendment asking for the matter to be decided upon when the electoral laws would be framed was lost. Thus, the Advisory Committee missed a chance to link reserved seats, which till then had been frowned upon as enabling the majority community to ensure the election of a candidate from a minority community who would toe its line, and the notion of 'authentic representation' via the device of cumulative voting.

Munshi further moved that there should be no stipulation that a candidate from a minority community should not be declared elected unless he or she secures a certain minimum proportion of the votes of his community.[192] The general drift towards reservations even before the 3 June Plan can be seen in K.M. Panikkar and S.P. Mookerjee's replies to a questionnaire circulated by Sir B. N. Rau, the Constitutional Advisor to the Assembly.[193] Only Mookerjee was explicit about the nature of constituencies. He preferred single-member ones and asked that wherever seats are sought to be reserved the constituencies should be multi-member ones.[194]

The same issues were debated in the replies to the questionnaires circulated by the Provincial Constitution Committee. Amrit Kaur argued for PR on the grounds that it would obviate the need for any special institutional measures to protect the minorities. She also specified that her proposal would naturally entail multi-member constituencies.[195] However, the general trend was in favour of reservations for certain specified minority groups, that too, on a population basis, and for single-member constituencies. Only those constituencies where seats were to be reserved were to be multi-member. Cumulative voting was supported by B.G. Kher, the Bombay Premier, and Dr P. Subbaroyan, while Mrs. Hansa Mehta supported PR-STV. Both these methods were to be applied in multi-member seats.[196] Communal electorates were, of course, out of question.

The report on Minority Rights was presented to the Constituent Assembly on 27 August 1947 by Sardar Vallabhbhai Patel. This provided an opportunity to debate the emerging contours of the electoral system in India. Joint electorates were seen as a means by which the caste Hindus and the minorities would come together to work for the country, while the right of the minorities to contest unreserved seats was seen as a sign of goodwill on part of the majority.[197] However, the cause of separate electorates was not lost. B. Pocker Sahib Bahadur, a Muslim League member from Madras, moved an amendment asking for a continuation of communal electorates for the Muslims. He argued that the only way the minorities could be kept satisfied was to give them an effective voice in the legislatures and that could be achieved by ensuring that those representating the minorities 'really represents that community'. Bahadur resorted to the old arguments against reserved seats by arguing that a successful candidate from such a seat belonging to a given minority community might well have been elected on the votes of the majority. Thus Bahadur laid stress on the notion of 'authentic representation'. He even raised the spectre of Muslims, whom he described as 'strong and well-organised' becoming 'desperate' if denied adequate and effective representation.[198] Pocker Bahadur's amendment, as was expected, was defeated.

Those emphasising 'authentic representation' now changed tack. The report had stipulated that a candidate from a minority community elected from a seat reserved for that particular community need not have secured a given percentage of votes from the voters of that community to be successful. S. Nagappa and K.T.M. Ahmed Ibrahim Sahib Bahadur moved amendments asking that a candidate from a reserved seat be elected only if he or she had secured a certain percentage of votes from the community for whom the seat has been reserved. Nagappa feared that in the absence of such a provision only 'show-boys of the general community' might be elected,[199] while Sahib Bahdur claimed that his amendment would ensure that the elected member would actually command the confidence of the minorities.[200] This demand was opposed by another member, Mrs. D. Velayudhan, who pointed out that such a provision would reduce the votes of the majority in a reserved constituency to a nullity,[201] while H.J. Khandekar feared that it would permanently marginalise the Scheduled Castes.[202] These amendments were even attacked as bringing in separate electorates by the back door. Ultimately, Nagappa withdrew his amendment while the second one was defeated. Moreover, there was opposition even to reserved seats. Mahavir Tyagi describing the system of reservations as a compromise opined that this was a step to far.[203]

The report also stipulated that the system of voting would be distributive and that cumulative voting would not be permitted. Cumulative voting was seen as encouraging voting on communal lines or even communal electorates in disguise. There was hardly any debate on this. Only one member, D.H. Chandrashekharaiya, representing the princely State of Mysore, urged PR-STV on the grounds that it would ensure the representation of all shades of public opinion. He reminded the Assembly that this system would ensure the representation of minorities and added that for him, minorities were primarily political. He added that despite wide-spread illiteracy, the system would work in India.[204] This was opposed by A.P. Jain who argued that this was bringing in separate electorates by the backdoor.

Rau's draft of the Constitution of India again reflected the consensus arrived at in both the Union and Provincial Constitution Committees. Seats were reserved for the Muslims and the Scheduled Castes in all the provinces, for the Scheduled Tribes in some, while Indian Christians were extended a similar concession only in Bombay and Madras.[205] The Draft Constitution did not mention any preference for a method of election. The details were to left to the Parliament and the state legislatures to decide. However, it did recommend reservations in line with Rau's draft constitution besides reflecting the consensus arrived on the issue of representation of the Anglo-Indian community.[206]

The Draft Constitution was then submitted to the Assembly which made it public for comments and suggestions. The electoral provisions of the Constitution evoked varied reactions. Reservations for minorities were regarded as being inconsistent with India's status as a 'non-communal secular state'.[207] The Socialist Party, however, welcomed reserved seats but denounced single-member constituencies as being artificial and liable to manipulation besides depriving the minorities of representation. Dismissing PR as being too complicated for India, the party advocated multi-member seats with cumulative voting as the best system.[208] However, D.R.Gadgil supported PR and provided extended arguments in its support. Pointing out that it was being argued on the basis of the American and the British that single-member or small multi-member constituencies lead to political stability and to the emergence of a two-party system, he claimed that the choice of electoral system had very little to do with these developments which were a consequence of other factors. Citing the instance of inter-war France, Gadgil argued that the adoption of single-member constituencies had not led to political stability. He further argued that since it was necessary to represent the minorities, which he described as being religious, social, linguistic and even political in nature, PR was the best system. He added that the assumption that a single-member system would lead to political integration in India was misplaced and that the most likely outcome was some form of the dominance of the majority and the subsequent resentment being felt on part of the minorities. He also added that unlike reservations, which would have to be placed on a statutory basis, PR might also assist in social and political integration of the population without resorting to legalities. He proposed the consideration of the list system in this context. But Gadgil was well aware of the contemporary political realities and concluded his discussion by noting that his suggestions would not endear themselves to the party in power, the Congress, whose leaders he noted had stressed the need for a strong one-party government.[209]

Meanwhile, the Constituent Assembly appointed a Special Committee under the chairmanship of Pandit Jawaharlal Nehru to examine the Draft Constitution.[210] At its insistence, the Drafting Committee proposed an amendment which stipulated that the elections to the Parliament and the state legislatures should be held on the basis of joint electorates. It was argued that since the nitty-gritty of the electoral structure was to be constructed by the Parliament and the state legislature, it was necessary to explicitly embody the Constituent Assembly's decision to reject separate electorates in the Draft Constitution.[211] Presumably, it was feared that any such absence would have left the doors open for communal representation.

The consideration of the question of communal electorates for the Sikhs in the Punjab had been postponed till the effects of the Partition were known. In early 1948, the Advisory Committee on Minorities rejected Sikh demands for communal electorates on grounds that the Sikhs could well hold their own given reserved seats and the right to contest unreserved seats. It was argued that the right to contest unreserved seats would in fact enable the community to obtain representation in excess of its share in population. In response, the Sikh members of the East Punjab Assembly asked for abolition of reserved seats for all minorities.[212] Meanwhile, movement against reservations for the religious minorities gathered strength. Suggestions made by a group of Assembly members, including one Muslim member, asked for abolition of reservations for both the Muslims and the Indian Christians.[213] By late 1948, the mood seems to have been shifted against reserved seats. In May 1949, the Sikh leaders agreed to give up reserved seats if the Sikh Scheduled Castes were treated on an equal basis as the Hindu Scheduled Castes. In the same month, the Advisory Committee adopted a resolution with one dissentient that reservations for all communities except the Scheduled Castes be abolished, and that the Sikh Scheduled Castes be included in the category of Scheduled Castes,[214] a clear trade-off. The revised Draft Constitution, however, bracketed the Scheduled Tribes with the Scheduled Castes as the two communities who would be entitled to reservations.[215]

In the meantime, the Draft Constitution was laid before the Assembly on 5 November 1948. It stipulated a system of joint electorates with reservations. Kazi Karimuddin once again discussed the merits of alternative electoral systems in terms of the advantages that they would have for the minorities. He argued that reserved seats in the absence of any stipulation that the successful candidate must have secured a certain minimum percentage of votes from the community for which the seat is reserved would serve no purpose, as far as the minorities were concerned. He claimed that this would not ensure that the individual elected would be the 'real representative' of the minority. Hence, he proposed PR with multi-member constituencies and cumulative voting as the best method to protect the minorities, both communal and political.[216] Similar sentiments were expressed by M.A.B. Sahib Bahadur and B. Pocker Sahib Bahadur.

A more extended argument was made by Z.H. Lari. He argued that single-member constituencies would lead to the disenfranchisement of the political minorities. In order to avoid such a scenario, he suggested PR with either STV or cumulative voting. To the critics who claimed that PR led to a proliferation of political parties, Lari pointed out that France had numerous parties even without PR.[217] Hussain Imam went even further when he claimed that PR was necessary to avoid India traversing the road to Fascism.[218] Mohammad Ismail Sahib reiterated that while the Muslims had accepted reservations, he was still of the opinion that separate electorates would return individuals who would express the views of the community.[219] However, all these arguments constituted, in a sense, special pleading. PR was merely being proposed to safeguard the political interests of the Muslims.

However, there was hardly any debate on the merits of a system of PR during the discussion on the Draft Constitution. The general argument was that PR was complicated, and given high rates of illiteracy unsuitable for India. M.A. Ananthashayanam Ayyangar reminded his fellow members that even they made mistakes when electing members of the Standing Committees by PR-STV in their capacity as members of the Constituent Assembly (Legislative) and hence it was evident that the average illiterate Indian voter would so the same.[220] Ambedkar cited illiteracy to oppose PR. However, he made an even more curious argument when he claimed that PR was opposed to the parliamentary system of government and cited the conclusion of the Royal Commission on Electoral Systems of 1910 in his support. Ambedkar argued that PR would obviously lead to a proliferation of political parties making governments unstable. An even stranger argument against PR was made by Ambedkar when he claimed that it was harmful to the minorities. He claimed that reservations would give the minorities a definite guaranteed quantum of representation, while PR would merely give them a voice in the election of their representatives.[221] This indicates a fundamental misunderstanding of the workings of PR.

There were, of course, members like K.T. Shah who suggested PR-STV for elections to the House of the People, only to have their amendments defeated. Cumulative voting also did not find favour with the Assembly. One member, Thakur Das Bhargava, argued that this was nothing but separate electorates in disguise,[222] while H.J. Khandekar claimed that it would encourage communalism.[223] V.L. Muniswami Pillai argued that distributive voting would in fact bring the various communities together.[224]

The only occasion PR found wide-spread favour was when it was stipulated as the method of elections for the Council of States. Many members, particularly Pandit H.N. Kunzru and Mahavir Tyagi, supported PR for the same on grounds that it would ensure the representation of the opposition parties.[225] Ultimately, the clause dealing with the Council of States was amended to state that elections to it would be held by PR-STV.[226] Neither was there much debate on the question of whether the constituencies for the lower house, the House of the People, should be single-member or not. Only Sardar B.S.Mann made a mention that multi-member seats would assist the minorities in getting elected.[227]

The Partition of India, it seems, had created an anti-Muslim and, by extension, an anti-reserved seats mood among some members of the Assembly. Pandit Lakshmi Kanta Maitra and Ramnarayan Singh explicitly cited the creation of Pakistan as the reason to deny reserved seats to the Muslims.[228] N.G. Ranga claimed that the Muslims were no longer a 'helpless community' and hence did not require reservations.[229] However, this was in keeping with the overall sentiment that no institutional guarantees be provided for the minorities. S. Nagappa reflected this feeling when he hoped that that not all minorities required safeguards.[230] Even some members from the minority communities expressed their opposition to reservations. R.K. Sidhwa trumpeted the fact that his community, the Parsis, had rejected any such safeguards and invited the other minorities to do the same,[231] while Sardar Hukum Singh and Giani Gurmukh Singh Musafir feared that they might perpetuate communalism.[232]

On 25 May 1949, the report of the Advisory Committee on Minorities, recommending the abolition of reservations for all communities, except the Scheduled Castes and the Scheduled Tribes, was laid before the Assembly. Patel's speech on moving the report explicitly stated that the abolition of reservations was a consequence of the changed political situation. The debate on the report primarily revolved on the question of how the representation of the minorities was to be ensured in the absence of any institutional arrangements. This debate again saw members take up Institutionalist versus Processualist positions.

B. Pocker Sahib Bahadur and Muhammad Ismail Sahib, both from Madras, strongly advocated retention of reservations without which, they felt, minorities would fail to get elected.[233] Syed Muhammad Saadullah, the former Prime Minister of Assam, supported reservations as having a psychological advantage for the Muslims.[234] He also warned that in the absence of any institutional arrangements for the representation of minorities, India might degenerate into an oligarchy. Proportional representation once again was advocated as an institutional arrangement to ensure the presence of the minorities. Z.H. Lari urged a system of multi-member seats with cumulative voting and no community being granted reservations.[235] In fact, he quoted the opinions of the Socialists and the Communists in favour of PR to bolster his case. Lari further recommended that since the legislature should reflect all shades of opinion prevalent in the society, PR was the best method to ensure it.

Not all members of the minorities were in favour of any institutional arrangements. Reservations were attacked as perpetuating the differences between communities and preventing them from coming together. Some like Dr H.C. Mookerjee, Father Jerome D'Souza, Mohammad Ismail Khan and Begum Aizaz Rasul argued that the minorities should now trust the majority to secure their rights. Rasul pointed out that in any democratic system, it would be difficult for the majority to ignore the minorities and hence there was all the possibility that candidates belonging to the minority community would be elected.[236] Any suggestions of proportional representation in any form were dismissed as being unsuitable to India once again on grounds of wide-spread illiteracy. However, Mahavir Tyagi supported cumulative voting as against STV. He claimed that while STV was complicated, the former was simple enough to be understood by the average Indian voter. He argued that this would ensure the representation of minorities, whether religious, economic or political.[237]

In support of the Muslim case, Lari had pleaded that since the Scheduled Castes had been granted reservations there was no reason why this option could not have been exercised in the case of the Muslims. This equation of the Scheduled Castes with the Muslims brought a furious response from S. Nagappa. He reminded the Assembly and particularly the Muslim members that his community had not migrated from Arabia and nor were invaders of India. It was the oldest inhabitants of the country and had been badly treated for many centuries, and hence the reservations.[238]

The Assembly formally passed Article 292 that provided for reservations only for the Scheduled Castes and the Scheduled Tribes in the House of the People on 23 August 1949, and in the provincial Legislative Assemblies the next day, thus closing the issue. But this success, partially, brought to the fore the question of whether members elected from reserved seats were 'authentic representatives' of their community. H.J. Khandekar replied in the negative and hence suggested that as far as the Scheduled Castes were concerned, seats should be reserved only in those areas where the community forms a majority to prevent the purpose of reservations from being defeated.[239]

It was stipulated that the reserved seats would continue only upto a period of 10 years from the commencement of the Constitution. There was a demand that in the case of the Scheduled Tribes, the period be extended since the community was backward. There was, of course, opposition expressed to the very idea of reservations. Critics claimed that capable individuals like Dr Ambedkar would be elected irrespective of their social background and without the aid of reservations. This Processualist argument was merely rhetoric.

However, this did not decide whether the constituencies were to be single- or multi-member. In the debates in the Constituent Assembly, after reservations for religious minorities had been abolished, Thakur Das Bhargava raised the issue. He recommended that all reserved seats be single-member ones. He claimed that multi-member constituencies would be large and unwieldy and hence his proposal.[240] Bhargava's amendment, however, was rejected by the Assembly without much debate.

While the Constituent Assembly had decided upon the broad outline of India's electoral system, the details were left to be filled in by legislation. This was done by the Provisional Parliament, the successor to the Constituent Assembly, by enacting two laws, the Representation of the Peoples Act, 1950 and the Representation of the Peoples Act, 1951. The debate on these laws demonstrate that while many members regarded the entire issue as foreclosed by the decisions taken by the Constituent Assembly, there were many who continued to propose alternatives. Their concern was once again motivated by the protection of minorities, however defined.

The bill to enact the first Act was introduced in the Provisional Parliament in April 1950 and dealt with delimitation as well as the qualifications for voters among other matters. There were protests from members on a wide variety of issues. Hossain Imam protested that the bill did not specify whether the constituencies were to be single-member or multi-member nor did it stipulate the method of voting. He argued that the First Past the Post voting (FPTP) system would lead to a situation where an individual securing only a minority of the votes would be elected.[241] Presumably, Imam meant that this fact would make the individual in question unrepresentative of the voters. The point about the voting systems overlooked the fact that the Constituent Assembly had already decided in favour of distributive voting. Ambedkar responded by saying that a second bill would deal with the issue raised by him,[242] reiterating an assurance given by the Prime Minister, Pandit Nehru. However, the government's clarifications did not satisfy the members, and G.V. Mavalankar, the Speaker, intervened to suggest an informal meeting which seems to have prevented a possible deadlock.

However, many members were still not satisfied. The key issue was whether constituencies wherein a seat was to be reserved for the Scheduled Castes and Scheduled Tribes were to be single-member or not. If they were single-member ones it would have naturally meant that those who did not belong to these communities would have no chance of contesting elections. It was these concerns that prompted A.P. Jain to move an amendment asking that all constituencies where seats for the Scheduled Castes are reserved be multi-member ones.[243] He clarified in response to a query from the Government that this amendment covered only the Scheduled Castes, and not the Scheduled Tribes since they 'live in particular areas'. This was a recognition that the constituencies reserved for the Scheduled Tribes were those where the community constituted a large majority of the population, while in the case of those for the Scheduled Castes, it may or may not constitute a majority. Thus Jain's amendment was actuated by a concern to ensure that the caste Hindus in constituencies where a seat was reserved for the Scheduled Castes had the opportunity to elect one of their 'own' rather than being solely represented by an individual belonging to the Scheduled Castes. Jain seemed to have realised that the purport of his amendment might prove controversial, for he was quick to claim the single-member constituencies were the best option and claimed the Constituent Assembly Debates gave the impression that single-member constituencies were to be the rule.[244] J.R. Kapoor went a step further when he moved an amendment asking for all reserved constituencies not to be single-member ones.[245] On the other hand, a member from Assam, Surendra Burgohain, asked that all constituencies reserved for Scheduled Tribes in Assam be single-member ones.[246]

Ambedkar declared that the two amendments were not acceptable to the Government and reiterated his promise that a second bill would deal with all the issues raised by the members.

The second bill as promised was introduced in the Provisional Parliament in December 1950. This prompted a renewed debate on the question of single- versus multi-member constituencies. Ambedkar mentioned that the bill provided for two-member constituencies since due to reservations they were an inevitability. He added that voting was to be distributive[247] to which Thakur Das Bhargava questioned the fact of inevitability. However, Bhargava and N.G. Ranga supported the idea of two-member constituencies, with Ranga explicitly stating that he wished that one of two seats be a general one.[248] It was left to Chaudhari Ranbir Singh to question the idea that single-member reserved constituencies would lead to the political exclusion of those communities who did not fall within the purview of reservations. He demanded that reserved constituencies should be single-member ones and made two points in support. Firstly, he claimed that not all constituencies would have Scheduled Castes and Scheduled Tribes representatives. By this he meant that if the non-reserved communities would feel excluded in single-member reserved seats, then reverse would be the case in non-reserved constituencies wherein the Scheduled Castes and Scheduled Tribes might feel excluded since members from these communities were unlikely to be elected from non-reserved constituencies. Secondly, Singh argued that there was no reason to suppose that Scheduled Caste and Scheduled Tribe representatives would not represent the non-reserved communities. He argued that multi-member constituencies would perforce be geographically large and hence would constitute a 'punishment' for the Scheduled Caste and Scheduled Tribes candidates.[249] The bill was then referred to a Select Committee. The entire question was clarified by Dr Ambedkar when he stated that constituencies where seats were reserved were perforce made two-member ones to prevent 'a complete disenfranchisement of the general population.'[250]

The bill as amended by the Committee was moved by Dr Ambedkar in May 1951. During his speech, he told the members that the Provisional

Parliament was not debating on a 'clean slate' and further reminded them of the Constituent Assembly resolution favouring distributive voting.[251] Yet, H.N. Kunzru argued that it might be desirable to permit cumulative voting in three-member constituencies. He contested the claim that cumulative voting encouraged communalism. Kunzru argued that for an individual to be elected in a given three-member constituency, he or she would have to secure at least 25 per cent of the votes and that since there would no instance of a community in any future constituency constituting more than 25 per cent of the electorate, there was no chance of anyone getting elected on the votes of a single community. He further argued that the Provisional Parliament was a sovereign body and was not bound by the decisions of the Constituent Assembly.[252] This was a strange argument by itself and was obviously not taken seriously. A further amendment moved by Sarangdhar Das asking for cumulative voting in multi-member constituencies was defeated. He too supported cumulative voting so as to enable the representation of minorities. He clarified that he meant political minorities. Das also asked for single-member constituencies whether reserved or not and pointed out that representatives belonging to the Scheduled Castes and Scheduled Tribes could well represent the non-reserved communities. He charged that two-member constituencies were being introduced to 'appease the non-scheduled electors'.[253] The question of reserved seats cropped up once again. Upendranath Burman asked that wherever the areas where the population of the Scheduled Castes or the Scheduled Tribes was in excess of 60 per cent the constituency may be a single-member reserved one.[254]

In June 1951, the second bill was passed to become the Representation of the Peoples Act, 1951. With this the construction of the electoral system was complete and the debate on political representation closed. It had travelled a long way from nominations to nearly completely elected legislatures, from communal electorates to seats reserved only for the deprived sections of the Indian society, and from indirect to direct elections. The only changes that took place was the abolition of the multi-member constituencies in the 1960s[255] and the subsequent repeal of the law that abolished such constituencies in the first decade of the twenty-first century. While the Indian electoral system has remained unchanged despite tectonic political transformations, the repeal of the Two-Member Constituencies (Abolition) Act, 1961 in 2001 has opened up a chance to reconstruct it, albeit within the letter and spirit of the constitution.

6

Delimitation and Electoral Qualifications

The present chapter deals with two relatively minor, albeit, crucial aspects of the debate over the question of political representation. The first is the process by which the geographical boundaries of constituencies are drawn, popularly referred to as delimitation in India. The second is the fixing of qualifications for the voters as well as the candidates.

In modern democracies, population is generally taken as the basis for the drawing of boundaries of constituencies. However, in colonial India both the context and basis was, of course, neither population nor the number of voters since the franchise was severely restricted. The thrust of the scheme of delimitation was to ensure that the legislature was representative of the society at large and this concern was evident even in the constituencies which were not earmarked for any specific community. Furthermore, two issues emerged with the advent of reservations for certain specified social categories. The first one was that all those communities which were included in a given category had a more or less equal chance of securing representation from the reserved seats, and secondly, ensuring that those communities which had not been granted reservations were not deprived of a fair chance of securing representation.

In the case of qualifications for the voters or the franchise qualifications, adult franchise was never seriously considered as a feasible or practical option in the colonial period, though there were periodic pious pronouncements that it was an ideal to be attained sometime in the distant future. If the colonial regime dismissed adult franchise, the nationalist movement was at times enamoured of it, albeit it seems for a variety of reasons.

The debate over the qualification of candidates saw the articulation of what were previously described as Institutionalist and Processualist positions. Should the voters be trusted to elect the 'right' kind of candidates? Or was it better to lay down specifications to ensure the election of 'suitable' candidates.

Delimitation

The problem of how exactly to delimit constituencies was not an issue during the Morley–Minto reforms since the system of representation stipulated by these changes rested on indirect elections to the provincial legislative councils as well as the all-India legislature, formally known as the Governor-General's Legislative Council. The local self-government institutions—the district boards and the municipalities which covered the rural and the urban areas respectively—constituted the electorates for the general constituencies, i.e. those not set aside for any particular community or for special interests like the landlords or the business community. Since more than one seat had been allotted in each provincial council to these local bodies, the only issue was how to group them to form suitable constituencies.

With the Montagu–Chelmsford reforms came legislative bodies which were predominatly elective, thus necessitating a full-fledged scheme of delimitation of constituencies. The Southborough Committee prepared an outline of such a scheme, while the Government of India proposed a detailed one. The Joint Select Committee was empowered to decide upon the delimitation proposals made by the Government of India. In only one instance did it change the proposals. This was in the case of the Bombay Presidency where it had been proposed that one seat in the multi-member constituency of Bombay City be reserved for the Maratha and the Allied Castes. The committee abolished the reserved seat on the grounds that the community did not have the numbers to justify reservations but, more importantly, for the reason that it would deprive the 'important and influential' Parsis of a chance to secure representation.[1] This is a clear instance of delimitation being regarded as an Institutional device to ensure a certain pattern of political representation.

In Bombay, the real contestation in the case of delimitation was about which constituencies were to be allotted the reserved seats as per the provisions of the 1935 Act. Dr Ambedkar objected to the manner in which the Maratha reserved seats were allotted. He claimed that the purpose of reservations to the Maratha and Allied castes was to ensure a minimum quantum of reservations and not to enable the communities to augment their legislative strength. He had objected to the official plan by claiming that it had allotted seats reserved for the community to those constituencies where it was numerically weak rather than where it was numerically strong. Ambedkar argued that this plan provided an unfair advantage to the Maratha and Allied Castes since the members of the community would not only be elected as a consequence of reservations from such seats where it was numerically weak but also would be elected from those non-reserved seats where it was numerically strong by virtue of its sheer numbers. This would naturally increase the number of representatives belonging to the Maratha and Allied Castes and thus the community would enjoy a double advantage. Ambedkar preferred that the community be granted reserved seats where it was strong in numbers. Thus, in this instance for Ambedkar, reservations were a limiting device rather than one which secured a guaranteed minimum quantum of political representation. He does not seem to have made clear why he took this position. One wonders if Ambedkar would have opposed such a scheme had it been proposed in the case of the Scheduled Castes.

The Government and the committee refuted this claim and stated that this was not indeed the case. In some instances, the community had a plurality while in others it was not strong. But in any case, the purpose of reservations was to enable the community to elect, where it had a reasonable chance of doing so, someone from within itself, irrespective of its numerical strength in the concerned constituencies.[2] The principle adopted in distributing the Scheduled Caste reserved seats was somewhat different. The Government stated that the entire allotment was done in a manner to ensure that the smaller castes among the broader category of Scheduled Castes had a reasonable chance of securing political representation. It added that it had been warned that an inequitable allotment would result in certain numerically strong communities within the Scheduled Castes monopolising representation granted to the category as a whole. Since some of these smaller castes were predominantly urban, it was proposed to allot some of these seats to the urban areas.[3]

With the Constituent Assembly adopting adult franchise, the terrain of the debate shifted. Population was now to determine the number of seats. The Constitution had provided that as far as the House of the People was concerned, there would not less than one member for every 5,00,000 and not more than one member for every 7,50,000 of the people in the case of the Part A and the Part B states. For the Legislative Assemblies of these states, one seat was to be allotted for every 75,000 of the population and their strength was not to exceed 500. Dr Ambedkar announced while introducing in Parliament the bill that became the Representation of the People Act, 1950, that this criterion would be altered in the case of the Part C states. He added that the government was trying to correct the anomalies whereby some states who had not received any representation on a population basis would secure it.[4] The population figures were estimates derived from the Constitution (Determination of Population Order) 1950. These figures were disputed by some members and the methodology used to arrive at them was termed faulty.[5]

The entire issue of delimitation now became the focus of discussion. H.N. Kunzru reminded the Provisional Parliament that 'on the manner in which constituencies are delimited would depend the representative character of Parliament'.[6] There were protests that the government had decided upon the number of constituencies without carrying out the process of delimitation. Dr Ambedkar clarified that delimitation, with which elected representatives would be associated, would be carried out by a Presidential Order which would then be placed before Parliament which would debate it.[7] It was evident that delimitation was regarded as an Institutionalist measure to achieve a certain pre-determined political goal. S.L. Saxena asked in mid-1951 that the constituencies be delimited in a manner so that no single caste dominates its electorate.[8]

Once the Delimitation Orders were laid before the House, amendments were moved to it. The most significant was the one proposed by R.K. Sidhwa which asked that all cantonments be grouped together to form single Parliamentary constituencies. Since most cantonments were cosmopolitan areas where the minority communities predominated, this was perhaps an attempt to secure them guaranteed representation. These amendments were not accepted and geographical contiguity became the accepted criterion for delimitation of constituencies.

Franchise

Given that the Morley–Minto reforms primarily rested on a system of indirect elections, the question of franchise qualifications did not quite arise. The question became pertinent only during the Montagu–Chelmsford reforms which recommended direct elections. Adult franchise was, of course, out of the question. The Report on Indian Constitutional Reforms, popularly referred to as the Montagu–Chelmsford Report after its principal authors, lamented that the absence of spread of education prevented a general extension of the franchise.[9] Yet it acknowledged that the proposed franchise had to be as broad as possible, at least as far as the provincial councils were concerned.[10] The report further recommended that the entire question of franchise qualifications and other related matters be examined by a specially constituted committee.[11] This was the Southborough Committee which naturally decided upon on property and income-based franchise qualifications.[12] Suggestions had been made that an educational qualification be introduced in order to bolster the electorate but the committee did not recommend any such qualification. Apparently, this suggestion had been made to enable the junior members of the Hindu joint families to qualify as voters.[13] The argument was that any property or income qualifications would qualify only the heads of such families but not other male members as voters even though the amount of tax paid by these families or their income exceeded the minimum stipulation to such an extent that remaining male members of the family could easily satisfy this stipulation and thus be eligible to enrol themselves as voters.

The impact of relying on income or property qualifications was assessed by the Simon Commission. It conceded that this state of affairs had led to 'predominance and sometimes a monopoly in the vote to certain classes of the population'. It also admitted that the junior members of undivided, i.e. joint Hindu, families were disenfranchised since they did not possess any property or income in their name so as to enable them to qualify as voters.[14] The Commission's recommendation was that the franchise qualifications should be such as would enfranchise only about 10 per cent of the adult population.[15] This meant that income and property would obviously form the principal basis for these qualifications. It also suggested that since hardly any women could qualify as voters in their own right as they lacked the required qualifications, the wives and widows of qualified male voters could be enfranchised. The Commission also recommended educational qualifications for both men and women.[16] These were to be the basis for all future proposals.

These proposals evoked a range of reactions. Dr Ambedkar was sharply opposed to property or income being the sole basis of franchise, for he feared that such restrictions would mean that the poor would be deprived of any chance to influence their political future. Pointing out that 'Franchise means the right to determine the terms of associated life', he rather exaggeratedly claimed that 'Property may as well dull the edge of intelligence'.[17] The Government of India seemed to be wary of the implications of the proposal to enfranchise women on the basis of their husbands' qualifications. It noted that the end result of such a provision would be that while women belonging to a cross-section of Indian society would become voters, only those from the 'low-caste' Hindu backgrounds would be able to freely cast their votes, presumably due to the relative social freedom that they enjoyed. On the other hand, upper caste Hindu as well as Muslim women would find it difficult to come out in public to vote. This, as the government put it, would give a double vote in the hands of the 'Hindu low castes'.[18] Clearly, the Raj preferred upper-caste Hindus and the Muslims as collaborators in their constitutional schemes. But soon it did change its mind. By 1933, the Government of India supported the enfranchisement of women on their husband's property qualifications.[19]

In the meantime, the franchise question was prominently discussed at the first Round Table Conference held in London. The Maharaja of Alwar hit the constitutional and communal nail on the head when he pointed out that the issue of franchise was at the root of the friction between the various communities in India.[20] Among the various sub-committees appointed by the conference was one on franchise. It was charged with devising the principles on which the franchise was to be based whose details were to be worked out by a separate expert committee.[21] But it did see a debate on the issue of what should constitute the basis for franchise. Joshi wanted income qualifications to replace a property-based one, presumably since it would enfranchise the working classes.[22] Sir Henry Gidney, representing the Anglo-Indians, opposed property qualifications on the grounds that his community hardly possessed any.[23] Rao Bahadur Pannir Selvan opposed educational qualifications, for he feared that it would enhance the influence of the Brahmins.[24]

The expert committee charged with devising a detailed scheme of franchise was the Indian Franchise Committee known as the Lothian Committee after its chairman, Lord Lothian. It recommended the continuation of property- and income-based qualifications besides an educational one. In the last instance, it made a distinction between men and women. While the former could qualify as voters if they had attained a given educational level, women could be enfranchised if they were literate. It also suggested that if uniform franchise qualifications for all communities led to an outcome wherein the case of any one or more community the ratio of voters to the total population was markedly different from the rest, then this should be rectified by differential franchise qualification for the concerned community or communities.[25] It also considered the question of on what basis could women be enfranchised for it desired that 'an adequate number of women' should be a part of the electorate. In addition to literacy, it recommended that women could be enfranchised on the basis of their husbands' qualifications, a suggestion originally made by the Simon Commission.

The suggestion made by the Simon Commission as to the way to enfranchise women was opposed by many. The Government of Madras expressed its opposition, while the Madras Provincial Franchise Committee opined that this would merely increase the husbands' votes,[26] thus implying that politically speaking women would vote the way their husbands' directed. But it was Ramabai Tambe, a member of the Central Provinces Franchise Committee, who offered a defence of this method of enfranchising women. She refuted the claim that accepting this proposal would in reality mean two votes for the male voter. She claimed that instead of wives being influenced by their husbands, it could well be the other way round.[27] Moreover, there was also opposition to women being granted the right to vote. B.G. Khaparde from the Central Provinces alleged Indian women were simply not capable of intelligently exercising the right to vote.[28]

Educational attainments as a condition for enfranchisement were supported by a majority of the Madras Provincial Committee, as well as the United Provinces Government.[29] But the Government of Bombay opposed it by sharply commenting that educational qualifications were no guarantee of an intelligent exercise of the vote.[30] Sardar Sir Jogendra Singh, the Minister for Agriculture of the Punjab, argued that high property qualifications would ensure the 'representation of a responsible and stable element in the Council',[31] thus once again reflecting a distrust of the masses.

Towards Adult Franchise

While many involved in the process of constructing a system of representation for India opined that they desired adult franchise in the abstract, hardly anyone demanded its immediate introduction. There were rare voices like Vitthalbhai Patel who asked for it. In his evidence before the Joint Committee in his capacity as a representative of the Indian National Congress, he demanded universal suffrage and argued that it could be easily implemented.[32] This was perhaps the first time that any leading nationalist figure had openly and explicitly referred to it.

These voices gathered strength as time went by. Chittranjan Das and Bhagvan Das's 'Outline Scheme of Swaraj', prepared sometime in the early 1920s, provided for adult franchise, though its proposals entailed direct elections only at the local level.[33] It was the All-Parties Report, known as the Nehru Report after its chairman, Pandit Motilal Nehru, which strongly advocated adult franchise. It deployed both a pragmatic as well as a thorough-going democratic argument in its support. Deploying the the democratic argument, it opined that any restriction on franchise was anti-democratic and hence adult franchise was necessary. It added that the right to vote would constitute a valuable means of political education and securing political experience. It also disposed of all objections of administrative difficulties stating the government machinery could easily cope with the responsibility of conducting elections based on adult franchise. But the Nehru Committee had pragmatic grounds for its position. It had done away with communal electorates and had, most reluctantly, supported reserved seats for minorities.[34] It now had to find an alternative by which the minorities could obtain a quantum of representation close to, if not equal to, their share in the population, without resorting to any contrived measures like differential franchise qualifications for different communities that would then ensure that each community's share in the electorate would be the same as their percentage in the overall population. The easiest answer to this was adult franchise, a fact that was admitted by the committee itself.[35] Others like Lord Lothian, who in the early 1930s was to chair the Indian Franchise Committee, recognised the logic that lay behind the Nehru Committee's acceptance of adult franchise. He pointed out that the Committee advocated it since it seemed the simplest way of dealing with the communal problem.[36] But not all sections of nationalist opinion regarded adult franchise with such ease. S. Srinivasa Iyengar's constitutional scheme known as the Swaraj Constitution dismissed it as impractical and substituted literacy as a franchise qualification. It was claimed that this would provide a boost to elementary education.[37]

The Congress formally adopted adult franchise as its goal at its Karachi session in 1931. However, it was not a participant in the process of constitutional reforms. Among those who participated, Dr Ambedkar was a powerful but lonely voice calling for adult franchise, a point acknowledged by the Simon Commission.[38] The Indian Central Committee opined that adult franchise was an ideal to be aimed at but thought it to be impractical at the present.[39] But a memorandum signed by a minority of the members recommended its immediate introduction in Bengal to ease communal tension. It clarified that this measure was likely to solve the knotty question of the quantum of representation for both the Hindus and the Muslims.[40] The Madras Provincial Committee appointed to collaborate with the Simon Commission took an even stronger negative stand. Apart from the usual arguments about administrative and logistical difficulties, it claimed that adult franchise would mean the right to vote being granted to 'persons lacking in political experience and ability'.[41] The Bengal Committee also condemned it as 'neither desirable nor practical'. For it, the greatest obstacle was the illiteracy of the masses.[42] Dr Shafaat Ahmed Khan, a member of the United Provinces committee, was even more explicit in his opposition. He argued that the people of India were simply not ready for it because they lacked training and education, were poorly organised and, more importantly, were 'enveloped in the Cimmerian fog of superstition'.[43] Clearly, they doubted or perhaps even feared the masses.

The Assam Committee, however, did at least consider adult franchise as a feasible alternative, albeit from a purely pragmatic viewpoint. It cited its multiple advantages which were that it did away with the need for special representation for backward communities, made bribery difficult by increasing the number of voters and made the legislature more representative.[44] But it was Dr Ambedkar who made an extended argument in favour of adult franchise. He claimed that apart from considerations of what he termed 'political justice', there were also pragmatic considerations in its favour. He pointed out that adult franchise could easily prove to be a feasible alternative to communal electorates, for it would enable the minorities to elect a candidate from among themselves on the strength of their own votes and prevent the election of someone who belong to the minority communities but did not quite command their confidence. He also accused the majority community, i.e. the Hindus, of not even considering adult franchise.[45] But there were ambiguities in Dr Ambedkar's position on adult franchise. He claimed that this should not be granted to the 'criminal tribes', for he alleged that they were only interested in their own communities and that were 'not very particular about the means whereby they earn their living'. But Ambedkar saw no harm in granting adult franchise to the 'aboriginals'.[46]

The pragmatic reasons for adult franchise were cited by some witnesses who gave evidence to the Simon Commission. S.K. Bole, a prominent non-Brahmin leader from Bombay, thought that its introduction would enable the doing-away with of reservations, communal electorates and nominations.[47] Interestingly, the All-India Muslim League also supported adult franchise, albeit only for the provincial councils.[48] But there were the usual voices like Pandit Nanak Chand from the Punjab who opposed it on grounds of being impractical at present.[49]

The Round Table Conferences once again saw a renewed debate on adult franchise. N.M. Joshi strongly advocated it at the first conference.[50] The discussion on adult franchise largely took place in the Franchise Sub-Committee. Joshi reiterated his demand.[51] There was opposition to it too. A.K. Fazl-ul-Haq, the veteran Muslim leader from Bengal, argued that indebtedness of the peasantry and illiteracy made its introduction impossible. Similarly, Rao Bahadur Pannir Selvan warned that adult franchise would increase the influence of the landed classes, for the peasantry was under their sway.[52] There were also those who thought that adult franchise was fraught with dangers. Sir Cowasji Jehagir claimed that it would lead to autocracy since the country was not ready for it, while Sir Hubert Carr warned of dangers of 'ochlocracy'.[53] Distrust of the masses was quite clear. Thus, those who advocated these positions desired that the legislative bodies be representative without necessarily being democratic. For them, representation and democracy did not quite go together.

These arguments were strongly countered by Dr Ambedkar who reiterated his support for adult franchise. He pointed out that only a system of universal suffrage would entail real political, responsible governance in India, for it would entail the executive being responsible to a genuinely representative legislature. Ambedkar added that adult franchise also had the potential of solving the thorny communal question.[54] The second point meant that the proportion of all communities, including the Scheduled Castes, in the electorate would be equal to their share of the population. This would dispel fears that 'backward' majority communities would be swamped by 'advanced' and prosperous 'minorities' who would constitute a larger share of the electorate than that which their numbers entitled them to by virtue of educational and property qualifications. But more importantly for Ambedkar, adult franchise would enhance the political and electoral strength of the Scheduled Castes, for it would be a reflection of their numbers.

The draft report of the sub-committee admitted that adult franchise was an ideal to be ultimately attained but not something that was to be immediately introduced.[55] To this, Joshi, Ambedkar and Srinivasan submitted a joint note of dissent calling for immediate introduction of adult franchise.[56] Ambedkar and Joshi continued their advocacy of adult franchise once the entire conference had reconvened to discuss the reports of the sub-committees. Despite this advocacy, the general trend of the conferences was against adult franchise. This attitude was also seen in the proceedings of the second Round Table Conference. At this conference, Mahatma Gandhi reiterated the Congress's commitment to adult franchise but on pragmatic grounds. He argued that it could 'satisfy all reasonable aspirations' of all communities in India. This implied that since the share of any particular community in the electorate would be more or less equal to its proportion in the population, it could potentially secure a quantum of political representation close, if not equal, to its numerical strength. Thus, for Gandhi, adult franchise obviated the need for any institutional mechanisms to guarantee the political representation of the minorities. Yet Gandhi added if certain groups went unrepresented by the electoral process, their representatives should be co-opted into the legislatures.[57] The cause of adult franchise found a surprising supporter in Sayajirao

Gaikwad, the Maharaja of Baroda.[58] This was in a sense surprising coming from a ruling prince but perhaps was a reflection of his progressive-mindedness which had already been demonstrated by the steps he had taken to further education, particularly of the backward communities and Scheduled Castes.

By the early 1930s, the tide seemed to be turning in favour of adult franchise. The Lothian Committee declared that it was a goal that was to be ultimately attained and listed a number of reasons in favour. It pointed out that adult franchise had the potential of ensuring representation of all sections of society, albeit to what extent would depend on the exact electoral system adopted. The committee also cited the example of Ceylon where adult franchise had been adopted. However, it was quick to argue against it on grounds of logistical difficulties in India besides the perennial claim that a predominantly illiterate electorate made adult franchise extremely difficult.[59] The responses of the provincial government and the provincial franchise committee were also largely unenthusiastic about adult franchise. The routine argument of administrative difficulties was trotted out. Adult franchise found only sporadic support from the witnesses who appeared before the committee. Only one witness, Kotieth Krishnan from the Madras Presidency, pointed out that since adult franchise had worked successfully in French India it could easily succeed in British India.[60] Other witnesses also supported adult franchise for many other reasons. Dr S. Muthulakshmi Reddiar, a leading women's activist from the Madras Presidency, advocated it to save women from the ignominy of qualifying as voters on the basis of their husbands' property.[61] The Bihar Provincial Muslim League also supported it on grounds that it would solve to a certain extent the problem of the representation of minorities.[62]

The constitutional schemes devised in the 1940s to deal with the political future of India supported adult franchise, at least for the lower houses of the provincial and the all-India legislature.[63] Though M.N. Roy's scheme did not explicitly mention adult franchise, its provisions were based on it.[64] Dr Ambedkar's 1945 address, known as the 'The Communal Deadlock and the Way to Solve It', also makes no explicit mention of it but given his earlier advocacy of adult franchise it can be safely assumed that he had not changed his position on it. His 1947 work 'States and Minorities', of course, advocated adult franchise.[65] K.G. Mashruwala's Gandhi-inspired scheme of 1946 also proposed adult franchise,[66] while Shriman Narayan Agarwal's Gandhian Constitution advocated adult franchise which would form the basis of a system of indirect elections.[67]

Despite the Congress's commitment to adult franchise, not all Congress leaders desired that it should be introduced immediately after independence or should be qualified by certain conditions. B.G. Kher, the Prime Minister (as the Chief Ministers were known then) of Bombay, in his reply submitted in mid-1947 to the questionnaire issued by the Provincial Constitution Committee, appointed by the Constituent Assembly, asked that a literacy test be introduced for at least the next decade.[68] Rohini Kumar Chaudhury, a member of the Assembly from Assam, supported adult franchise limited by educational or property qualifications to be introduced.[69] But the overall consensus was still on the side of adult franchise.

The desirability of adult franchise was also debated in the Constituent Assembly. While there were many who defended it, its critics were aplenty. The main thrust of many of these critics was widespread illiteracy made adult franchise a difficult proposition. Biswanath Das warned that introducing it in a largely illiterate society was fraught with risks which he described as 'a very highly inflammable class of people who have up to date no experience either of propaganda or of voting'.[70] Similarly, H.V. Kamath asked for adult education to precede adult franchise, for the second would be meaningless without the first.[71] Some like Thakur Das Bhargava wanted adult franchise to be qualified by a literacy test, albeit only for the first 10 years. He claimed that this would solve the enormous administrative and logistical difficulties associated with conducting elections on this basis and would provide a fillip to education as well since individuals desirous of voting would educate themselves.[72] Even no less a person than Dr Rajendra Prasad, the President of the Constituent Assembly, was reported to have expressed misgivings about adult franchise.[73]

On the other hand, there were those like H.N.Kunzru who wanted adult franchise to be achieved over a period of time by stages. He claimed that its immediate introduction would be inimical to democracy, for the electorate was more likely than not to be an ill-informed one. A progress by stages would also help spread political awareness and education.[74] Then there were others like Mahavir Tyagi, Loknath Misra and M. Thirumala Rao who warned of the dangers of adult franchise but seemed resigned to its introduction and hence offered no constructive alternatives.[75]

Some defenders of adult franchise defended it arguing not on the basis of the political capacity of the masses but rather by claiming that going back on it would a breach of a solemnly given promise. It was Alladi Krishnaswami Ayyar who provided the most eloquent defence of adult franchise. He pointed out that while its adoption was an experiment, it was adopted with 'abundant faith in the common man' and with 'the full realisation of its implications'. Ayyar added that any diminution of the principle would be antithetical to democracy itself and added that qualification based on property and income was bound to be arbitrary. He further expressed the hope that adult franchise would help eliminate electoral corruption.[76]

The strongest and the most consistent opposition to adult franchise came from Brajeshwar Prasad of Bihar. In his first but brief remarks on it, he claimed that adult suffrage was opposed to democracy. He claimed that adult franchise presupposed what he termed an enlightened electorate and that its absence entailed the failure of democracy.[77] Furthermore, he claimed that the Indian electorate was not only 'illiterate but narrow-minded, steeped in fanaticism and superstition'. He added that it was his belief that power should rest with those who were not only literate but wise too.[78] Prasad was even more vehement when he described adult franchise as 'a grand leap in the dark' which would unleash forces of violence and disorder on an unimaginable scale.[79] But his was an isolated voice, and adult franchise became an integral feature of the Indian political system.

Qualifications of Candidates

The regulations, made under the Morley–Minto reforms, contained the usual stipulations about the qualifications of candidates. Women, those who were not British subjects, those below 25 years of age, insolvents and individuals of unsound mind were excluded. However, the list of disqualifications did not end here. Those who had been dismissed from Government service, or had been sentenced to six-month imprisonment, or had been ordered to furnish security for good behaviour, or had been debarred from practising as lawyers, and lastly had declared by the Government 'to be of such reputation and antecedents' so as to render his election against the public interest were barred from contesting. These disqualifications were the same for the all-India legislature as well for the provincial councils. The curious fact of these second set of disqualifying rules was that the Government had powers to waive them.[80] The reasons for this are hard not to find.

The purpose of these reforms was to bolster the Moderate nationalists and reduced the influence of the Extremists. Many of the Extremists, and some of the former, had at one time or the other found themselves entangled with the Raj, and thus would have been subject to these disqualifications. The government, of course, did not wish to lose an opportunity to draw such individuals into the councils. The best illustration of this approach of the government is Surendranath Banerjea, who had served as the president of the Indian National Congress. As is well known, Banerjea had joined the elite Indian Civil Service only to find himself dismissed. The circumstances of his dismissal evoked a controversy. But this was fortuitous for him since that enabled him to embark on a political career which encompassed the membership of both the all-India and the Bengal council. Banerjea himself regarded these regulations as an attempt by the Government to impose restrictions on the concessions that it had made.[81] His own account of why and how the disqualifications were waived in his case make interesting reading. In 1913, he contested the elections to both the Bengal and the all-India council. In the first case, the waiver came quickly by the Lieutenant-Governor, Sir Edward Baker. In the second case, the illness of the then Viceroy, Lord Hardinge, delayed matters. An enquiry was started as regarded the 'suitability' of Banerjea. This delay made Baker's successor, Lord Carmichael, anxious, for he feared that this would provoke an agitation. As Banerjea himself commented, such a prevarication was patently absurd, for if he was suitable for one legislative body, then he was obviously suitable for another. The waiver came soon and the matter ended to the relief of everyone concerned.[82] The government had elicited the opinions of many non-officials on the reforms scheme and it was opined that candidates must be 'men of substance and property, having some real interests and stake in the country'.[83]

The Montagu–Chelmsford Report did not make any concrete suggestions about the qualifications for the membership of the proposed legislatures. It did recommend that the qualifications for the members of the Council of State, the proposed upper chamber of the all-India legislature, be such that they would be persons of status and position befitting the body's role as the supreme legislative body for crucial issues and the revising chamber in relation to legislation.[84] But the same question had to be tackled by the Southborough Committee. A majority held that dismissal from government service should constitute a disqualification which, however, could be waived by the government. But three members, the chairman himself, Surendranath Banerjea and V.S. Srinivasa Sastri, argued that this would amount to limiting the choice of the electorate on the basis of what they described as a decision taken by the executive.[85] Thus, they adopted a Processualist position. It also suggested minor changes in the case of the other provisions regarding disqualification.

The question of qualifications for candidates did not figure prominently during the examination of witnesses by the Southborough Committee. Only R.N. Mudholkar, a former president of the Indian National Congress, asked for the qualifications for candidates to be of a higher order than those for the voters to enable the election of a 'more responsible type' of individuals to the proposed councils.[86] R.P. Paranjpye presented a detailed proposal in this regard. Candidates were to be over 25 years of age, fluent in English and, more significantly, to have an income exceeding a certain limit or a share in immovable property worth more than a specified amount. In his oral evidence, Paranjpye stressed command over English. His argument that the property- or income-based qualification for the candidates should be more than that for the voters so that the former would not be tempted to take advantage of their position was quite novel.[87]

Apparently, there was a proposal that knowledge of English be laid down as a stipulation for the potential candidates. Pandit Malaviya opposed it arguing that this would deprive the provincial councils of many able men and further suggested that their proceedings could be conducted in the local language.[88] On the other hand, A.P. Sen suggested that the candidates must know English so that they would be able to follow the council debates,[89] a demand also made by the Maratha Aikyechhu Sabha, as well as H.N. Apte, the well-known Marathi novelist, representing the moderate Deccan Sabha.[90] V.S. Naik added to this argument that knowledge of English would enable a member to 'intelligently' participate in the proceedings.[91]

The Government of India was not in favour of the modifications, suggested by the Southborough Committee, of the disqualifications. In the case of each of the proposed changes, it claimed that they could be hardly termed as improvements and hence desired a maintenance of the status quo. Clearly, this meant that it had no strong views on the matter. In the case of dismissal from government service, the Joint Committee upheld the minority view in declining to stipulate it as a disqualification for candidature. But it recommended that conviction for a criminal offence entailing more than six months of imprisonment be regarded as a disqualification for a period of five years from the date on which the sentence came to an end.[92] The question of qualifications for the candidates did not figure prominently in the proceedings of the committee.

The rules made under the Government of India Act, 1919 laid down the qualifications as well as disqualifications for the candidates. Apart from the usual disqualifications, lawyers who had been barred by any competent court from practising were prohibited from contesting the elections. However, the local government in the case of provincial legislatures and the Governor-General-in-Council in the case of both the houses of the all-India legislature were granted the powers to waive this disqualification. The demand that candidates to the provincial councils and the all-India legislature should possess certain qualifications emerged once before the Reforms Enquiry Committee. N.K. Kelkar from the Central Provinces supported higher qualifications for candidates while lamenting that their absence had proved to be an obstacle in the attainment of responsible government.[93] He reiterated this demand which he stated was necessary to prevent what had happened during the Non-Cooperation Movement, wherein illiterate candidates had been elected to the local council in order to discredit the reforms.[94]

The issue of qualification of candidates did not prominently figure in the evidence before the Simon Commission. The question of qualifications for candidates did figure in the Constituent Assembly debates. As mentioned earlier, the Bordoloi sub-committee had recommended that there was no need for reservations for tribals in the areas of Assam where the community numerically dominated. However, it stipulated that the non-tribals be prohibited from contesting from constituencies in these areas arguing that their financial strength would enable them to electorally overwhelm the tribals.[95] This was nothing but reservations by the backdoor. One wonders why the sub-committee did not recommend reservations in the first place.

There were many who urged the need for specified qualifications for those who wished to contest the elections and become members of the legislatures. The overall thrust of their argument was that merely being qualified to become a voter could not automatically make an individual a suitable representative. As R.R. Diwakar argued, 'It is no doubt a superstition with western democratic method that each one who has a vote is also eligible for becoming a candidate.' He wanted only those who could shoulder the responsibility of integrating the country to become representatives.[96] On the other hand, there were some who wished to exclude certain kinds of persons from becoming representatives. K.M. Tripathi from Orissa wanted non-income tax payers and those who held less than 100 acres of agricultural land to be prevented from contesting. This he claimed would enable the villagers of India to enter the legislatures.[97]

K.T. Shah moved an amendment suggesting that those wishing to contest elections should be literate and fluent in the language of the province from where they wished to become candidates and within a period of 10 years should be literate and fluent in the National Language of India. Shah also made a broader argument in favour of qualifications. He argued that representatives must be capable of understanding the issues before them so as to enable them to legislate effectively.[98] In response, Dr Ambedkar moved an amendment to the Draft Constitution seeking to insert an article that would, among others, empower the Parliament to make a law prescribing qualifications for the candidates. He agreed that it was desirable that the future representative should posses 'some higher qualifications than merely being a voter'.[99] But this power granted to the future Parliament was objected to by S.L. Saxena who feared that the executive might misuse it to disqualify its political opponents.[100] It was perhaps this fear that led Naziruddin Ahmed to suggest that the qualifications and disqualifications for candidates be stipulated in the Constitution itself rather than in future legislation.[101]

Later, Ambedkar moved another amendment which empowered the provincial legislatures to enact legislation to prescribe qualifications for their membership.[120] This once again evoked criticism. Purnima Banerji expressed the fear that this would be used to introduce property qualifications for candidates, thus restricting the membership of the legislatures to the monied classes,[103] something that was immediately dispelled by Dr Ambedkar. K.T. Shah once again asked literacy be a qualification for candidates.[142] His unspoken fear seemed to be that given that the mass of the voters were illiterate there was always a possibility that they would elect a fellow illiterate. Dr Ambedkar brushed aside his suggestion by claiming that if the provincial legislatures found it necessary they would include such a provision in the law that they would enact. Brajeshwar Prasad, the implacable foe of adult franchise, while arguing for educational qualifications for candidates argued that the task of the legislator was a specialised one and hence necessitated the relevant training and expertise. He claimed that if India desired to have 'a decent system of government', educational qualifications were necessary.[105] Loknath Misra was not as extreme as Prasad but did plead for some stipulated qualifications for candidates. He claimed that the appropriate kind of individuals were necessary to make parliamentary democracy a success in India and this could be achieved by suitable qualifications.[106]

This issue did not emerge again till much after the framing of the Constitution of India. The Government had promised a bill dealing with qualifications of candidates and accordingly in December 1950, Dr Ambedkar introduced what would become the Representation of the People Act, 1951. He clarified at the outset that residential qualifications for candidates had been eliminated. Ambedkar told the Provisional Parliament that since India was now a united nation there was no need for any barriers and that now individuals who were otherwise qualified to be candidates could contest from anywhere in the country.[107] The bill was then referred to a Select Committee.

The Select Committee reported back in May 1951. It added four new disqualifications for the candidates. They were holding of a contract issued by the Government, holding of a licence to deal in commodities on which price or movement controls have been imposed by the Government, directorship in a company in which the Government was a shareholder or dismissal from Government service for corruption.[108] Gokulbhai Bhatt had objected to the first provision, while Ramnath Goenka had objected to the first two. Dr Ambedkar brushed aside their notes of dissent. He explained that while the business community must have all the opportunity to enter and influence politics, he did not wish Parliament to be converted into a 'stock exchange'.[109] There had been a demand for debarring Princes from contesting that was rejected by Dr Ambedkar.

Meanwhile, K.T. Shah reiterated his demand that all those contesting elections must have certain qualifications. He regretted that no positive qualifications had been prescribed in the bill. He asked that knowledge of English, Hindi and another Indian language be made compulsory.[110] The entire debate saw the participant divided on Processualist and Institutionalist lines. If K.T. Shah sought to debar Princes and expropriated zamindars on the grounds that their presence in the legislatures would be mischievous, then Raj Bahadur wanted *jagirdars* to be barred arguing that they were privileged.[111] But C.D. Pande argued that people should be left to choose their representatives and that since they have good sense they would not elect unsuitable people.[112] P.Y. Deshpande took an even extreme stance when he asked that even criminals be permitted to contest. He questioned the very need for disqualifications, for he wanted the people to choose. He pointed out that the Constitution had adopted what he termed a 'quantitative democracy' and that any attempts to make it 'qualitative' by adopting disqualifications would fail.[113] He further argued that any restrictions could be justified only if they ensured 'better conditions for free expression on the sovereign will of the people'.[114] Objections were also expressed to certain specific disqualifications.

As the debate trundled to its conclusion, a few amendments were moved asking for additional qualifications for the candidates. Dr Ambedkar rejected all of them saying that that would reduce the number of eligible candidates and thus might lead to a monopoly of a certain class of individuals.[115] The bill was passed by mid-1951 and this completed the architecture of the electoral system of India.

7

Conclusion

As the preceding chapters have demonstrated, the extensive and at times the rather raucous debate over political representation in India that began in the first decade of the twentieth century came to a close with the construction of the country's post-independence electoral system after having traversed a period of a little more than four decades. The vibrancy of the debate is evident from the wide range of institutional alternatives that were put forth, as has been discussed earlier. But that very vibrancy more often than not came to resemble a cacophony of voices not talking to but talking past each other. However, this entire debate can be and here has been reduced at the cost of some simplification to two broad political-cum-intellectual positions, the first one being the Institutionalist and other being the Processualist.

Their respective arguments have been sketched out in detail previously. Despite their seemingly mutually exclusive character, these opposing viewpoints had a shared objective. This was to ensure that the representative bodies in India, which also discharged legislative functions, were generally speaking representative of Indian society at large. Similarly, they conceived of representation as an activity where the representative was supposed to articulate and to protect as well as further the interests, however defined, of those whom he or she represented. Where they differed was how this representativeness of these bodies was to be ensured, and whether groups could be effectively represented by non-members. Underlying these differences lay their divergent perceptions of the electoral process and the outcomes that it led to, and more significantly those of Indian society as well.

For the Institutionalists, the electoral process had an inherently majoritarian bias. For them, it privileged the majority community and led to the exclusion of the minorities, thus reinforcing the existing structures of dominance. This was a position largely adopted by the political leadership of the Muslim community at the all-India level. They demanded institutional safeguards and mechanisms to ensure adequate (or rather what they thought as being adequate) numerical representation of the community. They argued that in the absence of such institutional safeguards, the Hindus would dominate the political scene. They were joined in the 1930s and the 1940s by the spokespersons of the Dalits, notably Dr Babasaheb Ambedkar, as well as those of a few other minority communities. But this was not the only argument put forth by the Institutionalists. They also believed that well-organised and strong minorities could exploit their entrenched positions to exclude poor and unorganised majorities, thus once again reinforcing existing patterns of social dominance. This was a position mainly adopted by the Non-Brahmin movement in the Madras and the Bombay provinces, as well as the Muslim leadership in the Punjab, Bengal and the Sindh region of Bombay. Hence, the talk that numerical strength was illusionary in nature. Thus, the Institutionalists made the claim of elections being both anti-minority and anti-majority at the same time. At the heart of these superficially contradictory positions was the desire that no single social segment should dominate these legislatures.

This seemingly untenable claim about the electoral process can be understood only if it is acknowledged that it consisted of two distinct arguments, which had equally distinct reference points. In the first instance, the reference point was Indian society, and thus on religious grounds, Hindus were the majority and the Muslims were the minority. In the second instance, the reference point was the Hindu community in the case of the non-Brahmin claims, and in the case of the Punjab, Bengal and Sindh, it was the provincial or regional society taken as a whole. In these cases, those who were demanding institutional safeguards were a numerical majority. But their spokespersons argued that numerical strength need not always translate into political power. For if the non-Brahmins were apprehensive of an entrenched, educated and economically powerful minority—the Brahmins—dominating the electoral process by virtue of these of their very strengths, the Muslims in the three regions mentioned above feared Hindu domination on the basis of the same strengths. It was the logic of the social situation that determined how these Institutionalist claims were framed, and the safeguards demanded included separate electorates or at the least reserved seats.

Yet, one common factor uniting these two positions within the Institutionalist argument was an insistence on 'descriptive representation'. For them, a legislative body could not be described as being properly representative unless all sections of the society for which it was to legislate were present in it. Thus, they were talking of what Anne Phillips evocatively called the 'politics of presence'. One could reasonably argue, like the Processualists would do, that the safeguards or institutional mechanisms need not be necessary to secure the presence of all sections of society, and that the electoral process would naturally more or less lead to such an outcome.

But in the Indian context, the Institutionalists were also concerned with 'authentic' representation. It was not enough that an individual should share the social attributes and characteristics of the group that he was representing but that the very group should regard him or her as one of them and that no one but the group should have played a role in electing this person. An individual who belonged to a given group but had succeeded in getting elected not just by the votes of that group but by those of others as well lacked 'authenticity' in the eyes of that group. This was at the core of the arguments put forth by the advocates of separate electorates. Presumably, only an 'authentic' representative could be trusted to protect a group's interests. That this could lead to issues of accountability, as Hanna Pitkin pointed out, did not figure in the Indian debates. No one seems to have paid serious attention to the possibility that a wayward representative might get away with anything and everything if he or she succeeded in convincing the electors, who possessed the same social attributes as the said representative, that what was being done in their name would benefit them. The representative could always claim that it was inconceivable that he or she would ever betray the interests of the group to which he or she belonged, for he or she was 'one of them' and hence could justify any action. The Processualists also never paid serious attention to the issue of accountability. This was a crucial omission in the entire debate.

Meanwhile, counter-arguments to the notion of 'authenticity' were stated by the Processualists. This category largely consisted of the leadership of the nationalist movement. Firstly, they disputed the claims that the electoral process was exclusionary in character or that it enabled strong minorities to dominate weak majorities. At the second Round Table Conference, Gandhi argued that there was no reason to suppose that members of the minority communities would not be elected by voters belonging to the majority community. He said that anyone who won the trust of the electorates on the strength of their political commitment towards the masses would succeed in getting elected, irrespective of his or her social background. This meant that the logic of the electoral process could overcome entrenched social biases which in turn supported the argument that safeguards were not required. But this, to the Institutionalists, meant that the political representation of the minorities or backward majorities would be dependent on the goodwill of the majority or the dominant minority, and this was something they detested. Moreover, they were also sceptical of the potential of the democratic processes to diminish the salience of social biases and ensure a representative legislature.

Furthermore, the Processualists argued that there was no reason to suppose that elected representatives belonging to the majority community would not represent the interests of the minorities. The opponents of the non-Brahmin demand for separate electorates who argued that Brahmin members of the legislative council had always advocated the public interests and not their own sectional interests made a similar version of this argument. This was an extension of the denial of the claim that it was essential that a representative body should reflect the composition of this society in which it was located. For the Processualists, it seems what mattered was whether the interests of all sections of society were represented, articulated and protected in the legislative body and not whether individuals belonging to these very sections were actually present.

It was these differing perceptions that determined the choice of institutional models preferred by the proponents of these two standpoints. Yet, there was consensus on one point. The Processualists generally preferred territorial representation derived from western models. Representatives were to represent specified areas rather than specific sections of society. Throughout the debate on political representation in India, the Processualists never wavered from their preference for geographically-based representation. Curiously, the Institutionalists also favoured territorial representation but with a qualification. Communities whom the electoral process might exclude would be represented through separate or communal electorates. These too were to be organised on a territorial basis. Thus, communal electorates demanded in India were never imagined as other than being geographically rooted. This preference for territory-based representation demonstrated that there was a significant overlap among these two positions.

But communal electorates were a novel proposition and as the Montagu–Chelmsford Report stated that similar arrangements were to be found only in 'Austria, some of the smaller German states and Cyprus'[1]. Such electorates were also to be found in Poland and Greece in the period between the two World Wars as well as in two British colonies, Sri Lanka and Burma till they were abolished there in the 1930s.[2] In this sense, communal electorates were an Indian contribution, or rather one arising out of Indian circumstances, to the debate on political representation. The proponents of such electorates declined to perceive them as anomalies. While they did regard them as departures from the prevailing western norm of territorial representation, they also defended them by arguing that since even the advanced democracies were debating alternatives like functional representation there was no reasons for communal electorates to be ruled out. Yet, at the same time such electorates were described as being merely temporary measures.

This focus on institutional models emphasised the conception of representation as an activity. At its heart was that question as to whether the social attributes of a representative would determine how effective would representation as an activity be. The Institutionalists regarded 'authenticity' as a *sine qua non* for effectiveness, and hence pressed for institutional safeguards, particularly communal electorates, to ensure it, while the Processualists questioned this equation of the sharing of social attributes with authenticity and preferred the how of the act of representing rather than the who. However, this is not to say that the Processualists never accepted the need for some kind of safeguards. The nationalist leadership did accept, at times grudgingly, the need for reservations as can been seen in the pre-independence schemes of political representation devised by the Congress, and the granting of reservations to the Scheduled Castes and Scheduled Tribes as well as the provision of nominations for the miniscule Anglo-Indian community in independent India. The only instance of the nationalist leadership supporting the cause of separate electorates was the Lucknow Pact of 1916, which was soon disowned and hence can be regarded as a political aberration.

But the Processualists contested the need for institutional mechanisms, particularly the one for communal electorates, not by amplifying their 'theory' of representation but on the terrain of nationalism and political community. Here the question was how to perceive Indian society and, more particularly, what were the political implications of India's visible and undeniable diversity. Here, the Processualists seemed to be talking of the idea of the Indian nation. While not denying the religious, ethnic, linguistic and caste-based differences in Indian society, they asserted that this in no way meant that the various sections of this very society had some fundamentally divergent interests that needed to be protected through the political and administrative structure. It was thus that the Processualists opposed separate electorates as being antithetical to the idea of an Indian nation. This was seen in the opposition expressed by the Congress leaders to communal electorates in the evidence given to the Southborough Commission, in the Nehru Report, Gandhi's speeches at the Round Table Conference and the proceedings of the Constituent Assembly. This position, if not self-serving, was certainly naive. It overlooked the deep-rooted hierarchies in Indian society, which would have led to the neglect of marginalised groups.

Curiously, for the Processualists, this Indian nation had not yet come into existence in its entirety but was in the process of becoming or making. It had not yet achieved a degree of homogeneity required to constitute a nation. An implicit assumption in the Processualist argument was that any institutional safeguards for specified communities would strengthen social identities and bring them into the domain of politics, and that this would adversely affect the process of the formation of the nation. The Processualists apparently believed that a certain level of homogeneity was essential for India to become a nation.

These claims were again countered by the Institutionalists deploying arguments which cannot be easily dismissed. For instance, Dr Ambedkar more often than not argued that the institution of caste permeated the Indian scene to such an extent that it almost made healthy social and associational life impossible. He added that this fact meant that the concept of the majority in India was social and not political or as he put it, the majority in India was communal in nature. This meant that the majority community would coalesce together and thus would always dominate the political system and that the minorities would then be deprived of opportunities to occupy positions of power. Hence, Dr Ambedkar's vehement insistence on institutional safeguards. Thus, the Institutionalists emphasised the deep-rooted strength of the Indian social structure and feared an electoral process without institutional mechanisms to tackle its biases would led to political marginalisation of many. They were not opposed to the claim that India could constitute a viable political community and hence a nation. But they were not willing to concede this claim before seeking satisfactory answers to the question as to what would be the status of various communities in this nation once the colonial regime came to the end.

The debates on political representation reflected the competing visions of what India was or perhaps was not. It must be clarified that the two competing viewpoints identified throughout cannot be truly described as clear-cut and water-tight positions. The debate on political representation in India was more in the nature of a continuum. If at the extreme end of the Institutionalist side were those who talked of Hindus and Muslims being separate nations or India being a mere geographical entity, there were those among the same viewpoint who looked at institutional safeguards as being an evil necessary for the time being. Among the Processualists too, there were those who conceded the necessity of safeguards, sometimes out of conviction and at times due to practical considerations.

During the colonial period, it was the Institutionalist viewpoint that was dominant. Initially, nominations by the Government and then later separate electorates were provided to ensure the representativeness of the legislative body. The notion that the nominated members could not possibly represent those whom they had been charged with representing since the latter had no role in determining who their representatives would be came a little later. This led to questions being raised about whether such nominated members did or could actually represent those whom they were asked to represent, and the consequent ruling-out of nominations as a method of representation.

Furthermore, it was soon recognised that carrying the Institutional argument for representativeness of legislative bodies to its logical end would mean ensuring the representation of all those sections of Indian society who claimed that the electoral system would exclude them, and that this would lead to the ridiculous outcome of a majority of the members of these bodies being elected through either reserved seats or communal electorates. Thus, despite being faced with demands for political representation made from all and sundry, the colonial regime was careful only to concede such claims which would either win them potential collaborators or prevent resentment emerging among the existing ones. By the 1930s, one can discern a slight change in the British position on communal electorates. There seems to be increased reluctance to extend them any further. At the same time, those communities which had been granted such electorates were not willing to concede the same to sub-groups within them, indeed at times questioning the very existence of such sub-groups.

It must be remembered that the electorate during the period was always a limited one. This led to the question of adult suffrage. The colonial regime always argued that the large size of India coupled with an equally large population meant that conducting elections based on adult franchise was fraught with enormous administrative and logistical difficulties, and hence, the necessity of a limited electorate which in turn meant that elaborate qualifying criteria had to be devised to keep it so. These were mainly educational and economic. Given the differential levels of education and economic strength of the various Indian communities, it was evident that the more advanced ones would predominate in the electorate. This in turn would have in the absence of safeguards, for the Institutionalists, further magnified the in-built biases of elections per se. This fact strengthened the case for these very safeguards. Adult franchise would have solved these vexed issues, as Dr Ambedkar more often than not pointed out. But not many were enthusiastic about it. It was often accepted in principle but not in practice.

The Processualist viewpoint was somewhat on the defensive during this same period. It had no real answer to the arguments that in any electoral system with a limited electorate, the organised minorities or numerically strong majorities would predominate, thus making the legislatures unrepresentative. Hence, measures like reservations for the non-Brahmins and later for the Dalits were accepted albeit with great reluctance. The standard Processualist position was that such safeguards were not really necessary. This very same period also saw rising political consciousness among diverse sections of Indian society which led to demands for political representation through institutional safeguards. It is at this juncture that adult franchise came to be adopted by the Processualists as a means to head off these demands. It is a moot point whether those who advocated adult franchise did so out of conviction or for pragmatic reasons.

But with the Partition of the subcontinent on religious lines, the Processualist viewpoint came to predominate. The dominant argument, as can be seen in the debates in the Constituent Assembly, did not focus so much on the strengths of the Processualist approach but rather on the perceived drawbacks of the Institutionalist viewpoint. Any institutional safeguards in the electoral system were seen as inherently divisive and antithetical to, and their absence conducive to the post-independence project of building a more integrated Indian society. There was a disinclination to provide any institutional opportunity to the minorities to organise themselves politically and thus secure representation. The constitution makers explicitly excluded any other means, which would have corrected the majoritarian tendencies of the electoral system. Multi-member seats, cumulative voting and proportional representation were ruled out, more often than not without any reasoned debate. The only exception was the provision for reserved seats for the Scheduled Castes and Scheduled Tribes.

It was on the backdrop of this objective in mind and the exclusion of other electoral alternatives that a predominantly single-member constituency system coupled with a plurality criterion was adopted in India, known as the FPTP system. Only those constituencies which had a seat reserved for either the Scheduled Castes or the Scheduled Tribes were two-member ones. Yet, it would be wrong to suggest that the single-member constituency was adopted for merely these reasons. The adoption was also a consequence of an historical legacy. By the mid-1880s itself, the United Kingdom had moved towards this system and the traditional double-member constituency became an exception. The electoral system in the United Kingdom finally became a uniformly single-member one by 1950.[3] Moreover, the electoral system in India that had come about as a consequence of the Montagu–Chelmsford reforms was also on the same lines. The colonial regime had not adopted it as a result of any reasoned debate but rather as a matter of administrative convenience.

The same system was carried forward into post-1947 India. The priority of the constitution-makers was to heal the scars of the violence generated by the process of Partition and to create a more integrated society. Any return to the electoral safeguards and devices of the colonial period might have meant that there was no means by which communities could be encouraged to collaborate politically. The single-member constituency perhaps fulfilled this very need. Given a heterogeneous society, it was evident that for any candidate to be successful in such a constituency, he or she could not depend on the basis of the votes of a single community, at least not at the parliamentary level. He or she would have had to build at least what William Riker described as a minimum winning coalition. The logic of the FPTP meant that to emerge victorious, a given candidate had perforce to appeal to many, if not all, sections of society and thus facilitate political integration. One could reasonably argue that the double-round election model could have even strengthened the process of political integration. But that would have necessitated the formation of a much larger coalition at the constituency level and that was perhaps the reason that the Congress which dominated the constitution-making process wished to avoid. Moreover, one other aspect of the electoral system was purposely designed to facilitate the project of national integration. This was the abolition of residential qualifications or the stipulation that an individual to qualify as a candidate for a given constituency had to be a resident of the same. In fact, it was explicitly stated there was no need for such a residential qualification, for India now was an integrated nation, a case of a goal sought to be achieved being presented as an accomplished fact.

That the FPTP would serve to reinforce the dominance of the Congress was recognised quite early by distinguished economist D.R. Gadgil. To be fair, he noted that the leaders of the party had stressed the need for a strong one-party government and noted that FPTP tended to produce this outcome.[4] Recent theoretical literature on the choice of electoral systems has noted that the interests and perception of the established elites, rather than any reasoned debate on merits of systemic alternatives, does play an important role in determining the nature of the system ultimately adopted.[5]

Thus, the debate on political representation in India was won by the Processualists. The actual choice of the system of representation and elections was determined by a combination of historical legacy, the need of political stability and integration, and sheer self-interest. Moreover, there is no doubt that to some extent that the social composition of Indian state legislatures has changed, a process that has been described as a 'Silent Revolution' or 'The Rise of the Plebeians', the two terms which have been used denote the increasing proportion of the 'backward castes' or peasant castes and the concurrent decline of the share of the 'upper castes' in the politics of many Indian states.[6] This is can be cited as a virtue of the Indian electoral process. The very objective of diversity of legislative bodies that PR could have brought about was secured through the workings of FPTP. Thus, it could be reasonably argued that both political integration and the social diversity of political representation were achieved by adopting FPTP.

The internal dynamics of Indian society have led to a proliferation of political parties, which in turn have led to fragmented legislatures and unstable coalitions, notwithstanding the results of the 2014 General Elections. Thus, FPTP has not entirely demonstrated the principal virtue claimed for it, the creation of a legislative majority so as to ensure a strong executive. The vices attributed to PR and its sub-types, namely an increase in number of parties, and smaller parties becoming unduly important, and a structural incentive for fringe elements to emerge, have occurred in India despite FPTP. It would be perhaps out of place here to discuss the relative merits of alternative electoral systems.

But what is more evident in recent times, FPTP has not quite succeeded in ensuring that the Indian legislatures continue to remain representative, a virtue long claimed for it. The recent election results have shown that no member of India's largest religious minority, the Muslims, has been elected to the Lok Sabha from the country's electorally most decisive state, Uttar Pradesh. Members of the minority communities no longer necessarily find a place in the political executives. Maharashtra does not have a single Muslim minister at this point of time. Furthermore, in many states, the levers of political power have been monopolised by dominant sections of society, some of whom came to power through the 'Silent Revolution'. If in states like Maharashtra, Haryana and the undivided Andhra Pradesh, the locally dominant Hindu peasant castes have dominated, then in Bengal, the Hindu upper castes have retained power irrespective of the ideological composition of the party or parties in power there. Increasingly, questions have been raised as to whether representatives elected from reserved constituencies truly represent the communities they belong to, or are they merely yes-men or puppets in the hands of the dominant communities. Numerically, smaller communities have a feeling of being left out and even systematically excluded from the political arena. These outcomes certainly would not encourage social integration.

Thus, there is a pressing need to re-imagine political representation and the electoral system in India, and it is here that some of the alternatives articulated in the colonial times can come in useful to tackle problems post-independence India. Thus, the debates surrounding these options are not merely of historical interest but of contemporary relevance as well. Some of these alternatives like communal electorates cannot be even considered, not just for reasons of national integration but also because they are constitutionally barred. But other options discussed in the pre-independence period, for instance the various varieties of PR or multi-member constituencies with or without reservations, might lead to more representative legislative bodies in terms of social character and diversity. This would in turn strengthen the Indian political system by making it inclusive and also by broadening access to power. It must be noted that by themselves these options would not ensure more effective and responsive legislatures but that is a matter of a different debate altogether.

Endnotes

Chapter 1

1 Raja Sekhar Vundru, *Ambedkar, Gandhi and Patel, The Making of India's Electoral System* (Bloomsbury: New Delhi, 2018).

2 Francesca R. Jensenius, 'Mired in Reservations: The Path-Dependent History of Electoral Quotas in India', *Journal of Asian Studies*, vol. 74, no. 1 (2015): 85–105.

3 Christophe Jaffrelot, *India's Silent Revolution: The Rise of the Lower Castes in Northern India* (Permanent Black: Ranikhet, 2002); Christophe Jaffrelot and Sanjay Kumar, eds, *Rise of the Plebeians? The Changing Face of the Indian Legislative Assemblies* (Routledge: New Delhi, 2009).

Chapter 2

1 David Plotke, 'Representation is Democracy', *Constellations*, vol. 4, no. 1 (1997).

2 Bernand Manin, Adam Przeworksi and Susan C. Stokes, 'Elections and Representation', in *Democracy, Accountability and Representation*, eds. Adam Przeworki, Susan C. Stokes and Bernard Manin (Cambridge University Press: Cambridge, 1999), 29.

3 Hanna Fenichel Pitkin, *The Concept of Representation* (The University of California Press: Berkeley, 1972 [1967]).

4 Hanna Fenichel Pitkin, 'Representation', in *Political Innovation and Conceptual Change*, eds. Terence Ball, James Farr and Russell L. Hanson (Cambridge University Press: Cambridge, 1985).

5 Monica Brito Viera and David Runciman, *Representation* (Polity Press: Cambridge, 2008).

6 Bernard Manin, *The Principles of Representative Government* (Cambridge University Press: Cambridge, 2002).

7 Pitkin, *The Concept of Representation*, 8–9.

8 Suzanne Dovi, 'Political Representation', in *The Stanford Encyclopaedia of Philosophy*, ed. Edward N. Zalta (Winter, 2017 Edition), URL: https://plato.stanford.edu/archives/win2017/entries/political-representation/ (Accessed on 2 September 2018).

9 Pitkin, *The Concept of Representation*, 144.

10 Viera and Runciman, *Representation*, 6.

11 Pitkin, *The Concept of Representation*, 4.

12 Ibid., 14–37.

13 Andrew Rehfeld, 'Towards a General Theory of Representation', *The Journal of Politics*, vol. 68, no. 1 (2006).

14 Pitkin, *The Concept of Representation*, 2–3.
15 Viera and Runciman, *Representation*, viii.
16 Manin, *The Principles of Representative Government*, 1–3.
17 Viera and Runciman, *Representation*, 12–4.
18 Carl Joachim Friedrich, 'Representation and Constitutional Reform in Europe', *Western Political Quarterly*, vol. 1, no. 2 (1948).
19 Viera and Runciman, *Representation*, 18–21.
20 Ibid., 45–50.
21 Hanna Fenichel Pitkin, 'Representation and Democracy: Uneasy Alliance', *Scandinavian Political Studies*, vol. 27, no. 3 (2004).
22 Manin, *The Principles of Representative Government*, and Nadia Urbinati, *Representative Government, Principles & Genealogy* (The University of Chicago Press: Chicago, 2008 [2006]).
23 Manin, *The Principles of Representative Government*, 83–7.
24 Pitkin, *The Concept of Representation*, 60–3; Viera and Runciman, *Representation*, 39.
25 Anne Phillips, *The Politics of Presence* (Clarendon Press: Oxford, 1995), Jane Mansbridge, 'Should Blacks represent Blacks and Women represent Women? A Contingent 'Yes'', *The Journal of Politics*, vol. 61, no. 3 (1999); Melissa Williams, *Voice, Trust, and Memory, Marginalized Groups and the Failings of Liberal Representation* (Princeton University Press: Princeton, 2000 [1998]).
26 Phillips, *The Politics of Presence.*
27 Melissa S. Williams, *Voice, Trust, and Memory, Marginalized Groups and the Failings of Liberal Representation*, 3.
28 Ibid., 5.
29 Mansbridge, 'Should Blacks represent Blacks and Women represent Women? A Contingent 'Yes''.
30 Suzanne Dovi, 'Preferable Descriptive Representatives: Will just any Woman, Black, or Latino do?', *American Political Science Review*, vol. 96, no.4 (2002).
31 Williams, *Voice, Trust, and Memory, Marginalized Groups and the Failings of Liberal Representation*, 14–7 and 177.
32 Pitkin, *The Concept of Representation*, 84–9.
33 Phillips, *The Politics of Presence*, 156 and 54–5.
34 René de Visme Williamson, 'The Fascist Concept of Representation', *The Journal of Politics*, vol. 3, no. 1 (1941).
35 Duncan Kelly, 'Carl Schmitt's Political Theory of Representation', *Journal of the History of Ideas*, vol. 65, no. 1 (2004).
36 Mark B. Brown, 'Survey Article: Citizen Panels and the Concept of Representation', *Journal of Political Philosophy*, 14, no. 2 (2006) and 'Fairly Balanced: The Politics of Representation on Government Advisory Committees', *Political Research Quarterly*, 61, no. 4 (2008).
37 Friedrich, 'Representation and Constitutional Reform in Europe', 127.
38 Pitkin, *The Concept of Representation*, 168.
39 Ibid., 173–74.

40 Viera and Runciman, *Representation*, 17–8.
41 Pitkin, *The Concept of Representation*, 192-96.
42 Ibid., 198-202.
43 Friedrich, 'Representation and Constitutional Reform in Europe', 128.
44 Enid Lakeman, *How Democracies Vote* (Faber and Faber: London, 1974).
45 George H. Horwill, *Proportional Representation, Its Dangers and Defects* (George Allen and Unwin: London, 1925).
46 F.A. Hermens, 'P.R. and Democracy,' *The Review of Politics*, vol. 4, no. 4 (1942); *Europe Between Democracy and Anarchy* (University of Notre Dame Press: Notre Dame, 1951).
47 *Report of the Royal Commission appointed to enquire into Electoral Systems, Cmd. 5163*, (His Majesty's Stationery Office: London, 1910).
48 Phillips, *The Politics of Presence*, 95.
49 Ibid., 170.
50 Viera and Runciman, *Representation*, 106.
51 Paul H. Douglas, 'Occupational Versus Proportional Representation', *The American Journal of Sociology*, vol. 29, no. 2 (1923).
52 Viera and Runciman, *Representation*, 105-109.
53 Burt L. Monroe, 'Understanding Electoral Systems: Beyond Plurality Versus PR', *PS: Political Science and Politics*, vol. 27, no.4 (1994).
54 Viera and Runciman, *Representation*, 117–19.
55 James Hogan, *Elections and Representation* (Cork University Press and B.H. Blackwell Ltd: Cork and Oxford, 1945).
56 Andrew Rehfeld, 'Silence of the Land: On the Historical Irrelevance of Territory to Congressional Districting and Political Representation in the United States', *Studies in American Political Development*, 15, Spring 2001 (2001).
57 Manin, *The Principles of Representative Government*, 95–119.
58 Ibid., 135.
59 Andrew Rehfeld, 'On Quotas and Qualifications for Office', in *Political Representation*, ed. Ian Shapiro, Susan C. Stokes, Elisabeth Jean Woods, Alexander S. Kirshner (Cambridge University Press: Cambridge, 2009), 236–70.
60 Pitkin, *The Concept of Representation*, 143.
61 Ibid., 115.
62 Viera and Runciman, *Representation*, 13 and 139.

Chapter 3

1. Arthur Berriedale Keith, *A Constitutional History of India, 1600–1935* (Methuen and Co.: London, 1937 [1936]).
2. Carl Bridge, *Holding India to the Empire, The British Conservative Party and the 1935 Constitution* (Oriental University Press: London, 1986).
3. Gurmukh Nihal Singh, *Landmarks in Indian Constitutional and National Development (1600–1919)* (The Indian Book Shop: Benares, 1933).
4. Sumit Sarkar, *Modern India, 1885–1947* (Macmillan: Delhi, 2009 [1983]); Bipin Chandra, Mridula Mukherjee, Aditya Mukherjee, K.N. Panikkar

and Sucheta Mahajan, *India's Struggle for Independence*, (Penguin: New Delhi, 1991 [1988]).

5. James Chiriyankandath, 'Democracy under the Raj: Elections and separate representation in British India', *Commonwealth and Comparative Politics*, vol. 30, no.1 (1992).
6. Farzana Shaikh, *Community and Consensus in Islam, Muslim Representation and Colonial India, 1860–1947* (Imprint One: New Delhi, 2012 [1989]).
7. Sekhar Bandyopadhyaya, *Caste, Protest and Identity in Colonial India: The Namasudras of Bengal, 1872–1947* (Oxford University Press: New Delhi, 2011); Chandra Mallampalli, *Christians and Public Life in Colonial South India, 1863–1937, Contending with Marginality* (RoutledgeCurzon: London, 2004).
8. Geraldine Forbes, *Women in Modern India, New Cambridge History of India, Vol. IV-2* (Cambridge University Press: Cambridge, 2004 [1996]).
9. A.K. Priyolkar, ed, *Lokahitwadikrut Nibandhasangraha* (Mumbai: Popular Prakashan (1996 [1967]), 59–60.
10. Keith, *A Constitutional History of India, 1600–1935*, 132.
11. Ibid., 138.
12. Ibid., 174.
13. Ibid., 182.
14. Thomas R. Metcalf, *The Aftermath of Revolt, India, 1857–1870* (Princeton University Press: Princeton, 1965), 263–66.
15. Ibid., 268.
16. R.J. Moore, *Liberalism and Indian Politics, 1872–1922* (Edward Arnold: London, 1966); 'The Twilight of the Whigs and the Reform of the Indian Councils, 1886–1892', *The Historical Journal*, vol. 10, no. 3 (1967); S. Gopal, *British Policy in India, 1858–1905* (Cambridge University Press: Cambridge, 2008 [1965]).
17. C.H. Philips, ed, *The Evolution of India and Pakistan, 1858 to 1947, Select Documents* (Oxford University Press: London, 1962), 60–2.
18. Sir Courtenay Ilbert, *The Government of India, Being a Digest of the Statute Law Relating Thereto with Historical Introduction and Explanatory Matter* (Clarendon Press: Oxford, 1907), 115–16.
19. M.V., *The Indian Councils Act and the Acts Amending It with All Official Papers Connected Therewith and The Rules for the Conduct of Business at the Meetings of the Council* (Madras, 1893), 59.
20. Syed Razi Wasti, *Lord Minto and the Indian Nationalist Movement, 1905–1910* (Clarendon Press: Oxford, 1964); Stanley Wolpert, *Morley and India, 1906–1910* (University of California Press: Berkeley, 1967); Stephen E. Koss, *John Morley at the India Office, 1905–1910* (Yale University Press: New Haven, 1969); Vina Mazumdar, *The Mind and the Medium, Explorations in the Evolution of Imperial Policy in India* (Three Essays Collective: Gurgaon, 2010); R.J. Moore, *Liberalism and Indian Politics, 1872–1922* (Edward Arnold: London, 1966); Francis Robinson, *Separatism among Indian Muslims : The Politics of the United Provinces' Muslims 1860–1923* (Cambridge University Press: Cambridge, 2008 [1974]).

21. John Morley, *Speeches on Indian Affairs*, G.A.Natesan & Sons: Madras, 1920), 159.
22. *East India (Advisory and Constitutional Reforms), Vol. I, Proposals of the Government of India and Despatch of the Secretary of State, Cd. 4426* (His Majesty's Stationery Office : London,1908), 8.
23. Ibid., 15.
24. Sir Courtenay Ilbert, *The Government of India, Supplementary Chapter (Indian Councils Act, 1909)* (Clarendon Press: Oxford, 1910), 418.
25. Ibid., 419.
26. Ibid., 414.
27. Ibid., 432–35.
28. *Report of The Proceedings of The Twenty-Fourth Indian National Congress Held at Lahore On the 27th, 28th and 29th December 1909* (Tribune Steam Press: Lahore, n.d.), 47.
29. Keith, *A Constitutional History of India, 1600–1935*, 285.
30. Peter Robb, *The Government of India and Reform, Policies Towards Politics and the Constitution, 1916–1921* (Oxford University Press: Oxford, 1976), 54–86.
31. Richard Danzig, 'The Announcement of August 20th 1917', *Journal of Asian Studies*, vol. 28, no.1 (1968); S.R. Mehrotra, 'The Politics Behind the Montagu Declaration of 1917' in *Politics and Society in India*, ed. C.H. Philips (George Allen and Unwin: London 1963).
32. B.R. Nanda, *Gokhale, The Indian Moderates and the British Raj* (Oxford University Press: New Delhi, 1998), 467–68.
33. *The Montagu–Chelmsford Reform Proposals with a Foreword by Annie Besant Together with the Text of the Memorandum of the Nineteen, the Congress-League Scheme and a Summary of the Indian Criticisms on the Proposal* (The Sons of India Ltd: Madras, n.d.), 136–37.
34. Hugh F. Owen, 'Negotiating the Lucknow Pact', *Journal of Asian Studies*, vol. 31, no. 3, (1972).
35. *Report of the Thirty-first Indian National Congress held at Lucknow on the 26th, 28th, 29th and 30th December, 1916* (The Reception Committee at Lucknow: Allahabad, 1917), 77.
36. *Report on Indian Constitutional Reforms* (Superintendent, Government Printing India: Calcutta,1918), 149.
37. Ibid., 175.
38. Ibid., 178.
39. Ibid., 149–150.
40. Robb, *The Government of India and Reform, Policies Towards Politics and the Constitution, 1916–1921,98–9.*
41. *Report of the Franchise Committee, 1918–19* (Superintendent, Government Printing India: Calcutta, 1919), 1.
42. Ibid., 7.
43. Ibid., 16.
44. Ibid., 9–10.
45. Ibid., 11.

46. Ibid., 6.
47. *Joint Select Committee on the Government of India Bill, 1919, Vol. I, Report and Proceedings of the Committee*(His Majesty's Stationery Office: London, 1919), 7.
48. Ibid., 46–7 and 63.
49. Ibid., 8.
50. Nihal Singh, *Landmarks in Indian Constitutional and National Development (1600–1919)*, 599.
51. Bridge, *Holding India to the Empire, The British Conservative Party and the 1935 Constitution*, and Andrew Muldoon, *Empire, Politics, and the Creation of the 1935 India Act* (Ashgate: Farnham, 2006).
52. S. Srinivasa Iyengar, *Swaraj Constitution*, (S. Ganesan: Madras, 1927).
53. *All-Parties Conference 1928, Report of the Committee appointed by the Conference to determine the principles of the Constitution for India, Together with the Summary of the Proceedings of the Conference held at Lucknow* (General Secretary, All-India Congress Committee: Allahabad, 1928).
54. Iyengar, *Swaraj Constitution, passim.*
55. *All-Parties Conference 1928, passim.*
56. *Indian Statutory Commission, Report, Vol-II, Recommendations, Cmd. 3569* (His Majesty's Stationery Office: London, 1930), 34–6.
57. Ibid., 54–55.
58. Ibid., 61–62.
59. Ibid., 63–64.
60. Ibid., 94.
61. Ibid., 113.
62. Ibid., 118.
63. R.J. Moore, *The Crisis of Indian Unity, 1917–1940* (Oxford University Press: Delhi, 1974), 41–43.
64. Ibid., *passim.*
65. *East India (Constitutional Reforms), Communal Decision, Cmd. 4147* (His Majesty's Stationery Office: London, 1932), 3.
66. Pyarelal, *The Epic Fast*, (Navajivan Press: Ahmedabad, 1932), 153–56; Ravinder Kumar, 'Gandhi, Ambedkar and the Poona Pact, 1932', *South Asia, Journal of South Asian Studies*, vol. 8, no. 1 (1985).
67. Tej Bahadur Sapru and others, *Constitutional Proposals of the Sapru Committee* (Kunwar Sir Jagadish Prasad: Moradabad, 1945).
68. D.V. Gokhale and others, *The Constitution of the Hindusthan Free State Act, 194_* (M.R. Dhamdhere: Poona, c.1944), iv and 41
69. B.R. Ambedkar, *Address by B.R. Ambedkar, M.A., Ph.D., D.Sc., Barrister-at-law, Member, Governor-General's Executive Council To the Session of the All-India Scheduled Caste Federation. Held in Bombay on May 6, 1945* (n.d, 1945), 23-4
70. Granville Austin, *The Indian Constitution: The Cornerstone of the Nation* (Clarendon Press: Oxford, 1966); Shibani Kinkar Chaube, *Constituent Assembly of India, Springboard of Revolution* (People's Publishing House: New Delhi, 1973).

71. B.R. Ambedkar, *States and Minorities, What Are Their Rights and How to Secure Them in the Constitution of Free India* (Thacker & Co.: Bombay, 1947).
72. Ornit Shani, *How India Became Democratic, Citizenship and the Making of Universal Franchise*, Penguin Random House India: Gurgaon, 2018).
73. Austin, *The Indian Constitution: The Cornerstone of the Nation*, Chaube, *Constituent Assembly of India, Springboard of Revolution*; Shefali Jha, 'Rights Versus Representation, Defending Minority Interests in the Constituent Assembly', *Economic and Political Weekly*, vol. 38, no. 16 (2003); E. Sridharan, 'The Origins of The Electoral System: Rules, Representation, and Power-sharing in Indian Democracy', in *India's Living Constitution, Ideas, Practices, Controversies*, ed., Zoya Hasan, E. Shridharan and R. Sudarshan (Permanent Black: Ranikhet, 2004).

Chapter 4

1 K.B. Krishna, *The Problem of Minorities or Communal Representation in India* (George Allen and Unwin: London, 1939), 28–31.
2 Shaikh, *Community and Consensus in Islam, Muslim Representation and Colonial India, 1860–1947*, 69 and 92.
3 Philips, ed, *The Evolution of India and Pakistan, 1858 to 1947, Select Documents*, 60–2.
4 *East India (Constitutional Reforms), Addresses presented in India to His Excellency The Viceroy and The Right Honourable The Secretary of State for India, Cmd.9178* (His Majesty's Stationery Office: London, 1918).
5 Shaikh, *Community and Consensus in Islam, Muslim Representation and Colonial India, 1860–1947, passim.*
6 Ibid., 132.
7 Philips, ed, *The Evolution of India and Pakistan, 1858 to 1947, Select Documents*, 191–92.
8 *East India (Advisory and Legislative Councils), Papers Relating to An Imperial Advisory Council and Provincial Advisory Councils; The Enlargement of The Legislative Councils; And the Discussion of the Budgets, Cmd. 3710*, His Majesty's Stationery Office: London, 1907), 10.
9 *East India (Advisory and Constitutional Reforms), Vol. I, Proposals of the Government of India and Despatch of the Secretary of State, Cd. 4426*, 14.
10 *Papers Relating to Constitutional Reform in India, Published Under the Authority of the Government of India, Vol. II* (Superintendent, Government Printing, India: Calcutta, 1908), 507.
11 Ibid., 95–118.
12 Ibid., 220.
13 *Papers Relating to Constitutional Reform in India, Published Under the Authority of the Government of India, Vol. III* (Superintendent, Government Printing, India: Calcutta, 1908), 743, 756, 1055, 1097 and 898.
14 Ibid., 1053.
15 Ibid., 759.
16 Ibid., 822–23 and 794.

17 Ibid., 912.
18 Ibid., 1022.
19 *Report of the Proceedings of the Twenty-seventh session of the Indian National Congress, Held at Bankipore, 26th, 27th and 28th December, 1912,* (n.d.), 19.
20 *Report on Indian Constitutional Reforms,* 149.
21 *First Despatch on Indian Constitutional Reforms, Government of India's Despatch of March 5th 1919, and Connected Papers* (Government of India, Central Publication Branch: Calcutta, 1928), 201.
22 Ibid., 234–35.
23 *Report of the Franchise Committee, 1918–19,* 158 and 207–08.
24 Ibid., 7.
25 *Reforms Committee (Franchise), Evidence Taken Before the Reforms Committee (Franchise), Vol. I* (Superintendent, Government Printing India: Calcutta, 1919), 276.
26 Ibid., 319.
27 *Reforms Committee (Franchise), Evidence Taken Before the Reforms Committee (Franchise), Vol. II* (Superintendent, Government Printing India: Calcutta, 1919), 433–34.
28 Ibid. 396.
29 *Joint Select Committee on the Government of India Bill, 1919, Vol. II, Minutes of Evidence* (His Majesty's Stationery Office: London, 1919), 60.
30 Ibid., 377.
31 *All-Parties Conference 1928,*35 and 48.
32 Shafaat Ahmed Khan, *What Are the Rights of the Muslim Minority in India?* (The Indian Press : Allahabad, 1928), 5.
33 *Indian Round Table Conference, 12th November, 1930–19th January, 1931, Proceedings of Sub-Committees (Volume III), [Sub-Committee No. III (Minorities)]* (Government of India, Central Publication Branch: Calcutta, 1931), 99.
34 Rezaul Karim, *For India and Islam,* (Chuckervertty, Chatterjee and Co.: Calcutta, 1937), 53–4 and 101.
35 Ibid., 49.
36 M.N. Dalal, *Whither Minorities?* (D.B. Taraporevala Sons and Co.:Bombay, 1940), 66.
37 *Constituent Assembly Debates,* Vol. VIII (Lok Sabha Secretariat: New Delhi, 2009), 337–38.
38 *Papers Relating to Constitutional Reform in India, Published Under the Authority of the Government of India, Vol. II,* 719.
39 *Papers Relating to Constitutional Reform in India, Published Under the Authority of the Government of India, Vol. III,*784.
40 Ibid, 786.
41 Ibid., 988.
42 *Report on Indian Constitutional Reforms,* 150.
43 *Report of the Franchise Committee, 1918–19,* 206–07.
44 Ibid., 211.

45 Ibid., 7.
46 *Reforms Committee (Franchise), Evidence Taken Before the Reforms Committee (Franchise), Vol. I*, 225.
47 Ibid., 236.
48 Ibid., 281.
49 *Joint Select Committee on the Government of India Bill, 1919, Vol. II, Minutes of Evidence*,170.
50 Ibid., 172.
51 *Joint Select Committee on the Government of India Bill, 1919, Vol. III, Appendices* (His Majesty's Stationery Office: London, 1919), 9.
52 *Indian Statutory Commission, Report, Vol-XVI, Selections from Memoranda & Oral Evidence by Non-Officials (Part-I)* (His Majesty's Stationery Office: London, 1930), 125.
53 *First Despatch on Indian Constitutional Reforms, Government of India's Despatch of March 5th 1919, and Connected Papers*, 140.
54 Ibid., 201–02 and 335.
55 *Report of the Franchise Committee, 1918-19*, 105.
56 Ibid., 7.
57 Ibid., 8.
58 *Joint Select Committee on the Government of India Bill, 1919, Vol. II, Minutes of Evidence*, 51.
59 *Joint Select Committee on the Government of India Bill, 1919, Vol. III, Appendices*, 9.
60 *Indian Statutory Commission, Report, Vol-XVI, Selections from Memoranda & Oral Evidence by Non-Officials (Part-II)* (His Majesty's Stationery Office: London, 1930), 334.
61 *East India (Constitutional Reforms) Indian Franchise Committee, Volume IV, Selections from Memoranda and Oral Evidence (Madras, Bombay, Bengal and The United Provinces)* (His Majesty's Stationery Office: London, 1932), 117.
62 Ibid., 221–22.
63 Ibid., 231.
64 *Constituent Assembly Debates*, Vol. XI (Lok Sabha Secretariat: New Delhi, 2009), 857–58.
65 *Papers Relating to Constitutional Reform in India, Published Under the Authority of the Government of India, Vol. II*,5.
66 Ibid., 288.
67 Ibid., 260.
68 Ibid., 287.
69 Ibid., 213.
70 Ibid., 128.
71 *East India (Advisory and Constitutional Reforms), Vol. I, Proposals of the Government of India and Despatch of the Secretary of State, Cd. 4426*, 19.
72 *Papers Relating to Constitutional Reform in India, Published Under the Authority of the Government of India, Vol. II*, 418–19 and 423.
73 Ibid., 451.

74 Ibid., 459–60.
75 *Report on Indian Constitutional Reforms*, 150.
76 *Report of the Franchise Committee, 1918–19*, 105.
77 Ibid., 124–27.
78 Ibid., 142–43.
79 *Reforms Committee (Franchise), Evidence Taken Before the Reforms Committee (Franchise), Vol. II*, 663–65
80 Ibid., 749, 785 and 793.
81 Ibid., 640.
82 Ibid., 585.
83 Ibid., 707.
84 Ibid., 793.
85 Ibid., 725.
86 Ibid., 749.
87 Ibid., 591, 596 and 608.
88 D.G. Karve, and D.V. Ambekar, eds, *Speeches and Writings of Gopal Krishna Gokhale, Volume Two: Political* (Allied Publishers: Bombay, 1966), 315.
89 *Reforms Committee (Franchise), Evidence Taken Before the Reforms Committee (Franchise), Vol. II*,751–54.
90 Ibid., 618.
91 Ibid., 632 and 637.
92 Ibid., 731.
93 *Report of the Franchise Committee, 1918–19*, 8–9.
94 *East India (Constitutional Reforms: Lord Southborough's Committees), Views of the Government of India on the Reports of Lord Southborough's Committees, Cmd. 176* (His Majesty's Stationery Office: London, 1919), 11.
95 *Joint Select Committee on the Government of India Bill, 1919, Vol. I, Report and Proceedings of the Committee*, 8.
96 *Joint Select Committee on the Government of India Bill, 1919, Vol. II, Minutes of Evidence*,89.
97 Ibid., 79 and 495
98 Ibid., 7.
99 Ibid., 47–8.
100 Ibid., 178 and 180.
101 Ibid., 387.
102 Ibid., 336.
103 Ibid., 338–39.
104 Ibid., 552.
105 Ibid., 299.
106 *Joint Select Committee on the Government of India Bill, 1919, Vol. III, Appendices*, 140–41.
107 *East India (Constitutional Reforms) Reforms Enquiry Committee, 1924, Appendix 6 to the Report, Oral Evidence (Part I)* (His Majesty's Stationery Office: London, 1925), 273.
108 *Indian Statutory Commission, Report, Vol-I, Survey, Cmd. 3568* (His Majesty's Stationery Office : London, 1930), 37.

109 *Indian Statutory Commission, Report, Vol-II, Recommendations, Cmd. 3569*, 64.

110 *Indian Statutory Commission, Report, Vol-III, Report of the Committees appointed by the Provincial Legislative Councils to co-operate with the Indian Statutory Commission,Cmd. 3572* (His Majesty's Stationery Office: London, 1930), 19.

111 Ibid., 43.

112 Ibid., 116.

113 *Indian Statutory Commission, Report, Vol-VI, Memorandum Submitted by the Government of Madras to the Indian Statutory Commission* (His Majesty's Stationery Office: London, 1930), 10.

114 *Indian Statutory Commission, Report, Vol-VII, Memorandum Submitted by the Government of Madras to the Indian Statutory Commission* (His Majesty's Stationery Office: London, 1930), 419.

115 *East India (Constitutional Reforms) Indian Franchise Committee, Volume I, Report of the Indian Franchise Committee, Cmd. 4080* (His Majesty's Stationery Office: London, 1932), 151.

116 *East India (Constitutional Reforms) Indian Franchise Committee, Volume IV, Selections from Memoranda and Oral Evidence (Madras, Bombay, Bengal and The United Provinces)*, 439.

117 *East India (Constitutional Reforms), Addresses presented in India to His Excellency The Viceroy and The Right Honourable The Secretary of State for India, Cmd.9178*, ii.

118 Ibid., 70.

119 *First Despatch on Indian Constitutional Reforms, Government of India's Despatch of March 5th 1919, and Connected Papers*, 140.

120 *Report of the Franchise Committee, 1918–19*,105 and 107.

121 Ibid., 257.

122 Ibid., 136.

123 *Reforms Committee (Franchise), Evidence Taken Before the Reforms Committee (Franchise), Vol. I*, 24.

124 Ibid., 111.

125 Ibid., 292.

126 *Reforms Committee (Franchise), Evidence Taken Before the Reforms Committee (Franchise), Vol. II*, 637.

127 *Reforms Committee (Franchise), Evidence Taken Before the Reforms Committee (Franchise), Vol. I*, 46.

128 *Reforms Committee (Franchise), Evidence Taken Before the Reforms Committee (Franchise), Vol. II*, 388, 434, 437 and 465.

129 Ibid., 652-653.

130 *Reforms Committee (Franchise), Evidence Taken Before the Reforms Committee (Franchise), Vol. I*, 279.

131 *Reforms Committee (Franchise), Evidence Taken Before the Reforms Committee (Franchise), Vol. II*, 739.

132 Ibid., 677.

133 *Indian Round Table Conference, 12th November, 1930-19th January, 1931, Proceedings* (Government of India, Central Publication Branch : Calcutta, 1931), 126.

134 *Indian Statutory Commission, Report, Vol-I, Survey, Cmd. 3568*, 41

135 *Indian Statutory Commission, Report, Vol-II, Recommendations, Cmd. 3569*, 65.

136 *Government of India's Despatch on proposals for Indian Constitutional Reforms* (Government of India: Simla, 1930), 31.

137 *Report of the Depressed Classes and Aboriginal Tribes Committee* (Government of Bombay: Bombay, 1930), 8.

138 *Indian Statutory Commission, Report, Vol-III, Report of the Committees appointed by the Provincial Legislative Councils to co-operate with the Indian Statutory Commission,Cmd. 3572*, 125.

139 *Indian Statutory Commission, Report, Vol-XVI, Selections from Memoranda & Oral Evidence by Non-Officials (Part-I)*, 54.

140 *Indian Statutory Commission, Report, Vol-X, Memorandum Submitted by the Government of the Punjab to the Indian Statutory Commission* (His Majesty's Stationery Office : London, 1930), 8.

141 *Indian Statutory Commission, Report, Vol-XVI, Selections from Memoranda & Oral Evidence by Non-Officials (Part-I)*, 348.

142 Ibid., 352.

143 *Indian Statutory Commission, Report, Vol-XVI, Selections from Memoranda & Oral Evidence by Non-Officials (Part-II)*, 90.

144 Ibid., 288-289.

145 *Indian Round Table Conference (Second Session), 7th September, 1931-1st December, 1931, Proceedings of the Federal Structure Committee and Minorities Committees* (His Majesty's Stationery Office: London, 1932), 586.

146 Ibid., 621.

147 Ibid., 564.

148 *East India (Constitutional Reforms) Indian Franchise Committee, Volume I, Report of the Indian Franchise Committee, Cmd. 4080*, 113–14.

149 Ibid., 210–11.

150 Ibid., 219.

151 Ibid., 119.

152 *East India (Constitutional Reforms) Indian Franchise Committee, Volume II, Memoranda Submitted by the Local Governments and Provincial Franchise Committees (Madras, Bombay, Bengal and The United Provinces)*(His Majesty's Stationery Office : London, 1932), 211–12.

153 Ibid., 230–31.

154 Ibid., 184.

155 Ibid., 230.

156 Ibid., 252–53.

157 *East India (Constitutional Reforms) Indian Franchise Committee, Volume III, Memoranda Submitted by the Local Governments and Provincial Franchise Committees (Punjab, Bihar and Orissa, Central Provinces, Assam, North-West Frontier Province, Coorg and Ajmer-Merwara)* (His Majesty's Stationery Office: London, 1932), 35–6.

158 Ibid., 35.

159 Ibid., 63.

160 Ibid., 49–50.

161 Ibid., 81–8.
163 Ibid., 129–30.
163 Ibid., 322–23.
164 Ibid., 327–28.
165 Ibid., 337–47.
166 *East India (Constitutional Reforms) Indian Franchise Committee, Volume IV, Selections from Memoranda and Oral Evidence (Madras, Bombay, Bengal and The United Provinces)*, 93–4.
167 Ibid., 350.
168 Ibid., 357.
169 *Report of the Depressed Classes and Aboriginal Tribes Committee*, 8.
170 *East India (Constitutional Reforms) Indian Franchise Committee, Volume IV, Selections from Memoranda and Oral Evidence (Madras, Bombay, Bengal and The United Provinces)*, 183.
171 Ibid., 843.
172 Ibid., 725.
173 Ibid., 581.
174 *East India (Constitutional Reforms) Indian Franchise Committee, Volume V, Selections from Memoranda and Oral Evidence (Punjab, Bihar and Orissa, Central Provinces, Assam, North-West Frontier Province, Delhi and Miscellaneous Memoranda)* (London: His Majesty's Stationery Office: London, 1932), 533.
175 Ibid., 34.
176 *Proposals for Indian Constitutional Reforms* (Manager of Publications: Delhi, 1933), 115–19.
177 *Joint Committee on Indian Constitutional Reform (Session 1932-1933), Volume IIC, Minutes of Evidence given before the Joint Committee on Indian Constitutional Reform* (His Majesty's Stationery Office: London, 1934), 1362–64.
178 *Constituent Assembly Debates,* Vol. I (Lok Sabha Secretariat: New Delhi, 2009), 139-140.
179 *Constituent Assembly Debates,* Vol. II (Lok Sabha Secretariat: New Delhi, 2009), 298–300.
180 *Constituent Assembly Debates,* Vol. X (Lok Sabha Secretariat: New Delhi, 2009), 344.
181 Ibid., 235.
182 Ibid., 247.
183 *Parliamentary Debates, Parliament of India, Official Report, Volume X, No.1, Part-II, Proceedings Other Than Questions and Answers* (The Manager of Publications: New Delhi, 1951), 7054.
184 Ibid., 7059.
185 Ibid., 7096–97.
186 Ibid., 7095–96.
187 *Parliamentary Debates, Parliament of India, Official Report, Volume XII, No.1, Part-II, Proceedings Other Than Questions and Answers* (The Manager of Publications: New Delhi, 1951), 9130.
188 *Indian Statutory Commission, Report, Vol-I, Survey, Cmd. 3568*, 161.

189 *Indian Statutory Commission, Report, Vol-XV, Extracts from Oral Evidence (Official)* (His Majesty's Stationery Office: London, 1930), 273 and 274.
190 *East India (Constitutional Reforms) Indian Franchise Committee, Volume III, Memoranda Submitted by the Local Governments and Provincial Franchise Committees (Punjab, Bihar and Orissa, Central Provinces, Assam, North-West Frontier Province, Coorg and Ajmer-Merwara)*, 205.
191 *Joint Committee on Indian Constitutional Reform (Session 1932–1933), Volume IIA, Minutes of Evidence given before the Joint Committee on Indian Constitutional Reform* (His Majesty's Stationery Office: London, 1934), 332.
192 *Joint Committee on Indian Constitutional Reform (Session 1932–1933), Volume IIB, Minutes of Evidence given before the Joint Committee on Indian Constitutional Reform* (His Majesty's Stationery Office: London, 1934), 1225.
193 *Joint Committee on Indian Constitutional Reform (Session 1932–1933), Volume IIC, Minutes of Evidence given before the Joint Committee on Indian Constitutional Reform*, 2363 and 2382.
194 Ambedkar, *Address by B.R. Ambedkar, M.A., Ph.D., D.Sc., Barrister-at-law, Member, Governor-General's Executive Council To the Session of the All-India Scheduled Caste Federation. Held in Bombay on May 6, 1945*, 25.
195 *Constituent Assembly Debates*, Vol. I, 143–45.
196 *Constituent Assembly Debates*, Vol. VIII, 120.
197 Ibid., 156 and 159.
198 *Constituent Assembly Debates*, Vol. IX, (Lok Sabha Secretariat: New Delhi, 2009), 985–86.
199 Ibid., 999.
200 *Papers Relating to Constitutional Reform in India, Published Under the Authority of the Government of India, Vol. II*, 1208.
201 *Report on Indian Constitutional Reforms*, 150.
202 *First Despatch on Indian Constitutional Reforms, Government of India's Despatch of March 5th 1919, and Connected Papers*, 202.
203 Ibid., 337–38.
204 *Report of the Franchise Committee, 1918–19*, 135.
205 *Reforms Committee (Franchise), Evidence Taken Before the Reforms Committee (Franchise), Vol. II*, 380, 391 and 755.
206 Ibid., 423 and 455.
207 Ibid., 786.
208 *Report of the Franchise Committee, 1918–19*, 7-8.
209 Ibid., 8.
210 Ibid., 8.
211 Frank Anthony, *Britain's Betrayal In India, The Story of the Anglo-Indian Community* (Allied Publishers: Bombay, 1969), 2.
212 *Report of the Franchise Committee, 1918–19*, 91.
213 Ibid., 91.
214 Ibid., 186.
215 *Reforms Committee (Franchise), Evidence Taken Before the Reforms Committee (Franchise), Vol. II*, 365.
216 Ibid., 451.

217 Ibid., 713.
218 *Reforms Committee (Franchise), Evidence Taken Before the Reforms Committee (Franchise), Vol. I*, 111.
219 *Reforms Committee (Franchise), Evidence Taken Before the Reforms Committee (Franchise), Vol. II*, 391.
220 *Reforms Committee (Franchise), Evidence Taken Before the Reforms Committee (Franchise), Vol. I*, 125.
221 Ibid., 211.
222 *Reforms Committee (Franchise), Evidence Taken Before the Reforms Committee (Franchise), Vol. II*, 587.
223 *Joint Select Committee on the Government of India Bill, 1919, Vol. III, Appendices*, 9.
224 *Report of the Indian Central Committee* (Government of India, Central Publication Branch: Calcutta, 1929), 46–47.
225 *Indian Statutory Commission, Report, Vol-XVI, Selections from Memoranda & Oral Evidence by Non-Officials (Part-I)*, 273.
226 *Indian Round Table Conference, 12th November, 1930–19th January, 1931, Proceedings*, 67–9.
227 *East India (Constitutional Reforms) Indian Franchise Committee, Volume IV, Selections from Memoranda and Oral Evidence (Madras, Bombay, Bengal and The United Provinces)*, 76–7.
228 *Joint Committee on Indian Constitutional Reform (Session 1932–1933), Volume IIA, Minutes of Evidence given before the Joint Committee on Indian Constitutional Reform*,450.
229 *Joint Committee on Indian Constitutional Reform (Session 1932–1933), Volume IIC, Minutes of Evidence given before the Joint Committee on Indian Constitutional Reform*, 1948.
230 Ibid., 1981.
231 Anthony, *Britain's Betrayal In India, The Story of the Anglo-Indian Community*, 4.
232 *Papers Relating to Constitutional Reform in India, Published Under the Authority of the Government of India, Vol. II*, 104.
233 *Reforms Committee (Franchise), Evidence Taken Before the Reforms Committee (Franchise), Vol. II*, 752.
234 Ibid., 673 and 792.
235 *East India (Constitutional Reforms) Reforms Enquiry Committee, 1924, Appendix 6 to the Report, Oral Evidence (Part I)*, 70.
236 *Indian Statutory Commission, Report, Vol-XVI, Selections from Memoranda & Oral Evidence by Non-Officials (Part-I)*, 58.
237 *Indian Round Table Conference, 12th November, 1930-19th January, 1931, Proceedings of Sub-Committees (Volume II), [Sub-Committee No. II (Provincial Constitution)]* (Government of India, Central Publication Branch: Calcutta, 1931), 49.
238 Khan, *What Are the Rights of the Muslim Minority in India?, passim.*
239 *Indian Round Table Conference (Second Session), 7th September, 1931-1st December, 1931, Proceedings of the Federal Structure Committee and Minorities Committees*, 544.

240 Ibid., 531.
241 Ibid., 548.
242 *Joint Committee on Indian Constitutional Reform (Session 1932–1933), Volume IIB, Minutes of Evidence given before the Joint Committee on Indian Constitutional Reform*, 1206.
243 Ambedkar, *States and Minorities, What Are Their Rights and How to Secure Them in the Constitution of Free India*, 46–7.
244 Nicholas Mansergh, ed, *Constitutional Relations Between Britain and India, The Transfer of Power 1942–47, Volume 1*, (HMSO: London, 1970), 476.
245 Ibid., 552.
246 B. Shiva Rao, ed, *The Framing of India's Constitution, Select Documents, Vol.II* (Indian Institute of Public Administration: New Delhi, 1967), 325–31.
247 *Constituent Assembly Debates,* Vol. I, 98.
248 Ibid., 105–6.
249 Ibid., 139.
250 Ibid., 144.
251 *Constituent Assembly Debates,* Vol. III (Lok Sabha Secretariat: New Delhi, 2009), 503.
252 *Constituent Assembly Debates,* Vol. V (Lok Sabha Secretariat: New Delhi, 2009), 228.
253 *Constituent Assembly Debates,* Vol. I, 91–2.
254 *Constituent Assembly Debates,* Vol. V, 218.
255 *Constituent Assembly Debates,* Vol. VII (Lok Sabha Secretariat: New Delhi, 2009), 361.
256 *Constituent Assembly Debates,* Vol. V, 283.
257 *Constituent Assembly Debates,* Vol. VII, 39.
258 *Constituent Assembly Debates,* Vol. VIII, 333.
259 *Constituent Assembly Debates,* Vol. I, 296, and *Constituent Assembly Debates,* Vol. VII, 226 and 229.
260 Shiva Rao, ed, *The Framing of India's Constitution, Select Documents, Vol.II*, 393.
261 *Constituent Assembly Debates,* Vol. VII, 155.
262 *Representation of Muhammadans on Legislative Councils, Cd. 4652* (His Majesty's Stationery Office: London, 1909), 4.
263 *East India (Constitutional Reforms: Lord Southborough's Committees), Views of the Government of India on the Reports of Lord Southborough's Committees, Cmd. 176*, 10.
264 Ibid., 18–9.
265 *Report of the Franchise Committee, 1918–19*, 206–7.
266 *Reforms Committee (Franchise), Evidence Taken Before the Reforms Committee (Franchise), Vol. II*, 737 and 748.
267 *East India (Constitutional Reforms) Reforms Enquiry Committee, 1924, Appendix 5 to the Report, Written Evidence* (His Majesty's Stationery Office: London, 1925), 328.
268 *All-Parties Conference 1928*, 52.
269 *Indian Statutory Commission, Report, Vol-I, Survey, Cmd. 3568*, 25.

270 *Indian Statutory Commission, Report, Vol-II, Recommendations, Cmd. 3569*, 63.

271 Ibid., 66–7.

272 Ibid., 71.

273 *Report of the Indian Central Committee*, 42–3.

274 *Indian Statutory Commission, Report, Vol-III, Report of the Committees appointed by the Provincial Legislative Councils to co-operate with the Indian Statutory Commission,Cmd. 3572*, 126–27.

275 *Indian Round Table Conference, 12th November, 1930–19th January, 1931, Proceedings of Sub-Committees (Volume III), [Sub-Committee No. III (Minorities)]*,79.

276 *Indian Statutory Commission, Report, Vol-III, Report of the Committees appointed by the Provincial Legislative Councils to co-operate with the Indian Statutory Commission,Cmd. 3572*, 415–18.

277 Ibid., 456–7.

278 *Indian Statutory Commission, Report, Vol-XVI, Selections from Memoranda & Oral Evidence by Non-Officials (Part-I)*, 109.

279 Ibid., 125.

280 *Indian Round Table Conference, 12th November, 1930-19th January, 1931, Proceedings of Sub-Committees (Volume III), [Sub-Committee No. III (Minorities)]*, 51.

281 Ibid., 15.

282 Ibid., 172.

283 Ambedkar, *Address by B.R. Ambedkar, M.A., Ph.D., D.Sc., Barrister-at-law, Member, Governor-General's Executive Council To the Session of the All-India Scheduled Caste Federation. Held in Bombay on May 6, 1945*, 23.

284 Ambedkar, *States and Minorities, What Are Their Rights and How to Secure Them in the Constitution of Free India*, 21–2.

285 Ibid., 43.

Chapter 5

1 Shaikh, *Community and Consensus in Islam, Muslim Representation and Colonial India, 1860–1947*, 63–4.

2 *East India (Advisory and Constitutional Reforms), Vol. I, Proposals of the Government of India and Despatch of the Secretary of State, Cd. 4426*, 10 and 13.

3 *Papers Relating to Constitutional Reform in India, Published Under the Authority of the Government of India, Vol. II*, 70, 104, 108, 157 and 354, and *Papers Relating to Constitutional Reform in India, Published Under the Authority of the Government of India, Vol. III*, 743 and 1476.

4 *Papers Relating to Constitutional Reform in India, Published Under the Authority of the Government of India, Vol. III*, 814, 864, 934 and 949–50.

5 *Papers Relating to Constitutional Reform in India, Published Under the Authority of the Government of India, Vol. II*, 883, and *Papers Relating to Constitutional Reform in India, Published Under the Authority of the Government of India, Vol. III*, 1260.

6 *Report on Indian Constitutional Reforms*, 150–51.
7 *Joint Select Committee on the Government of India Bill, 1919, Vol. I, Report and Proceedings of the Committee*, 8.
8 *Report of the Franchise Committee, 1918–19*, 8.
9 Ibid., 7–8.
10 Ibid., 16.
11 Ibid., 16.
12 *First Report from the Joint Select Committee on the Government of India Act, 1919, (Draft Rules)* (His Majesty's Stationery Office: London, 1920), 5.
13 *Report on Indian Constitutional Reforms*, 147.
14 Ibid., 178–79.
15 Ibid., 175–76.
16 *East India (Constitutional Reforms: Lord Southborough's Committees), Views of the Government of India on the Reports of Lord Southborough's Committees, Cmd. 176*, 17.
17 *Report of the Franchise Committee, 1918–19*, 16.
18 Ibid., 16.
19 *East India (Constitutional Reforms: Lord Southborough's Committees), Views of the Government of India on the Reports of Lord Southborough's Committees, Cmd. 176*, 16.
20 *Joint Select Committee on the Government of India Bill, 1919, Vol. I, Report and Proceedings of the Committee*, 9–10.
21 *Indian Statutory Commission, Report, Vol-II, Recommendations, Cmd. 3569*, 113.
22 *Indian Round Table Conference, 12th November, 1930-19th January, 1931, Proceedings of Sub-Committees (Volume I), [Sub-Committee No. I (Federal Structure)]* (Government of India, Central Publication Branch: Calcutta, 1931), 315–17.
23 Ibid., 656.
24 *Indian Round Table Conference, 12th November, 1930-19th January, 1931, Proceedings of Sub-Committees (Volume II), [Sub-Committee No. II (Provincial Constitution)]*, 193–95.
25 *Indian Round Table Conference (Second Session), 7th September, 1931-1st December, 1931, Proceedings of the Federal Structure Committee and Minorities Committees*, 59–60.
26 *East India (Constitutional Reforms) Indian Franchise Committee, Volume III, Memoranda Submitted by the Local Governments and Provincial Franchise Committees (Punjab, Bihar and Orissa, Central Provinces, Assam, North-West Frontier Province, Coorg and Ajmer-Merwara)*, 342.
27 Ibid, 158.
28 Ibid, 241 and 262.
29 *East India (Constitutional Reforms) Indian Franchise Committee, Volume IV, Selections from Memoranda and Oral Evidence (Madras, Bombay, Bengal and The United Provinces)*, 93–4.
30 *Proposals for Indian Constitutional Reforms*, 74.
31 Ibid., 75.

32 Ibid., 77.

33 Ibid., 78 and 103.

34 *Joint Committee on Indian Constitutional Reform (Session 1932-1933), Volume IIC, Minutes of Evidence given before the Joint Committee on Indian Constitutional Reform*, 2382.

35 *Joint Committee on Indian Constitutional Reform (Session 1933–1934), Volume I (Part II), Proceedings*(His Majesty's Stationery Office: London, 1934), 367.

36 Ibid., 372.

37 Ibid., 382.

38 *Joint Committee on Indian Constitutional Reform (Session 1933-1934), Volume I (Part I), Reports* (His Majesty's Stationery Office : London, 1934), 110 and 112.

39 Ibid., 69.

40 *Report of the Committee appointed in connection with the Delimitation of Constituencies and connected matters, Volume I, The Report, Cmd. 5099* (His Majesty's Stationery Office: London, 1936), 222.

41 M.N. Roy, *Constitution of India, A Draft* (Radical Democratic Party: No Place of Publication, c. 1945), 16–25.

42 Shriman Narayan Agarwal, *Gandhian Constitution for India* (Kitabistan: Allahabad, 1946), 100.

43 Sir Maurice Gwyer and A. Appadorai, eds, *Speeches and Documents on the Indian Constitution, 1921-1947, Vol. II* (Oxford University Press : Bombay, 1957), 582.

44 Shiva Rao, ed, *The Framing of India's Constitution, Select Documents, Vol.II*, 404.

45 Ibid., 581.

46 Ibid., 628.

47 *Constituent Assembly Debates*, Vol. III, 377 and 385.

48 B. Shiva Rao, ed, *The Framing of India's Constitution, Select Documents, Vol. III* (Indian Institute of Public Administration : New Delhi, 1967), 22–3 and 50–2.

49 Ibid., 52.

50 *Draft Constitution of India, Prepared by the Drafting Committee* (Constituent Assembly of India: New Delhi, 1948), 27–9.

51 Ibid., 66-67.

52 *Constituent Assembly Debates*, Vol. VII, 156.

53 *Constituent Assembly Debates*, Vol. VIII, 82–3.

54 Ibid., 197.

55 *Constituent Assembly Debates*, Vol. IX, 660.

56 Ibid., 662.

57 *East India (Advisory and Constitutional Reforms), Vol. I, Proposals of the Government of India and Despatch of the Secretary of State, Cd. 4426*, 13, and *Papers Relating to Constitutional Reform in India, Published Under the Authority of the Government of India, Vol. II*, 548.

58 *Papers Relating to Constitutional Reform in India, Published Under the Authority of the Government of India, Vol. II*, 335–36.

59 *Report on Indian Constitutional Reforms*, 149.
60 *Reforms Committee (Franchise), Evidence Taken Before the Reforms Committee (Franchise), Vol. II*, 729–39.
61 Ibid., 731.
62 Ibid., 725, 774, 785 and 593–94.
63 V.S. Srinivasa Sastri, *The Congress-League Scheme, An Exposition* (Servants of India Society: Poona, 1917), 11–2.
64 *Joint Select Committee on the Government of India Bill, 1919, Vol. II, Minutes of Evidence*, 355.
65 *Reforms Committee (Franchise), Evidence Taken Before the Reforms Committee (Franchise), Vol. II*, 754, and *Reforms Committee (Franchise), Evidence Taken Before the Reforms Committee (Franchise), Vol. I*, 124.
66 *Reforms Committee (Franchise), Evidence Taken Before the Reforms Committee (Franchise), Vol. II*, 623.
67 *All-Parties Conference 1928*, 28.
68 *East India (Advisory and Constitutional Reforms), Vol. I, Proposals of the Government of India and Despatch of the Secretary of State, Cd. 4426*, 25.
69 *Papers Relating to Constitutional Reform in India, Published Under the Authority of the Government of India, Vol. III*, 798.
70 *Papers Relating to Constitutional Reform in India, Published Under the Authority of the Government of India, Vol. II*, 506.
71 *Report on Indian Constitutional Reforms*, 149.
72 *Report of the Franchise Committee, 1918–19*, 7.
73 Ibid., 7.
74 Ibid., 105–7.
75 Ibid., 9.
76 *Reforms Committee (Franchise), Evidence Taken Before the Reforms Committee (Franchise), Vol. II*, 633, 636-637, and 640.
77 *Report of the Franchise Committee, 1918–19*, 135–36.
78 *Reforms Committee (Franchise), Evidence Taken Before the Reforms Committee (Franchise), Vol. II*, 785.
79 Ibid., 756.
80 Ibid., 732.
81 *East India (Constitutional Reforms: Lord Southborough's Committees), Views of the Government of India on the Reports of Lord Southborough's Committees, Cmd. 176*, 10–1.
82 *Report of the Franchise Committee, 1918–19*, 6.
83 *Reforms Committee (Franchise), Evidence Taken Before the Reforms Committee (Franchise), Vol. I*, 109 and 242–43.
84 *Reforms Committee (Franchise), Evidence Taken Before the Reforms Committee (Franchise), Vol. II*, 750–51.
85 Ibid., 731.
86 *Joint Select Committee on the Government of India Bill, 1919, Vol. I, Report and Proceedings of the Committee*, 8.
87 *Reforms Committee (Franchise), Evidence Taken Before the Reforms Committee (Franchise), Vol. II*, 596, 613, and 776.
88 Ibid., 641, 727,and 744.

89 Ibid., 589.

90 Ibid., 611.

91 *Reforms Committee (Franchise), Evidence Taken Before the Reforms Committee (Franchise), Vol. I*, 111 and 319, and *Reforms Committee (Franchise), Evidence Taken Before the Reforms Committee (Franchise), Vol. II*, 411 and 435.

92 *Reforms Committee (Franchise), Evidence Taken Before the Reforms Committee (Franchise), Vol. II*, 443.

93 Ibid., 424.

94 Ibid., 641.

95 *First Report from the Joint Select Committee on the Government of India Act, 1919, (Draft Rules)*, 4.

96 *Report of the Reforms Enquiry Committee appointed by the Government of India and other connected papers, Cmd. 2360*, (His Majesty's Stationery Office: London, 1925), 189.

97 *All-Parties Conference 1928*, 38.

98 Ibid., 35–7.

99 Ibid., 95.

100 Iyengar, *Swaraj Constitution*, xxiii-xxiv.

101 Syed Tofail Ahmed, *Responsible Government and Solution of Hindu-Muslim Problem* (1928), 59–60.

102 Khan, *What Are the Rights of the Muslim Minority in India?*, 5, 91–2 and 94–5.

103 *Indian Statutory Commission, Report, Vol-II, Recommendations, Cmd. 3569*, 60.

104 Ibid., 66.

105 Ibid., 64.

106 Ibid., 61 and 86–7.

107 Ibid., 62.

108 *Indian Statutory Commission, Report, Vol-III, Report of the Committees appointed by the Provincial Legislative Councils to co-operate with the Indian Statutory Commission,Cmd. 3572*, 40–1.

109 Ibid., 464–66.

110 Ibid., 117–21.

111 *Indian Statutory Commission, Report, Vol-XVI, Selections from Memoranda & Oral Evidence by Non-Officials (Part-I)*, 54.

112 *Indian Statutory Commission, Report, Vol-II, Recommendations, Cmd. 3569*, 71–2.

113 *Indian Round Table Conference, 12th November, 1930-19th January, 1931, Proceedings of Sub-Committees (Volume III), [Sub-Committee No. III (Minorities)]*, 59.

114 Ibid., 78.

115 *Indian Round Table Conference, 12th November, 1930-19th January, 1931, Proceedings of Sub-Committees (Volume III), [Sub-Committee No. VI (Franchise)]* (Government of India, Central Publication Branch : Calcutta, 1931), 34.

116 *Indian Round Table Conference, 12th November, 1930-19th January, 1931, Proceedings of Sub-Committees (Volume III), [Sub-Committee No. III (Minorities)]*, 166.

117 Ibid., 166–67.

118 *Indian Round Table Conference (Second Session), 7th September, 1931-1st December, 1931, Proceedings of the Federal Structure Committee and Minorities Committees*, 59–60.

119 M.K. Gandhi, 'The Future of India', *International Affairs*, 10, no. 6 (1931).

120 *Indian Round Table Conference (Second Session), 7th September, 1931-1st December, 1931, Proceedings of the Federal Structure Committee and Minorities Committees*, 548.

121 Ibid., 537.

122 Ibid., 171.

123 Ibid., 45.

124 *East India (Constitutional Reforms) Indian Franchise Committee, Volume I, Report of the Indian Franchise Committee, Cmd. 4080*, 10 and 150.

125 Ibid., 151.

126 Ibid., 152.

127 Ibid., 150.

128 *East India (Constitutional Reforms) Indian Franchise Committee, Volume II, Memoranda Submitted by the Local Governments and Provincial Franchise Committees (Madras, Bombay, Bengal and The United Provinces*, 28.

129 Ibid., 70.

130 Ibid., 125.

131 Ibid., 184.

132 Ibid., 215.

133 Ibid., 191.

134 *East India (Constitutional Reforms) Indian Franchise Committee, Volume III, Memoranda Submitted by the Local Governments and Provincial Franchise Committees (Punjab, Bihar and Orissa, Central Provinces, Assam, North-West Frontier Province, Coorg and Ajmer Merwara)*, 87-88.

135 *East India (Constitutional Reforms) Indian Franchise Committee, Volume IV, Selections from Memoranda and Oral Evidence (Madras, Bombay, Bengal and The United Provinces)*, 426.

136 Ibid., 580.

137 *East India (Constitutional Reforms) Indian Franchise Committee, Volume V, Selections from Memoranda and Oral Evidence (Punjab, Bihar and Orissa, Central Provinces, Assam, North-West Frontier Province, Delhi and Miscellaneous Memoranda)*,191

138 Ibid., 492–94.

139 *East India (Constitutional Reforms) Indian Franchise Committee, Volume IV, Selections from Memoranda and Oral Evidence (Madras, Bombay, Bengal and The United Provinces)*, 699–700.

140 *East India (Constitutional Reforms) Indian Franchise Committee, Volume II, Memoranda Submitted by the Local Governments and Provincial Franchise Committees (Madras, Bombay, Bengal and The United Provinces*, 87–9.

141 *East India (Constitutional Reforms) Indian Franchise Committee, Volume III, Memoranda Submitted by the Local Governments and Provincial Franchise Committees (Punjab, Bihar and Orissa, Central Provinces, Assam, North-West Frontier Province, Coorg and Ajmer-Merwara)*, 322–23.

142 Ibid., 321.

143 Ibid., 813–14.

144 *East India (Constitutional Reforms) Indian Franchise Committee, Volume IV, Selections from Memoranda and Oral Evidence (Madras, Bombay, Bengal and The United Provinces)*, 438.

145 *East India (Constitutional Reforms) Indian Franchise Committee, Volume II, Memoranda Submitted by the Local Governments and Provincial Franchise Committees (Madras, Bombay, Bengal and The United Provinces)*, 140.

146 *East India (Constitutional Reforms) Indian Franchise Committee, Volume V, Selections from Memoranda and Oral Evidence (Punjab, Bihar and Orissa, Central Provinces, Assam, North-West Frontier Province, Delhi and Miscellaneous Memoranda)*, 291.

147 *East India (Constitutional Reforms), Communal Decision, Cmd. 4147*, (His Majesty's Stationery Office: London, 1932), 3.

148 Kumar, 'Gandhi, Ambedkar and the Poona Pact, 1932'.

149 Pyarelal, *The Epic Fast, passim.*

150 *Joint Committee on Indian Constitutional Reform (Session 1932–1933), Volume IIC, Minutes of Evidence given before the Joint Committee on Indian Constitutional Reform*, 1364.

151 Ibid., 1422.

152 Ibid., 2091 and 2104.

153 *Joint Committee on Indian Constitutional Reform (Session 1933–1934), Volume I (Part II), Proceedings*, 338–40.

154 Ibid., 111–12.

155 *Report of the Provincial Advisory Committee on the Delimitation of Constituencies 1933-34, Volume I (Parts I and II)* (Government of Bengal, Appointments Department, Reforms: Calcutta, 1934) 6–7.

156 Ibid., 7–8.

157 Ibid., 6.

158 *Report of the Government of Bombay on the Delimitation of Constituencies in the Presidency of Bombay and in Sind* (Government of Bombay : Bombay, 1935), 3.

159 *Report of the Committee appointed in connection with the Delimitation of Constituencies and connected matters, Volume I, The Report, Cmd. 5099*, 12–5.

160 Ibid., 16–9.

161 Ibid., 106.

162 Ibid., 44–5.

163 Ibid., 106.

164 Ibid., 106.

165 Ibid., 114.

166 Bidyut Chakravarty, 'The Communal Award and Its Implications in Bengal', *Modern Asian Studies*, vol. 23, no. 3 (1989).
167 *Report of the Committee appointed in connection with the Delimitation of Constituencies and connected matters, Vol.II, Proposals for the Delimitation of Constituencies* (His Majesty's Stationery Office: London, 1936), 175, and 190–91.
168 *Report of the Committee appointed in connection with the Delimitation of Constituencies and connected matters, Volume I, The Report, Cmd. 5099*, 222.
169 Ibid., 215.
170 Ibid., 228–29.
171 *Report of the Committee appointed in connection with the Delimitation of Constituencies and connected matters, Vol. III, Selections from Evidence* (His Majesty's Stationery Office: London, 1936), 1–3.
172 Ibid., 48.
173 Ibid., 48.
174 Ibid., 59 and 77.
175 Ibid., 70.
176 Ibid., 61.
177 Ibid., 78.
178 Ibid., 70.
179 Gokhale and others, *The Constitution of the Hindusthan Free State Act, 194*, 41.
180 Sapru and others, *Constitutional Proposals of the Sapru Committee*, 164.
181 Ambedkar, *Address by B.R. Ambedkar, M.A., Ph.D., D.Sc., Barrister-at-law, Member, Governor-General's Executive Council To the Session of the All-India Scheduled Caste Federation. Held in Bombay on May 6, 1945*, 45.
182 Ibid., 23.
183 Y.G. Krishnamurti, *Constituent Assembly and Indian Federation* (New Book Company: Bombay, 1940), 37–44; Dr G.S. Mahajani, *The Problem of Minorities and Constitutional Democracy as its Solution* (Bombay, 1941), 16.
184 Gwyer and Appadorai, eds, *Speeches and Documents on the Indian Constitution, 1921–1947, Vol. II*, 582.
185 Ambedkar, *States and Minorities, What Are Their Rights and How to Secure Them in the Constitution of Free India*, 22 and 25–6.
186 Ibid., 44–8.
187 *Constituent Assembly Debates*, Vol. I, 137.
188 Ibid., 150.
189 Shiva Rao, ed, *The Framing of India's Constitution, Select Documents, Vol.II*, 392–93.
190 Ibid., 396–98.
191 Ibid., 404.
192 Ibid., 408.
193 Ibid., 531.

194 Ibid., 531.
195 Ibid., 628.
196 Ibid., 628.
197 *Constituent Assembly Debates,* Vol. V, 203.
198 Ibid., 211–14.
199 Ibid., 260.
200 Ibid., 261.
201 Ibid., 264.
202 Ibid., 267.
203 Ibid., 219.
204 Ibid., 273–75.
205 Shiva Rao, ed, *The Framing of India's Constitution, Select Documents, Vol. III*, 22.
206 *Draft Constitution of India, Prepared by the Drafting Committee*, 139–40.
207 M. Venkatrangaiya, *Draft Constitution of India*, (Hind Kitabs Ltd.: Bombay, 1948), 48.
208 *Draft Constitution of Indian Republic* (Suresh Desai, General Secretary, Socialist Party: Bombay, 1948), 65–70.
209 D.R. Gadgil, *Some Observations on the Draft Constitution of India* (Gokhale Institute of Politics and Economics: Poona, 1948), 89–94.
210 Chaube, *Constituent Assembly of India, Springboard of Revolution*, 115–16.
211 B. Shiva Rao, ed, *The Framing of India's Constitution, Select Documents, Vol. IV* (New Delhi : Indian Institute of Public Administration: New Delhi, 1968), 141.
212 Ibid., 591 and 594.
213 Ibid., 355–59.
214 Ibid., 599.
215 Ibid., 869.
216 *Constituent Assembly Debates,* Vol. VII, 242-243 and 1233–35.
217 Ibid., 300.
218 Ibid., 303.
219 Ibid., 332.
220 Ibid., 1259.
221 Ibid., 1261–63.
222 Ibid., 1245.
223 Ibid., 1252.
224 Ibid., 1251.
225 Ibid., 1224–25 and 1222–23.
226 Ibid., 1231.
227 Ibid., 1249.
228 Ibid., 248 and 250.
229 Ibid., 351.
230 Ibid., 252.
231 Ibid., 267.
232 Ibid., 1249–50 and 1255.
233 *Constituent Assembly Debates,* Vol. VIII, 274–75.

234 Ibid., 305.
235 *Constituent Assembly Debates,* Vol. X, 283.
236 *Constituent Assembly Debates,* Vol. VIII, 301.
237 Ibid., 346.
238 Ibid., 291–93.
239 *Constituent Assembly Debates,* Vol. IX, 666–67.
240 Ibid., 649.
241 *Parliamentary Debates, Parliament of India, Official Report, Volume IV, No.1, Part-II-Proceedings Other Than Questions and Answers* (The Manager of Publications: New Delhi, 1950), 3046.
242 Ibid., 3053–54.
243 Ibid., 3059.
244 Ibid., 3060.
245 Ibid., 3060.
246 Ibid., 3066.
247 *Parliamentary Debates, Parliament of India, Official Report, Volume VII, No.1, Part-II, Proceedings Other Than Questions and Answers* (The Manager of Publications: New Delhi, 1950), 2286–87.
248 Ibid., 2294.
249 Ibid., 2311-2313.
250 *Parliamentary Debates, Parliament of India, Official Report, Volume X, No.1, Part-II, Proceedings Other Than Questions and Answers* (The Manager of Publications: New Delhi, 1951), 7021.
251 *Parliamentary Debates, Parliament of India, Official Report, Volume XI, No.1, Part-II, Proceedings Other Than Questions and Answers* (The Manager of Publications: New Delhi, 1951), 8359–66.
252 Ibid., 8605–06.
253 *Parliamentary Debates, Parliament of India, Official Report, Volume XII, No.1, Part-II, Proceedings Other Than Questions and Answers* (The Manager of Publications: New Delhi, 1951), 9245–49.
254 *Parliamentary Debates, Parliament of India, Official Report, Volume XI, No.1, Part-II, Proceedings Other Than Questions and Answers,* 8641.
255 Sridharan, 'The Origins of The Electoral System: Rules, Representation, and Power-sharing in Indian Democracy', 361.

Chapter 6

1 *First Report from the Joint Select Committee on the Government of India Act, 1919, (Draft Rules)*, 3-4.
2 *Report of the Government of Bombay on the Delimitation of Constituencies in the Presidency of Bombay and in Sind*, 6-7.
3 Ibid., 7.
4 *Parliamentary Debates, Parliament of India, Official Report, Volume IV, No.1, Part-II-Proceedings Other Than Questions and Answers*, 3002.
5 Ibid., 3007 and 3029.
6 Ibid., 3067.
7 Ibid., 3053.

8 *Parliamentary Debates, Parliament of India, Official Report, Volume XI, No.1, Part-II, Proceedings Other Than Questions and Answers*, 8503.
9 *Report on Indian Constitutional Reforms*, 129.
10 Ibid., 147.
11 Ibid., 146.
12 *Report of the Franchise Committee, 1918-19*, 4.
13 Ibid., 168.
14 *Indian Statutory Commission, Report, Vol-I, Survey, Cmd. 3568*, 191-192.
15 *Indian Statutory Commission, Report, Vol-II, Recommendations, Cmd. 3569*, 91-93.
16 Ibid., 93.
17 *Indian Statutory Commission, Report, Vol-XVI, Selections from Memoranda & Oral Evidence by Non-Officials (Part-I)*, 41.
18 *Government of India's Despatch on proposals for Indian Constitutional Reforms*, 24-25.
19 *Proposals for Indian Constitutional Reforms*, 19.
20 *Indian Round Table Conference, 12th November, 1930-19th January, 1931, Proceedings*, 44.
21 *Indian Round Table Conference, 12th November, 1930-19th January, 1931, Proceedings of Sub-Committees (Volume III), [Sub-Committee No. VI (Franchise)]*, 2.
22 Ibid., 88.
23 Ibid., 89.
24 Ibid., 91.
25 *East India (Constitutional Reforms) Indian Franchise Committee, Volume I, Report of the Indian Franchise Committee, Cmd. 4080*, 34-40.
26 *East India (Constitutional Reforms) Indian Franchise Committee, Volume II, Memoranda Submitted by the Local Governments and Provincial Franchise Committees (Madras, Bombay, Bengal and The United Provinces*, 12 and 27.
27 *East India (Constitutional Reforms) Indian Franchise Committee, Volume III, Memoranda Submitted by the Local Governments and Provincial Franchise Committees (Punjab, Bihar and Orissa, Central Provinces, Assam, North-West Frontier Province, Coorg and Ajmer-Merwara)*, 289.
28 *East India (Constitutional Reforms) Indian Franchise Committee, Volume V, Selections from Memoranda and Oral Evidence (Punjab, Bihar and Orissa, Central Provinces, Assam, North-West Frontier Province, Delhi and Miscellaneous Memoranda)*, 298.
29 *East India (Constitutional Reforms) Indian Franchise Committee, Volume II, Memoranda Submitted by the Local Governments and Provincial Franchise Committees (Madras, Bombay, Bengal and The United Provinces*, 27 and 295.
30 Ibid., 123.
31 *East India (Constitutional Reforms) Indian Franchise Committee, Volume III, Memoranda Submitted by the Local Governments and Provincial Franchise Committees (Punjab, Bihar and Orissa, Central Provinces, Assam, North-West Frontier Province, Coorg and Ajmer-Merwara)*, 26.

32 *Joint Select Committee on the Government of India Bill, 1919, Vol. II, Minutes of Evidence*, 113.
33 C.R. Das and Bhagvan Das, *Outline Scheme of Swaraj*, (No Place of Publication, No Year of Publication), 12.
34 *All-Parties Conference 1928*, 92-94.
35 Ibid., 92-93.
36 The Marquess of Lothian, 'India and the Franchise Problem', *International Affairs*, 11, no. 5 (1932).
37 Iyengar, *Swaraj Constitution*, xxvi.
38 *Indian Statutory Commission, Report, Vol-II, Recommendations, Cmd. 3569*, 90.
39 *Report of the Indian Central Committee*, 36.
40 Ibid., 155-156.
41 *Indian Statutory Commission, Report, Vol-III, Report of the Committees appointed by the Provincial Legislative Councils to co-operate with the Indian Statutory Commission,Cmd. 3572*, 17.
42 Ibid., 173.
43 Ibid., 303.
44 Ibid., 600.
45 Ibid., 105.
46 *Indian Statutory Commission, Report, Vol-XVI, Selections from Memoranda & Oral Evidence by Non-Officials (Part-I)*, 56.
47 Ibid., 31.
48 Ibid., 108.
49 Ibid., 103.
50 *Indian Round Table Conference, 12th November, 1930-19th January, 1931, Proceedings*, 104.
51 *Indian Round Table Conference, 12th November, 1930-19th January, 1931, Proceedings of Sub-Committees (Volume III), [Sub-Committee No. VI (Franchise)]*, 5.
52 Ibid., 12 and 18-19.
53 Ibid., 23 and 143.
54 Ibid., 33-34.
55 Ibid., 149.
56 Ibid., 150.
57 *Indian Round Table Conference (Second Session), 7th September, 1931-1st December, 1931, Proceedings of the Federal Structure Committee and Minorities Committees*, 59-60.
58 Ibid., 62.
59 *East India (Constitutional Reforms) Indian Franchise Committee, Volume I, Report of the Indian Franchise Committee, Cmd. 4080*, 10-21.
60 *East India (Constitutional Reforms) Indian Franchise Committee, Volume IV, Selections from Memoranda and Oral Evidence (Madras, Bombay, Bengal and The United Provinces)*, 156.
61 Ibid., 215.
62 *East India (Constitutional Reforms) Indian Franchise Committee, Volume V, Selections from Memoranda and Oral Evidence (Punjab, Bihar and*

Orissa, Central Provinces, Assam, North-West Frontier Province, Delhi and Miscellaneous Memoranda), 195.

63 Gokhale and others, *The Constitution of the Hindusthan Free State Act, 194*, iv, and Sapru and others, *Constitutional Proposals of the Sapru Committee*, 166.

64 M.N. Roy, *Constitution of India, A Draft, passim.*

65 Ambedkar, *States and Minorities, What Are Their Rights and How to Secure Them in the Constitution of Free India*, 22.

66 K.G. Mashruwala, *Some Particular Suggestions for the Constitution of Free India* (Hamara Hindustan : Bombay, 1946), 8.

67 Agarwal, *Gandhian Constitution for India*, 78.

68 Shiva Rao, ed, *The Framing of India's Constitution, Select Documents, Vol.II*, 624.

69 Ibid., 642.

70 *Constituent Assembly Debates*, Vol. VII, 1254-1255.

71 *Constituent Assembly Debates*, Vol. VIII, 134.

72 *Constituent Assembly Debates*, Vol. VII, 1245-1246.

73 Shani, *How India Became Democratic, Citizenship and the Making of Universal Franchise*, 106-107.

74 *Constituent Assembly Debates*, Vol. XI, 785-786.

75 Ibid., 963-964, 798, and 818.

76 Ibid., 835.

77 *Constituent Assembly Debates*, Vol. VIII, 931.

78 *Constituent Assembly Debates*, Vol. IX, 45.

79 Ibid., 482.

80 *East India (Executive and Legislative Councils), Regulations &c for Giving Effect to the Indian Councils Act, 1909, Cmd. 4987* (His Majesty's Stationery Office: London, 1910), *passim.*

81 Surendranath Banerjea, *A Nation In Making, Being Reminiscences of Fifty Years of Public Life* (Oxford University Press : London, 1925), 123.

82 Ibid., 292-293.

83 *Papers Relating to Constitutional Reform in India, Published Under the Authority of the Government of India, Vol. III*, 1355.

84 *Report on Indian Constitutional Reforms*, 179.

85 *Report of the Franchise Committee, 1918-19*, 12.

86 *Reforms Committee (Franchise), Evidence Taken Before the Reforms Committee (Franchise), Vol. I*, 284.

87 *Reforms Committee (Franchise), Evidence Taken Before the Reforms Committee (Franchise), Vol. II*, 752-753.

88 *Reforms Committee (Franchise), Evidence Taken Before the Reforms Committee (Franchise), Vol. I*, 111.

89 Ibid., 130.

90 *Reforms Committee (Franchise), Evidence Taken Before the Reforms Committee (Franchise), Vol. II*, 725 and 761.

91 Ibid., 774.

92 *Joint Select Committee on the Government of India Bill, 1919, Vol. I, Report and Proceedings of the Committee*, 8.

93 *East India (Constitutional Reforms) Reforms Enquiry Committee, 1924, Appendix 5 to the Report, Written Evidence*, 402.
94 *East India (Constitutional Reforms), Views of the Local Governments, on the Working of the Reforms, dated 1924, Cmd. 2362* (His Majesty's Stationery Office : London, 1925), 326.
95 *Constituent Assembly Debates*, Vol. VII, 119.
96 Ibid., 291.
97 Ibid., 368-369.
98 Ibid., 1319.
99 *Constituent Assembly Debates*, Vol. VIII, 89.
100 Ibid., 91.
101 Ibid., 140.
102 Ibid., 550.
103 Ibid., 551.
104 Ibid., 551-552.
105 Ibid., 573.
106 *Constituent Assembly Debates*, Vol. XI, 799.
107 *Parliamentary Debates, Parliament of India, Official Report, Volume VII, No.1, Part-II, Proceedings Other Than Questions and Answers*, 2285.
108 *Parliamentary Debates, Parliament of India, Official Report, Volume XI, No.1, Part-II, Proceedings Other Than Questions and Answers*, 8349.
109 Ibid., 8352.
110 Ibid., 8433-8438.
111 Ibid., 8466-8467 and 8433.
112 Ibid., 8474.
113 Ibid., 8490-8491.
114 Ibid., 8495.
115 Ibid., 8688.

Chapter 7

1 *Report on Indian Constitutional Reforms*, 148.
2 J.A. Laplonce, 'The Protection of Minorities by the Electoral System', *Western Political Quarterly*, vol. 10, no. 2 (1957).
3 D.E. Butler, *The Electoral System in Britain Since 1918* (Oxford University Press: Oxford, 1963 [1953]), 5 and 174.
4 Gadgil, *Some Observations on the Draft Constitution of India, passim.*
5 Amel Ahmed, *Democracy and the Politics of Electoral System Choice, Engineering Electoral Dominance* (Cambridge University Press: Cambridge, 2013); Carles Boix, 'Setting the Rules of the Game: The Choice of Electoral Systems in Advanced Democracies', *American Political Science Review*, vol. 93, no. 3 (1999); Bernard Ivan Tamas, 'A Divided Political Elite: Why Congress Banned Multimember Districts in 1842', *New Political Science*, vol. 28, no. 1 (2006).
6 Jaffrelot, *India's Silent Revolution: The Rise of the Lower Castes in Northern India*); Jaffrelot and Kumar, eds, *Rise of the Plebeians? The Changing Face of the Indian Legislative Assemblies.*

References

English

Official Publications

Constituent Assembly Debates, Vol. I, (2009), New Delhi: Lok Sabha Secretariat

Constituent Assembly Debates, Vol. II, (2009), New Delhi: Lok Sabha Secretariat

Constituent Assembly Debates, Vol. III, (2009), New Delhi: Lok Sabha Secretariat

Constituent Assembly Debates, Vol. IV, (2009), New Delhi: Lok Sabha Secretariat

Constituent Assembly Debates, Vol. V, (2009), New Delhi: Lok Sabha Secretariat

Constituent Assembly Debates, Vol. VII, (2009), New Delhi: Lok Sabha Secretariat

Constituent Assembly Debates, Vol. VIII, (2009), New Delhi: Lok Sabha Secretariat

Constituent Assembly Debates, Vol. IX, (2009), New Delhi: Lok Sabha Secretariat

Constituent Assembly Debates, Vol. X, (2009), New Delhi: Lok Sabha Secretariat

Constituent Assembly Debates, Vol. XI (2009), New Delhi: Lok Sabha Secretariat

Draft Constitution of India, Prepared by the Drafting Committee (1948), New Delhi: Constituent Assembly of India

East India (Advisory and Legislative Councils), Papers Relating to An Imperial Advisory Council and Provincial Advisory Councils; The Enlargement of The Legislative Councils; And the Discussion of the Budgets, Cmd. 3710 (1907), London: His Majesty's Stationery Office

East India (Advisory and Constitutional Reforms), Vol. I, Proposals of the Government of India and Despatch of the Secretary of State, Cmd. 4426 (1908), London: His Majesty's Stationery Office

East India (Constitutional Reforms), Addresses presented in India to His Excellency The Viceroy and The Right Honourable The Secretary of State for India,Cmd.9178 (1918), London: His Majesty's Stationery Office

East India (Constitutional Reforms: Lord Southborough's Committees), Views of the Government of India on the Reports of Lord Southborough's Committees, Cmd. 176 (1919), London: His Majesty's Stationery Office

East India (Constitutional Reforms) Reforms Enquiry Committee, 1924, Appendix 5 to the Report, Written Evidence (1925), London: His Majesty's Stationery Office

East India (Constitutional Reforms) Reforms Enquiry Committee, 1924, Appendix 6 to the Report, Oral Evidence (Part I) (1925), London: His Majesty's Stationery Office

East India (Constitutional Reforms), Views of the Local Governments, on the Working of the Reforms, dated 1924, Cmd. 2362 (1925), London: His Majesty's Stationery Office

East India (Constitutional Reforms) Indian Franchise Committee, Volume I, Report of the Indian Franchise Committee, Cmd. 4080 (1932), London: His Majesty's Stationery Office

East India (Constitutional Reforms) Indian Franchise Committee, Volume II, Memoranda Submitted by the Local Governments and Provincial Franchise Committees (Madras, Bombay, Bengal and The United Provinces) (1932),London: His Majesty's Stationery Office

East India (Constitutional Reforms) Indian Franchise Committee, Volume III, Memoranda Submitted by the Local Governments and Provincial Franchise Committees (Punjab, Bihar and Orissa, Central Provinces, Assam, North-West Frontier Province, Coorg and Ajmer-Merwara) (1932), London: His Majesty's Stationery Office

East India (Constitutional Reforms) Indian Franchise Committee, Volume IV, Selections from Memoranda and Oral Evidence (Madras, Bombay, Bengal and The United Provinces) (1932), London: His Majesty's Stationery Office

East India (Constitutional Reforms) Indian Franchise Committee, Volume V, Selections from Memoranda and Oral Evidence (Punjab, Bihar and Orissa, Central Provinces, Assam, North-West Frontier Province, Delhi and Miscellaneous Memoranda) (1932), London: His Majesty's Stationery Office

East India (Constitutional Reforms), Communal Decision, Cmd. 4147 (1932), London: His Majesty's Stationery Office

East India (Executive and Legislative Councils), Regulations &c for Giving Effect to the Indian Councils Act, 1909, Cmd. 4987 (1910), London: His Majesty's Stationery Office

First Despatch on Indian Constitutional Reforms, Government of India's Despatch of March 5th 1919, and Connected Papers (1928), Calcutta: Government of India, Central Publication Branch

First Report from the Joint Select Committee on the Government of India Act, 1919, (Draft Rules) (1920), London: His Majesty's Stationery Office

Government of India's Despatch on proposals for Indian Constitutional Reforms (1930), Simla: Government of India

Indian Round Table Conference, 12th November, 1930-19th January, 1931, Proceedings, (1931), Calcutta: Government of India, Central Publication Branch

Indian Round Table Conference, 12th November, 1930-19th January, 1931, Proceedings of Sub-Committees (Volume I), [Sub-Committee No. I (Federal Structure)], (1931), Calcutta: Government of India, Central Publication Branch

Indian Round Table Conference, 12th November, 1930-19th January, 1931, Proceedings of Sub-Committees (Volume II), [Sub-Committee No. II (Provincial Constitution)], (1931), Calcutta: Government of India, Central Publication Branch

Indian Round Table Conference, 12th November, 1930-19th January, 1931, Proceedings of Sub-Committees (Volume III), [Sub-Committee No. III (Minorities)] (1931), Calcutta: Government of India, Central Publication Branch

Indian Round Table Conference, 12th November, 1930-19th January, 1931, Proceedings of Sub-Committees (Volume III), [Sub-Committee No. VI (Franchise)] (1931), Calcutta: Government of India, Central Publication Branch

Indian Round Table Conference (Second Session), 7th September, 1931-1st December, 1931, Proceedings of the Federal Structure Committee and Minorities Committees, 1932, London: His Majesty's Stationery Office

Indian Statutory Commission, Report, Vol-I, Survey, Cmd. 3568 (1930), London: His Majesty's Stationery Office

Indian Statutory Commission, Report, Vol-II, Recommendations, Cmd. 3569 (1930), London: His Majesty's Stationery Office

Indian Statutory Commission, Report, Vol-III, Report of the Committees appointed by the Provincial Legislative Councils to co-operate with the Indian Statutory Commission,Cmd. 3572 (1930), London: His Majesty's Stationery Office

Indian Statutory Commission, Report, Vol-VI, Memorandum Submitted by the Government of Madras to the Indian Statutory Commission(1930), London: His Majesty's Stationery Office

Indian Statutory Commission, Report, Vol-VII, Memorandum Submitted by the Government of Bombay to the Indian Statutory Commission (1930), London: His Majesty's Stationery Office

Indian Statutory Commission, Report, Vol-VIII, Memorandum Submitted by the Government of Bengal to the Indian Statutory Commission (1930), London: His Majesty's Stationery Office

Indian Statutory Commission, Report, Vol-X, Memorandum Submitted by the Government of the Punjab to the Indian Statutory Commission (1930), London: His Majesty's Stationery Office

Indian Statutory Commission, Report, Vol-XV, Extracts from Oral Evidence (Official) (1930), London: His Majesty's Stationery Office

Indian Statutory Commission, Report, Vol-XVI, Selections from Memoranda & Oral Evidence by Non-Officials (Part-I) (1930), London: His Majesty's Stationery Office

Indian Statutory Commission, Report, Vol-XVII, Selections from Memoranda & Oral Evidence by Non-Officials (Part-II)(1930), London: His Majesty's Stationery Office

Joint Select Committee on the Government of India Bill, 1919, Vol. I, Report and Proceedings of the Committee (1919), London: His Majesty's Stationery Office

Joint Select Committee on the Government of India Bill, 1919, Vol. II, Minutes of Evidence,(1919), London: His Majesty's Stationery Office

Joint Select Committee on the Government of India Bill, 1919, Vol. III, Appendices, (1919), London: His Majesty's Stationery Office

Joint Committee on Indian Constitutional Reform (Session 1932–1933), Volume IIA, Minutes of Evidence given before the Joint Committee on Indian Constitutional Reform (1934), London: His Majesty's Stationery Office

Joint Committee on Indian Constitutional Reform (Session 1932–1933), Volume IIB, Minutes of Evidence given before the Joint Committee on Indian Constitutional Reform (1934), London: His Majesty's Stationery Office

Joint Committee on Indian Constitutional Reform (Session 1932–1933), Volume IIC, Minutes of Evidence given before the Joint Committee on Indian Constitutional Reform (1934), London: His Majesty's Stationery Office

Joint Committee on Indian Constitutional Reform (Session 1933–1934), Volume I (Part I), Reports (1934), London: His Majesty's Stationery Office

Joint Committee on Indian Constitutional Reform (Session 1933–1934), Volume I (Part II), Proceedings (1934), London: His Majesty's Stationery Office

Papers Relating to Constitutional Reform in India, Published Under the Authority of the Government of India, Vol. II (1908), Calcutta: Superintendent, Government Printing, India

Papers Relating to Constitutional Reform in India, Published Under the Authority of the Government of India, Vol. III (1908), Calcutta: Superintendent, Government Printing, India

Parliamentary Debates, Parliament of India, Official Report, Volume IV, No.1, Part-II-Proceedings Other Than Questions and Answers (1950), New Delhi: The Manager of Publications

Parliamentary Debates, Parliament of India, Official Report, Volume VII, No.1, Part-II, Proceedings Other Than Questions and Answers, (1950), New Delhi: The Manager of Publications

Parliamentary Debates, Parliament of India, Official Report, Volume X, No.1, Part-II, Proceedings Other Than Questions and Answers, (1951), New Delhi: The Manager of Publications

Parliamentary Debates, Parliament of India, Official Report, Volume XI, No.1, Part-II, Proceedings Other Than Questions and Answers, (1951), New Delhi: The Manager of Publications

Parliamentary Debates, Parliament of India, Official Report, Volume XII, No.1, Part-II, Proceedings Other Than Questions and Answers, (1951), New Delhi: The Manager of Publications

Proposals for Indian Constitutional Reforms (1933), Delhi: Manager of Publications

Reforms Committee (Franchise), Evidence Taken Before the Reforms Committee (Franchise), Vol. I (1919), Calcutta: Superintendent, Government Printing India

Reforms Committee (Franchise), Evidence Taken Before the Reforms Committee (Franchise), Vol. II(1919), Calcutta: Superintendent, Government Printing India

Report of the Depressed Classes and Aboriginal Tribes Committee (1930), Bombay: Government of Bombay

Report of the Franchise Committee, 1918–19 (1919), Calcutta: Superintendent, Government Printing India

Report of the Indian Central Committee (1929), Calcutta: Government of India, Central Publication Branch

Report on Indian Constitutional Reforms (1918), Calcutta: Superintendent, Government Printing India

Report of the Committee appointed in connection with the Delimitation of Constituencies and connected matters, Volume I, The Report, Cmd. 5099 (1936), London: His Majesty's Stationery Office

Report of the Committee appointed in connection with the Delimitation of Constituencies and connected matters, Vol.II, Proposals for the Delimitation of Constituencies (1936), London: His Majesty's Stationery Office

Report of the Committee appointed in connection with the Delimitation of Constituencies and connected matters, Vol.III, Selections from Evidence (1936), London: His Majesty's Stationery Office

Report of the Government of Bombay on the Delimitation of Constituencies in the Presidency of Bombay and in Sind (1935), Bombay: Government of Bombay

Report of the Provincial Advisory Committee on the Delimitation of Constituencies 1933-34, Volume I (Parts I and II) (1934), Calcutta: Government of Bengal, Appointments Department, Reforms

Report of the Reforms Enquiry Committee appointed by the Government of India and other connected papers, Cmd. 2360 (1925), London: His Majesty's Stationery Office

Report of the Royal Commission appointed to enquire into Electoral Systems, Cmd. 5163, (1910), London: His Majesty's Stationery Office

Representation of Muhammadans on Legislative Councils, Cd.4652 (1909), London: His Majesty's Stationery Office

Reports and Proceedings of Organisations

All-Parties Conference 1928, Report of the Committee appointed by the Conference to determine the principles of the Constitution for India, Together with the Summary of the Proceedings of the Conference held at Lucknow (1928), Allahabad: General Secretary, All-India Congress Committee

Draft Constitution of Indian Republic (1948), Bombay: Suresh Desai, General Secretary, Socialist Party

Report of The Proceedings of The Twenty-Fourth Indian National Congress Held at Lahore On the 27th, 28th and 29th December 1909, (n.d), Lahore: Tribune Steam Press

Report of the Proceedings of the Twenty-seventh session of the Indian National Congress, Held at Bankipore, 26th, 27th and 28th December, 1912, (n.d)

Report of the Thirty-first Indian National Congress held at Lucknow on the 26th, 28th, 29th and 30th December, 1916, (1917), Allahabad, Published by the Reception Committee at Lucknow

Books and Articles

Agarwal, Shriman Narayan (1946), *Gandhian Constitution for India*, Allahabad: Kitabistan

Ahmed, Amel (2013), *Democracy and the Politics of Electoral System Choice, Engineering Electoral Dominance*, Cambridge: Cambridge University Press

Ambedkar, B.R. (1945), *Address by B.R. Ambedkar, M.A., Ph.D., D.Sc., Barrister-at-law, Member, Governor-General's Executive Council To the Session of the All-India Scheduled Caste Federation. Held in Bombay on May 6, 1945*

Ambedkar, B.R. (1947), *States and Minorities, What Are Their Rights and How to Secure Them in the Constitution of Free India*, Bombay: Thacker & Co.

Anthony, Frank (1969), *Britain's Betrayal In India, The Story of the Anglo-Indian Community*, Bombay: Allied Publishers

Austin, Granville (1966), *The Indian Constitution: The Cornerstone of the Nation*, Oxford: Clarendon Press

Bandyopadhyaya, Sekhar (2011), *Caste, Protest and Identity in Colonial India : The Namasudras of Bengal, 1872–1947*, New Delhi: Oxford University Press

Banerjea, Surendranath (1925), *A Nation In Making, Being Reminiscences of Fifty Years of Public Life*, London: Oxford University Press

Boix, Carles (1999), 'Setting the Rules of the Game: The Choice of Electoral Systems in Advanced Democracies', *American Political Science Review*, 93 (3): 609–624

Bridge, Carl (1986), *Holding India to the Empire, The British Conservative Party and the 1935 Constitution*, London: Oriental University Press

Brown, Mark B. (2006), 'Survey Article: Citizen Panels and the Concept of Representation', *Journal of Political Philosophy*, 14 (2): 203–25

Brown, Mark B. (2008), 'Fairly Balanced: The Politics of Representation on Government Advisory Committees', *Political Research Quarterly*, 61 (4): 547–60

Butler, D.E. (1963 [1953]), *The Electoral System in Britain Since 1918*, Oxford: Oxford University Press

Chakravarty, Bidyut (1989), 'The Communal Award and Its Implications in Bengal', *Modern Asian Studies*, 23 (3): 493–523

Chandra, Bipin, Mridula Mukherjee, Aditya Mukherjee, K.N. Panikkar and Sucheta Mahajan (1991 [1988]),*India's Struggle for Independence*, New Delhi: Penguin

Chaube, Shibani Kinkar (1973), *Constituent Assembly of India, Springboard of Revolution*, New Delhi: People's Publishing House

Chiriyankandath, James (1992), "Democracy' under the Raj: Elections and separate representation in British India', *Commonwealth and Comparative Politics*, 30 (1): 39–63

Dalal, M.N. (1940), *Whither Minorities?* Bombay: D.B. Taraporevala Sons and Co.

Danzig, Richard (1968), 'The Announcement of August 20th 1917', *Journal of Asian Studies*, 28 (1) : 19–37

Das, C.R., and Bhagvan Das (No Year of Publication), *Outline Scheme of Swaraj*

Douglas, Paul H.(1923), 'Occupational Versus Proportional Representation', *The American Journal of Sociology*, 29 (2): 129–57

Dovi, Suzanne (2002), 'Preferable Descriptive Representatives: Will just any Woman, Black, or Latino do?', *American Political Science Review*, 96 (4): 729–43

Dovi, Suzanne (2017) 'Political Representation', in Edward N. Zalta (ed.) *The Stanford Encyclopaedia of Philosophy* (Winter, 2017 Edition), URL : https://plato.stanford.edu/archives/win2017/entries/political-representation/ (Accessed on 2 September 2018)

Fischer Williams, J. (1914), *Proportional Representation and British Politics*, London: John Murray

Forbes, Geraldine (2004 [1996]), *Women in Modern India, New Cambridge History of India, Vol. IV-2*, Cambridge: Cambridge University Press

Friedrich, C.J. (1948), 'Representation and Constitutional Reform in Europe', *Western Political Quarterly*, 1 (2): 124–30

Gadgil, D.R. (1948), *Some Observations on the Draft Constitution of India*, Poona: Gokhale Institute of Politics and Economics

Gandhi, M.K. (1931), 'The Future of India', *International Affairs*, 10 (6) : 721–39

Gokhale, D.V., and others (c.1944), *The Constitution of the Hindusthan Free State Act, 194_*, Poona: M.R. Dhamdhere

Gopal, S. (2008 (1965), *British Policy in India, 1858–1905*, Cambridge: Cambridge University Press

Gwyer, Sir Maurice and A. Appadorai (1957), *Speeches and Documents on the Indian Constitution, 1921–1947, Vol. II*, Bombay: Oxford University Press

Hare, Thomas(1857), *The Machinery of Representation*, London: W. Maxwell

Hare, Thomas (1873), *Election of Representatives, Parliamentary and Municipal, A Treatise*, London: Longmans, Green, Reader, and Dyer

Hermens, F.A. (1942), 'P.R. and Democracy,' *The Review of Politics*, 4 (4): 459-88

Hermens, F.A.(1951), *Europe Between Democracy and Anarchy*, Notre Dame: University of Notre Dame Press

Hoag, Clarence and George Hallett, Jr. (1926), *Proportional Representation*, New York: Macmillan and Co.

Hogan, James (1945), *Elections and Representation*, Cork and Oxford: Cork University Press and B.H. Blackwell Ltd

Horwill, George H.(1925), *Proportional Representation, Its Dangers and Defects*, London: George Allen and Unwin

Humphreys, John H. (1911), *Proportional Representation, A Study in the Method of Elections*, London: Methuen and Co.

Ilbert, Sir Courtenay (1907), *The Government of India, Being a Digest of the Statute Law Relating Thereto with Historical Introduction and Explanatory Matter*, Oxford: Clarendon Press

Ilbert, Sir Courtenay (1910), *The Government of India, Supplementary Chapter (Indian Councils Act, 1909)*, Oxford: Clarendon Press

Iyengar, S. Srinivasa (1927), *Swaraj Constitution*, Madras: S. Ganesan

Jaffrelot, Christophe (2002), *India's Silent Revolution: The Rise of the Lower Castes in Northern India*, Ranikhet: Permanent Black

Jaffrelot, Christophe and Sanjay Kumar, eds (2009), *Rise of the Plebeians? The Changing Face of the Indian Legislative Assemblies*, New Delhi: Routledge

Jensenius, Francesca R. (2015), 'Mired in Reservations: The Path-Dependent History of Electoral Quotas in India', *Journal of Asian Studies*, 74 (1): 85–105

Jha, Shefali (2003), 'Rights Versus Representation, Defending Minority Interests in the Constituent Assembly', *Economic and Political Weekly*, 38 (16): 1579–83

Karim, Rezaul (1937), *For India and Islam*, Calcutta : Chuckervertty, Chatterjee and Co.

Karve, D.G., and D.V. Ambekar, eds (1966), *Speeches and Writings of Gopal Krishna Gokhale, Volume Two: Political*, Bombay: Allied Publishers

Keith, Arthur Berriedale (1937 [1936]), *A Constitutional History of India, 1600–1935*, London: Methuen and Co.

Kelly, Duncan (2004), 'Carl Schmitt's Political Theory of Representation', *Journal of the History of Ideas*, 65 (1): 113–134

Khan, Shafaat Ahmed (1928), *What Are the Rights of the Muslim Minority in India?*, Allahabad: The Indian Press

Koss, Stephen E. (1969), *John Morley at the India Office, 1905–1910*, New Haven: Yale University Press

Krishna, K.B. (1939), *The Problem of Minorities or Communal Representation in India*, London: George Allen and Unwin

Krishnamurti, Y.G. (1940), *Constituent Assembly and Indian Federation*, Bombay: New Book Company

Kumar, Ravinder (1985), 'Gandhi, Ambedkar and the Poona Pact, 1932', *South Asia, Journal of South Asian Studies*, 8 (1): 87-101

Lakeman, Enid (1974), *How Democracies Vote*, London: Faber and Faber

Laplonce, J.A. (1957), 'The Protection of Minorities by the Electoral System', *Western Political Quarterly*, 10 (2): 318–339

Lothian, The Marquess of (1932), 'India and the Franchise Problem', *International Affairs*, 11 (5): 593–617

M.V. (1893), *The Indian Councils Act and the Acts Amending It with All Official Papers Connected Therewith and The Rules for the Conduct of Business at the Meetings of the Council*, Madras

Mahajani, Dr G.S. (1941), *The Problem of Minorities and Constitutional Democracy as its Solution*, Bombay

Mallampalli, Chandra (2004), *Christians and Public Life in Colonial South India, 1863-1937, Contending with Marginality*, London: RoutledgeCurzon

Manin, Bernard (2002), *The Principles of Representative Government*, Cambridge: Cambridge University Press

Manin, Bernand, Adam Przeworksi and Susan C. Stokes (1999), 'Elections and Representation', in Adam Przeworki, Susan C. Stokes and Bernard Manin (eds), *Democracy, Accountability and Representation*, 29–54.Cambridge: Cambridge University Press

Mansbridge, Jane (1999), 'Should Blacks represent Blacks and Women represent Women? A Contingent 'Yes' ', *The Journal of Politics*, 61 (3): 628–57

Mansergh, Nicholas, ed (1970), *Constitutional Relations Between Britain and India, The Transfer of Power 1942–47, Volume 1*, London: HMSO

Mashruwala, K.G. (1946), *Some Particular Suggestions for the Constitution of Free India*, Bombay: Hamara Hindustan

Mazumdar, Vina (2010), *The Mind and the Medium, Explorations in the Evolution of Imperial Policy in India*, Gurgaon: Three Essays Collective

Mehrotra, S.R. (1963), 'The Politics Behind the Montagu Declaration of 1917' in C.H. Philips (ed), *Politics and Society in India*, 71–96. London: George Allen and Unwin

Meisel, Joseph S. (2011), *Knowledge and Power, The Parliamentary Representation of Universities in Britain and Empire*, Chichester: Wiley-Blackwell

Metcalf, Thomas R.(1965), *The Aftermath of Revolt, India, 1857–1870*, Princeton: Princeton University Press

Monroe, Burt L. (1994), 'Understanding Electoral Systems: Beyond Plurality Versus PR', *PS: Political Science and Politics*, 27 (4): 677–82

Morley, John (1920), *Speeches on Indian Affairs*, Madras: G.A.Natesan & Sons

Moore, R.J. (1966), *Liberalism and Indian Politics, 1872–1922*, London: Edward Arnold

Moore, R.J. (1967), 'The Twilight of the Whigs and the Reform of the Indian Councils, 1886–1892', *The Historical Journal*, 10 (3) : 400–14

Moore, R.J. (1974), *The Crisis of Indian Unity, 1917–1940*, Delhi: Oxford University Press

Muldoon, Andrew (2006), *Empire, Politics, and the Creation of the 1935 India Act*, Farnham: Ashgate

Nanda, B.R. (1998), *Gokhale, The Indian Moderates and the British Raj*, New Delhi: Oxford University Press

Nihal Singh, Gurmukh (1933), *Landmarks in Indian Constitutional and National Development (1600–1919)*, Benares : The Indian Book Shop

Owen, Hugh F. (1972), 'Negotiating the Lucknow Pact', *Journal of Asian Studies*, 31 (3): 561–87

Philips, C.H., ed (1962), *The Evolution of India and Pakistan, 1858 to 1947, Select Documents*, London: Oxford University Press

Phillips, Anne (1995), *The Politics of Presence*, Oxford: Clarendon Press

Pitkin, Hanna Fenichel (1972 [1967]), *The Concept of Representation*, Berkeley: University of California Press

Pitkin, Hanna Fenichel (1985)'Representation', in Terence Ball, James Farr and Russell L. Hanson (eds), *Political Innovation and Conceptual Change*, 132–54, Cambridge: Cambridge University Press

Pitkin, Hanna Fenichel (2004), 'Representation and Democracy: Uneasy Alliance', *Scandinavian Political Studies*, 27 (3): 335–42

Plotke, David (1997), 'Representation is Democracy', *Constellations*, 4 (1): 19–34

Pyarelal (1932), *The Epic Fast*, Ahmedabad: Navajivan Press

Rehfeld, Andrew (2001), 'Silence of the Land: On the Historical Irrelevance of Territory to Congressional Districting and Political Representation in the United States', *Studies in American Political Development*, 15 (Spring 2001): 53–87

Rehfeld, Andrew (2006),'Towards a General Theory of Representation', *The Journal of Politics*, 68 (1): 1–21

Rehfeld, Andrew (2009), 'On Quotas and Qualifications for Office', in Ian Shapiro, Susan C. Stokes, Elisabeth Jean Woods, Alexander S. Kirshner (eds), *Political Representation*, 236–70,Cambridge: Cambridge University Press

Robb, Peter (1976), *The Government of India and Reform, Policies Towards Politics and the Constitution, 1916–1921*, Oxford: Oxford University Press

Robinson, Francis (2008 (1974)), *Separatism among Indian Muslims: The Politics of the United Provinces' Muslims 1860–1923*, Cambridge: Cambridge University Press

Roy, M.N. (c.1945), *Constitution of India, A Draft*, No Place of Psublication: Radical Democratic Party

Sapru, Tej Bahadur, and others (1945), *Constitutional Proposals of the Sapru Committee*, Moradabad: Kunwar Sir Jagadish Prasad

Sarkar, Sumit (2009 [1983]), *Modern India, 1885–1947*, Delhi: Macmillan

Sastri, V.S. Srinivasa (1917), *The Congress-League Scheme, An Exposition*, Poona: Servants of India Society

Shaikh, Farzana (2012 [1989]), *Community and Consensus in Islam, Muslim Representation and Colonial India, 1860–1947*, New Delhi: Imprint One

Shani, Ornit (2018), *How India Became Democratic, Citizenship and the Making of Universal Franchise*, Gurgaon: Penguin Random House India

Shiva Rao, B, ed (1967), *The Framing of India's Constitution, Select Documents, Vol.II,* New Delhi: Indian Institute of Public Administration

Shiva Rao, B, ed, (1967), *The Framing of India's Constitution, Select Documents, Vol.III,* New Delhi: Indian Institute of Public Administration

Shiva Rao, B, ed (1968), *The Framing of India's Constitution, Select Documents, Vol.IV,* New Delhi: Indian Institute of Public Administration

Sridharan, E.(2004) 'The Origins of The Electoral System: Rules, Representation, and Power-sharing in Indian Democracy', in Zoya Hasan, E. Shridharan and R. Sudarshan (eds), *India's Living Constitution, Ideas, Practices, Controversies*, 344–369. Ranikhet: Permanent Black

Tamas, Bernard Ivan (2006), 'A Divided Political Elite: Why Congress Banned Multimember Districts in 1842', *New Political Science*, 28 (1): 23-44

The Montagu–Chelmsford Reform Proposals with a Foreword by Annie Besant Together with the Text of the Memorandum of the Nineteen, the Congress-League Scheme and a Summary of the Indian Criticisms on the Proposal (n.d), Madras: The Sons of India Ltd

Tofail Ahmed, Syed (1928), *Responsible Government and Solution of Hindu-Muslim Problem*

Urbinati, Nadia (2008 [2006]), *Representative Government, Principles & Genealogy*, Chicago: The University of Chicago Press

Venkatrangaiya, M. (1948), *Draft Constitution of India*, Bombay: Hind Kitabs Ltd.

Viera, Monica Brito and David Runciman (2008), *Representation*, Cambridge: Polity Press

Vundru, Raja Sekhar (2018), *Ambedkar, Gandhi and Patel, The Making of India's Electoral System*, New Delhi: Bloomsbury

Wasti, Syed Razi (1964), *Lord Minto and the Indian Nationalist Movement, 1905 to 1910*, Oxford: Clarendon Press

Williams, Melissa (2000 [1998]), *Voice, Trust, and Memory, Marginalized Groups and the Failings of Liberal Representation*, Princeton: Princeton University Press

Williamson, René de Visme (1941), 'The Fascist Concept of Representation', *The Journal of Politics*, 3 (1): 29-41

Wolpert, Stanley (1967), *Morley and India, 1906–1910*, Berkeley: University of California Press

Marathi

Priyolkar, A.K, ed(1996 [1967]), *Lokahitwadikrut Nibandhasangraha*, Mumbai: Popular Prakashan

Index

D